MONEY ROCK

MONEY ROCK

A FAMILY'S STORY OF COCAINE, RACE, AND AMBITION IN THE NEW SOUTH

PAM KELLEY

THE
NEW
PRESS

NEW YORK
LONDON

Requests for permission to reproduce selections from this book should be mailed to: Permissions Department, The New Press, 120 Wall Street, 31st floor, New York, NY 10005.

"New Jack Hustler," words and music by Alphonso Henderson and Tracy Marrow. Copyright © 2012 WB Music Corp., Carrumba Music, Ammo Dump Music, Reach Global (U.K.) Ltd., and Rhyme Syndicate Music. All rights on behalf of itself, Carrumba Music, Ammo Dump Music. Administered by WB Music Corp. All rights reserved. Used by permission of Alfred Music.

"Ten Crack Commandments," words and music by Khary Kimani Turner, Chris Martin, and Christopher Wallace. Copyright © 1997 EMI April Music Inc., Weblife, Hertzrentatune, Gifted Pearl Music, and Justin Combs Publishing Company, Inc. All rights administered by Sony/ATV Music Publishing LLC, 424 Church Street, Suite 1200, Nashville, TN 37219. All rights reserved. Used by permission of Hal Leonard LLC.

"Freedom," words and music by Matthew Michael Bushard. Copyright © 2009 University Music—Brentwood Benson Publishing (ASCAP), City Bible Music (ASCAP). Administered by CapitalCMGPublishing.com. All rights reserved. Used by permission of Capital CMG Publishing.

"All Around," words and music by Aaron Lindsey, Curt Coffield, and Israel Houghton. Copyright © 2004—Integrity's Hosanna! Music, Integrity's Praise! Music (BMI), Sound of the New Breed (BMI), Like a Card (ASCAP). Administered by CapitalCMGPublishing.com. All rights reserved. Used by permission of Capital CMG Publishing.

Published in the United States by The New Press, New York, 2018
Distributed by Two Rivers Distribution

ISBN 978-1-62097-327-1 (hc)
ISBN 978-1-62097-328-8 (ebook)

CIP data is available.

The New Press publishes books that promote and enrich public discussion and understanding of the issues vital to our democracy and to a more equitable world. These books are made possible by the enthusiasm of our readers; the support of a committed group of donors, large and small; the collaboration of our many partners in the independent media and the not-for-profit sector; booksellers, who often hand-sell New Press books; librarians; and above all by our authors.

www.thenewpress.com

Book design and composition by dix! Digital Prepress
This book was set in Minion

Printed in the United States of America

10 9 8 7 6 5 4 3 2 1

For Trent, Jackson, and Emma

For to those who have, more will be given, and they will have an abundance; but from those who have nothing, even what they have will be taken away.

—Matthew 13:12

To be a poor man is hard, but to be a poor race in a land of dollars is the very bottom of hardships.

—W.E.B. Du Bois, *The Souls of Black Folk*

> With cocaine, my success came speedy
> Got me twisted, jammed into a paradox
> Every dollar I get, another brother drops
> Maybe that's the plan, and I don't understand
>
> —Ice-T, *New Jack Hustler*

CONTENTS

PROLOGUE

In May 1986, I made a trip to Central Prison in Raleigh, North Carolina, to meet Money Rock. He was an inmate, recently convicted; I was a reporter for the *Charlotte Observer*, hoping to get the inside story of a cocaine turf war between him and a guy named Big Lou. We sat across from each other in a visiting room, sparsely furnished with a large metal desk. Affixed to its front, unaccountably, was North Carolina's state seal, with female figures depicting Liberty and Plenty and the state's Latin motto, *Esse quam videri: To be rather than to seem*. The motto struck me as a promising omen.

I'd covered Money Rock's trial weeks earlier, watching him at the defendant's table from my seat in the courtroom. After his conviction, I'd requested an interview. When he agreed, I was hopeful that he wanted to come clean, and I'd get a great story. I was twenty-six, a middle-class white woman from Ohio listening to testimony about African American dealers battling over turf in Charlotte, North Carolina. It was all new to me—except for the cocaine. Coke had been big when I attended college at UNC Chapel Hill in the late 1970s. I'd tried it, and I'd known classmates who sold it. None of us had gotten caught.

That day of our first conversation, he wore prison-issued khaki and a patchy beard, a stark contrast to the Money Rock diamond rings and earring stud he'd worn in court. I shook his hand. He smiled. But almost as soon as we started talking, I could tell I wouldn't get the truth. His goal was to convince me he was innocent. Persecuted, even.

He wasn't a cocaine dealer. He was a Christian who made his money cleaning Hardee's restaurants. "The devil has put me here because of all my works and all the stuff I did to help people," he told me. "He done put me here to try my faith."

I doubt the interview lasted an hour, and while I left without my big story, there were memorable moments. One was his description of his nemesis, Big Lou, as a dinosaur. "You know," he told me, "little old brain, big old dinosaur." It made me smile. But when it became clear he wasn't going to tell me anything more about the shootout, I put away my pen, shut my notebook, and shook his hand goodbye.

My eventual front-page story, headlined "Moneyrock and Big Lou: Portrait of a Shootout," laid out many facts about cocaine, big money, and flashy jewelry, but offered little insight, no explanation why a public housing project in prosperous Charlotte, North Carolina, had become ground zero for a rapidly expanding drug economy.

A quarter century later, in 2011, I was still working at the *Charlotte Observer*, though I'd long ago left the courthouse beat, and stories about cocaine dealers had long ago disappeared from the front page. I hadn't thought of Money Rock in years. But one afternoon I happened to dip into rap artist Jay-Z's memoir, *Decoded*, a Christmas present I'd bought for my daughter. I found myself engrossed in Jay-Z's early years, before he'd recorded his first hit or married Beyoncé, when he was an unknown young crack dealer living in Marcy, a public housing project in Brooklyn:

> Guys my age, fed up with watching their moms struggle on a single income, were paying utility bills with money from hustling. So how could those same mothers sit them down about a truant report? Outside, in Marcy's courtyards and across the country, teenagers wore automatic weapons like they were sneakers. Broad-daylight shoot-outs had our grandmothers afraid to leave the house, and had neighbors who'd known us since we were toddlers forming Neighborhood Watches against us.[1]

The world Jay-Z described—the public housing, the weapons, the broad-daylight gunfire—transported me back to 1986, to the weeks I'd spent sitting through shootout trials, scribbling notes, watching a judge send cocaine dealers to prison. I got to wondering what happened to those Charlotte men who'd dealt cocaine, whether they'd lived to tell about it. And of course I remembered Money Rock. He hadn't told me much that was truthful or useful, but his charm had made an impression. I'd ended up liking the guy.

I had to look up my old stories to remember his real name, Belton Lamont Platt. The newspaper's researcher found his phone listing—in Conway, South Carolina, outside Myrtle Beach. On a whim, I called. Belton was out when I telephoned, but I left a message. He called back, pleased to hear from me.

That's how this book began, with a simple question: What happened to Money Rock? The question grew more complicated the more I researched, as I saw everything I'd missed the first time around. Money Rock's story began long before cocaine invaded the city of Charlotte. Today, years after the epidemic subsided, the city continues to feel its effects. These pages profile one of the city's flashiest drug dealers and his striving African American family, three generations swept up and transformed by cocaine. They're also the story of Charlotte, a New South boomtown that's finally beginning to confront the many ways its Jim Crow past lives on.

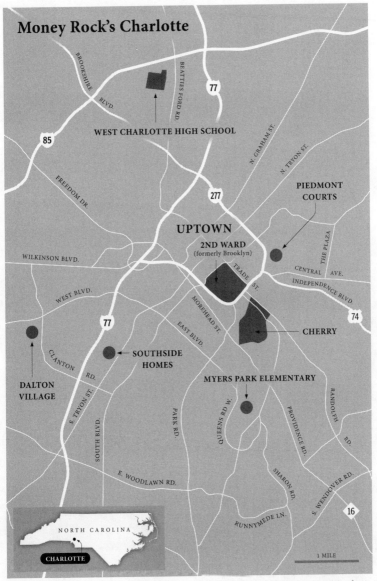

Money Rock's Charlotte

BROOKSHIRE BLVD.

BEATTIES FORD RD.

77

WEST CHARLOTTE HIGH SCHOOL

85

FREEDOM DR.

N. GRAHAM ST.

N. TRYON ST.

277

PIEDMONT COURTS

THE PLAZA

UPTOWN

2ND WARD
(formerly Brooklyn)

TRADE ST.

CENTRAL AVE.

WILKINSON BLVD.

INDEPENDENCE BLVD.

MORHEAD ST.

CHERRY

74

WEST BLVD.

77

EAST BLVD.

SOUTHSIDE HOMES

CLANTON RD.

MYERS PARK ELEMENTARY

RANDOLPH RD.

DALTON VILLAGE

S. TRYON ST.

SOUTH BLVD.

PARK RD.

QUEENS RD W.

PROVIDENCE RD.

E. WOODLAWN RD.

SHARON RD.

S. WENDOVER RD.

16

RUNNYMEDE LN.

NORTH CAROLINA

CHARLOTTE

1 MILE

Map by David Puckett

1

MONEY ROCK AND BIG LOU

Something was up in Piedmont Courts. Belton Lamont Platt was making an entrance, but not in his typical way. Usually, he steered his Cadillac to the curb of the main strip, where he'd greet familiar faces hanging around the public housing apartments, then slip inside the unit where he conducted business. This time, he'd chosen a back way. He and his three men approached on foot. They crossed a bridge over a trickling creek, then passed a neighborhood park, with its broken merry-go-round and glass shards thick under the monkey bars.[1] This time, he and his crew had gone to the trouble of dressing alike, in ball caps and plastic rain ponchos, which Belton had bought that morning at the Army-Navy surplus store. The caps obscured their identities. The dark green ponchos hid their guns.

The date was Saturday, November 30, 1985. After-Thanksgiving shoppers filled local malls; fragrant pines and firs, freshly cut from North Carolina's mountains, stocked Christmas tree lots.[2] It was gray and rainy, a lazy holiday weekend in Charlotte, but not for Belton, who dominated Piedmont Courts' cocaine trade and meant to keep it that way. He was twenty-two years old, with a sprinkling of brown freckles across his caramel-colored cheeks that would later be noted ("Freckles on face") in FBI descriptions. He ran on ego and ignorance, good intentions and greed, but he had a reputation in Piedmont Courts as a no-nonsense guy, out to make money, not trouble. He acknowledged older residents with *yes ma'ams* and *yes sirs*, and was careful to avoid profanity. Women went for him; his earnest nature put people at ease. When he smiled, his brown eyes lit up. Today, however, Belton wasn't smiling.

The reputation of cocaine and coke dealers has been so bad in America for so long that it's easy to forget that stretch of time in the 1970s, before Belton got into the game, when the drug was associated with rich white people, not black gangsters. In August 1977, when Belton was thirteen, the *Charlotte News* published a front-page feature whose casual treatment of cocaine now seems extraordinary. Labeled "Cocaine . . . drug of the rich," the story opened with a man it called Paul, a thirty-something manufacturer's representative who places his straw into a tiny mound of cocaine powder, lifts it to his nose, and inhales. "Cocaine," he said with a smile, "is probably the most sociable drug in the world."[3]

It was a nonaddictive stimulant, the *News* explained, that was being enjoyed by some of the city's most upstanding people "in the legal and medical community, in retail sales, insurance, real estate and finance."[4] The newspaper's sympathetic portrayal mirrored those of national publications, particularly *Newsweek*, which had written about cocaine three months earlier as if it were a fun new fad, akin to the advent of skateboarding or the growing popularity of quiche: "Among hostesses in the smart sets of Los Angeles and New York, a little cocaine, like Dom Pérignon and Beluga caviar, is now *de rigueur* at dinners. Some partygivers pass it around along with the canapes on silver trays."[5] The *News*, citing that *Newsweek* article, gave its story a headline that could have doubled as an advertisement for blow: "One Whiff and You've Joined the 'Smart Set.'"[6]

This lighthearted treatment was predicated on a belief that cocaine wasn't a dangerous drug. President Gerald Ford's administration had pronounced it nonaddictive in a 1975 position statement. President Jimmy Carter's drug policy adviser described it as benign.[7] In 1976, when an author named Robert Sabbag published one of the first books about cocaine smuggling, *Snowblind: A Brief Career in the Cocaine Trade*, he described an experiment in which rats were taught to press a lever for a reward. They repeated the behavior 250 times for caffeine, 4,000 times for heroin, and 10,000 times for cocaine. And yet he stressed that cocaine was not necessarily habit forming. "It has been demonstrated clinically that, since 1914, the greatest danger connected with the moderate use of cocaine is legal and not chemical."[8]

Sabbag was making this argument before the rise of crack cocaine or freebasing, when cocaine was seen as speed's gentler cousin. Sure, overuse could eat through your septum and cause a perpetually runny nose, but conventional wisdom said it could be enjoyed, in moderation, without worrisome repercussions. The drug wasn't physically addictive; you didn't throw up or shake or writhe in pain when you stopped using it. In that way, it was different from heroin. But what many users didn't appreciate—until they realized they had a habit—was the psychological craving. People did get addicted, and the price was high. A hundred bucks would buy a gram of powder, not even a teaspoon's worth. For a recreational user, it was enough to share with friends over a weekend. For an addict, it was gone within hours.

Cocaine's reputation was evolving by the time Belton began dealing in 1983. Hardcore users were freebasing—smoking a mixture of coke and ether. The intense high had caught on in Charlotte's poor, black neighborhoods and was hastening their decay. In Piedmont Courts, residents were accustomed to a certain level of lawlessness. Liquor houses—apartments where residents illegally sold alcohol—were as much a part of life as the white church volunteers who showed up to tutor Piedmont Courts' children. Drugs were freely bought and sold. Men fought, with fists or knives or sometimes guns. For years, however, a protocol had existed, an unwritten contract that said if you weren't involved you had little to fear. But by the autumn of 1985, as Piedmont Courts' tall oaks dropped their leaves onto bare-dirt front yards, the community's fragile equilibrium was shifting. A sixty-nine-year-old woman had shown a newspaper reporter the axe, pick, machete, and .22-caliber pistol she kept for safety near her bed.[9] The liberal white minister of Seigle Avenue Presbyterian Church, across the street from the project, had pleaded with police and city council members to do something. He even offered to raise money for under-cover drug buys, but found no takers. Violent crime had begun tick-ing upward nationally. The day before Belton walked into Piedmont Courts with his gun concealed under a poncho, the *New York Times* published its first front-page story about crack, an addictive, purified form of cocaine that had appeared in the Bronx and was spreading through the city.[10] Crack hadn't hit Charlotte yet, at least not in large quantities. That would soon change.

Charlotte leaders believed they already had a good plan to address rampant crime: a $6-million renovation that would demolish ten of the housing project's forty buildings. The new green space would make it harder for lawbreakers to hide.[11]

Some city leaders viewed Piedmont Courts' problems as a distrac-tion. Charlotte was focused on its future. Rust Belt refugees were arriving daily, drawn to Carolina blue skies and new jobs in shiny new office buildings. The term *world-class* had become the city's buzzword. Charlotte, population 350,000 and growing, longed for a world-class airport, a world-class business district, a world-class reputation.

This long-standing obsession with progress meant the city often had little use for history. Unless a person did some digging, it was easy to forget that the town had been part of the Confederacy, that it had been home to cotton plantations, and that in 1860 enslaved African Americans were 40 percent of the population.[12] No marble Civil War general sat astride his steed on a town square. And though Jefferson Davis held the final meeting of the Confederacy's full cabinet in a pri-vate home on North Tryon Street, that structure was long gone, re-placed by a Sears store, which eventually relocated to the burgeoning white suburbs.[13]

Charlotte's forward-looking zeal generally served the city well. In-tegration came more quickly than it did in much of the South; leaders realized a segregated community would never hit the big time. Many in this majority-white town were proud that they'd integrated their schools relatively peacefully, if not cheerfully, and that in 1983 they'd elected a handsome African American mayor named Harvey Gantt, an architect who'd been the first black student to enroll at South Carolina's Clemson University.

And yet Jim Crow's vestiges remained. You could see them in the city's segregated housing patterns, in the grinding poverty of many black neighborhoods. That was especially true in Piedmont Courts, which had come to embody Charlotte's civil rights history—segregation, integration, good intentions, blind spots—all bundled into a single public housing project. It had opened in 1941 for white people only, but when federal laws forced integration, whites fled. By 1985, it was home to one thousand residents, all black, living in two-story apartments squeezed onto little more than twenty acres. Statistics from a 1984 survey presented a grim picture: The average family income, $4,018, was the lowest of any Charlotte public housing complex. The unemployment rate, 81 percent, was the highest. Women headed 91 percent of the households. A third of the families didn't have a telephone.[14]

The apartments were unremarkable—red-brick buildings with cinder block walls and linoleum floors, torn screen doors and concrete stoops. The development, at Tenth Street and Seigle Avenue, was just east of downtown, a couple minutes' drive from police headquarters. Officers complained that multiple entrances and narrow streets made the area a nightmare to patrol. Dealers hung out on the street bisecting the complex, known even to cops as Hollywood Boulevard, probably because it was where the action took place. Users, both white and black, cruised the boulevard, lining up to sellers like customers at a drive-through window. The drug menu was varied, but cocaine had become Piedmont Courts' specialty.

By the time that Saturday in 1985 rolled around, Belton had become a skilled marketer. He stoked demand by giving out free samples. He made sure that his product's purity beat the competitors'. He sold all

The street known as Hollywood Boulevard in Charlotte's Piedmont Courts public housing development, days after the December 1985 shootout. Photo by Jeep Hunter, courtesy of the *Charlotte Observer*.

night, after other suppliers went to bed. Also, he never used cocaine, not only as a sound business practice, but because he was opposed to drug use.

He was rolling in cash. He had acquired the nickname Money Rock and was focusing his investments in gold jewelry. He wore enough, a police officer once quipped, to drown him in a swimming pool. He had purchased a nice ride, the Cadillac, light green. As he entered Piedmont Courts that wet fall day, he knew his friend Mitch would be arriving in that very ride momentarily.

Belton loved much of his work—the image, the money, the satisfaction he felt when he tossed cash at some lucky beneficiary. His mother had instilled in him a desire to do a good turn since childhood, even before he became a Boy Scout. He believed he was meant to be an entrepreneur as early as elementary school, when he bought candy and resold it at a markup to wealthier classmates.

Still, dealing wasn't easy. All he'd known about cocaine when he got into the game was that selling the bagged powder would be more lucrative than his janitorial business, which required lots of floor mopping and grill-hood scrubbing at fast-food restaurants. Now, though, he felt constant pressure: Score a kilo, cut it, bag it, sell it, score again. He had six children—one with his wife and five by four other mothers. Several of these women didn't know about the others. Stress played havoc with his weight. Two hundred pounds on a five-foot-eight frame, Belton carried the paunch and jowls of an older man. But his most immediate problem, the problem that brought him to Piedmont Courts on this particular afternoon, was Louis Samuels.

Samuels, known as Big Lou, also sold cocaine in Piedmont Courts. He'd been established first, but Lou lacked Belton's ability to engender good will. At age twenty-six, Lou had been charged with more than thirty crimes, many of them violent—raping two women, assaulting six women, hitting a child, shooting a man in the hip. His reputation, coupled with his size—six feet, 250 pounds—made people reluctant to testify against him, which had allowed him to avoid prison time.[15]

In the beginning, Belton's business hadn't cut into Big Lou's sales. Belton had once even helped Lou when he was broke, giving him free product so he could get himself back on his feet. But as Belton's fortunes rose, so had Big Lou's hostility. He'd had trouble with Lou the previous night, the Friday after Thanksgiving. They had argued, a police officer stepped in to break it up, Lou mouthed off and got arrested. Later, Belton was inside a Piedmont Courts apartment when three of Lou's men, angry about their boss's arrest, approached. One shot into the ground. Belton emerged, furious, and fired his .45. The Cadillac took a few bullets in the door. Police arrived again. Everyone scattered.

Afterward, Belton had headed to the Ranch, a rental townhouse where he counted money, bagged drugs, and entertained women. He was exhausted, not only from his skirmish, but from surgery earlier in the week to remove a fatty tumor below his left hip. It had been benign but sizable enough that he needed stitches. His doctor had instructed him to take it easy. So while a few guys smoked pot and drank beer downstairs, he and one of his girlfriends had retreated upstairs, which he'd designated smoke- and drug-free. He'd been lying down, carefully, on his side, when his pager roused him. It was a message from Carolyn, one of several Piedmont Courts residents who looked out for him. When he telephoned her, she sounded frantic. She told him Lou was shooting his mouth off, saying Money Rock's going to die tomorrow. She pleaded with him to stay away.

"I've never run from anybody," he told Carolyn. In this matchup, he saw himself as the good guy, generous and smart to Lou's mean and crazy. If he prevailed, he could finally conduct business without interference. He would be doing the community a favor. Maybe he'd be a hero. "I'll be there," he said.

He hung up and hatched a strategy. It was the boldest plan he'd ever conceived. It was also the dumbest.

The next morning, Saturday, November 30, Belton briefed his men before they passed Piedmont Courts' broken-down playground. He walked a few hundred yards, past clotheslines and garbage dumpsters, toward Hollywood Boulevard. His big brother, Al Platt, followed, as did his friends—William Hamilton, known as December, and Gerald Bernard Davis, known as Toot. His top salesman, Bernard Torrence, would meet up with them. The men were loyal to Belton and irate about Lou. All were in their twenties, but Belton, their leader, was youngest. Under his poncho, he wore a navy Adidas tracksuit and a necklace befitting his stature. It had a diamond-studded crown hanging from its gold rope chain.

A dealer with colder blood might have dispatched Big Lou with a shot to the head. That wasn't Belton's style. His .45 was always with him, even under his pillow while he slept, but only for protection. The idea wasn't to kill Lou, but to surprise him, confront him, and set him straight. Belton hadn't worked out exactly how he'd manage that. Mostly, he was focusing on the element of surprise, which was why he'd instructed his friend Mitch to drive the Cadillac into Piedmont Courts. Big Lou would assume Belton was driving. While Lou was distracted, Belton would sneak up on him.

That part of the plan actually worked. Just as Belton had figured, Big Lou was hanging out on Hollywood Boulevard with his men when Mitch drove up in Belton's car. Al, December, Toot, and Bernard had stationed themselves inside or beside a couple of nearby apartments, readying their weapons and awaiting further instructions. Belton approached Lou from behind, closing in, silent until he was a few yards away.

"What's up," he called to Lou. "You all looking for me?"

2

SHOWDOWN

Belton saw his miscalculation as soon as the words were out of his mouth. Big Lou held two pistols—a .357 Magnum in one hand, a .44 in the other. Belton, intent on surprising Lou, had made his own weapon inaccessible by holstering it at his shoulder, under his track-suit jacket and the rain poncho that had seemed such a good idea a few minutes earlier. His only move was to appeal to Lou's sense of honor: "Put down the guns and fight like a man."

Lou didn't buy it. They argued, and Belton decided not to risk in-citing an armed man. He ducked into a nearby apartment, knowing he'd be welcomed because he regularly gave money to the woman who lived there. He pulled off his poncho when he heard shouting out-side and ran to investigate. There was Gordon, his younger brother, standing like a statue on Hollywood Boulevard while one of Lou's men, Charles Locke, held him at gunpoint. Gordon had been visiting his girlfriend in Piedmont Courts when someone tipped him off that Money Rock and Big Lou were fighting. He hurried to find his big brother and instead encountered Locke, who stepped into his path, ordered him to halt, and fired near his feet.

Belton took cover behind a dumpster, unzipped his jacket, and reached for his gun. "Locke," he said, "if you shoot my brother, you're going to have to kill me."

Before Belton could draw, Lou reappeared and ordered Locke to hand over the .357. Even in Piedmont Courts, you weren't supposed to gun down someone for no good reason, and Lou's beef was with Money Rock, not his brother.

The arrival of Lou Samuels rarely defused a tense situation, but this time it did. This time, after Charles Locke headed off, Belton decided he'd had enough close calls for one day. He'd shown Lou that he couldn't be pushed around. He grabbed Gordon by the hand and pulled him toward the Cadillac.

It appeared that the beef was over. But Big Lou strode up to Belton, unarmed, as Belton had first requested. Now me and you can fight, he announced. With that, he landed a right to Belton's jaw, stunning him with both the blow and the disrespect. *I can't believe that nigga hit me*, Belton thought. He swung back.

As Belton and Lou flung fists and insults, Belton's men remained close, on the street or inside apartments, minding Belton's instructions not to act without his okay. Residents, meanwhile, pushed open screen doors and stepped onto porches. Money Rock and Big Lou were fighting. This was something to see.

Going nose to nose with Big Lou wasn't what Belton had imagined when he began selling cocaine. The goal—his only goal—had been to get rich. With new income, he'd remade his image. It was the early '80s. He bought tracksuits, Nike tennis shoes, and Kangol bucket hats. He owned a fine black leather jacket and dropped thousands at a west Charlotte jewelry store on custom-made diamond rings and gold jewelry designed to his specifications. For his wife, who'd been mopping floors since she was a teenager, he paid $10,000 for a fox and mink jacket that tickled her neck and made her look like a movie star. Gone was the Afro he'd worn in high school, replaced by a fade—a little on the top, close on the sides. This was the style of anyone who had style, the fashion of Run DMC and L.L. Cool J, hip-hop artists who drew inspiration from dealers who in turn modeled themselves after the artists. Belton adopted the look because he liked it, unaware he was donning what would become the dealer's uniform, a style that would be popularized in action movies and even comedy skits. In 1991, when Wesley Snipes played ruthless yet misunderstood Nino Brown in *New Jack City*, some of the film's wardrobe choices were right out of Belton's 1980s closet.

Belton's high-dollar image had spawned his nickname. As a teenager, he'd DJed at a local skating rink, where a friend dubbed him "Monty Rock," a play on Lamont, his middle name. Now, his friend changed a single letter, and he had a name to match his financial status. Monty Rock became Money Rock.

He also had loyal comrades. He and Bernard Torrence had forged a boyhood friendship on their neighborhood blacktop basketball court. Bernard admired Belton's jump shot and envied his family situation. Bernard's mother worked long shifts as a cook at Barclays Cafeteria in southeast Charlotte, the white upper-middle-class part of town; he seldom saw his father, who lived in Philadelphia. Belton, on the other hand, had a mom who baked chocolate-chip cookies and a stepdad she'd married when Belton was eight. "It gave you a sense of familyhood," Bernard told me decades later.

Bernard was two years older than Belton. He'd been newly discharged from the army after a stint in Korea when Belton pulled up one day in a two-tone Cadillac, wondering if Bernard was looking for work. Bernard recalled that he didn't hesitate. "Somebody going to be selling drugs. Why not us?"

They had many close calls. Once, heading to a housing project called Fairview Homes with Bernard in the passenger's seat, Belton spotted a police cruiser in his rearview mirror. Charlotte officers sometimes tailed Money Rock, but rarely pulled him over, perhaps figuring he wouldn't carry cocaine on him. Usually, they were right. But on this day, a thorough search would have yielded a windfall, thousands of dollars' worth of bagged product hidden in Bernard's underwear. As Belton pulled into the housing complex, Bernard threw open the car door and sprinted away. Belton rolled down his window and told the officer he had no idea why his passenger had fled. He'd simply been giving a stranger a ride.

In 2013, Bernard, fifty-two years old, with a shaved head and deep rumble of a voice, told this story with a chuckle. It had been decades since he carried cocaine in his pants or slept on Belton's couch with a cocked .357 Magnum beside his head. Over lunch at Wendy's, he recalled how Belton bought him and other employees clothing, cars— whatever they wanted. Cocaine was a blessing, he said, because it allowed him to give his mom $500 a week. As Bernard described his late mother's life—the low-paying jobs, the no-account boyfriends who smacked her around—he wiped a tear from his cheek with a paper napkin. Belton was the best boss he'd ever had, he told me. "Even though selling drugs is wrong, it was a true blessing to hang out with somebody like that."

In those first couple of years, Belton also found cocaine a blessing. He was breaking laws, sure, but they were white people's laws, and white people hadn't done anything for him. If he stopped selling, junkies would get coke somewhere else. Above all, he told himself, he was helping his community. He paid rents and grocery bills. He pulled out a wad of cash at a backyard fish fry and treated the whole crowd. And he bought dozens of pairs of shoes for kids in Piedmont Courts, because Belton remembered what it felt like to be the kid with the cheap sneakers. In 2012, a man named Tony who'd grown up there told me he still remembered his red Converse high-tops from Money Rock.

No one can say exactly how long Belton and Lou fought on that Saturday in 1985, but it was long enough to draw a crowd. One teenager would recall hearing the two arguing about "who had the most stuff— money, cars, whatever else."[1] Another man heard Lou calling Belton a snitch, followed by Belton's retort: "I don't have to snitch because they know what you do."[2]

Belton's confidence grew with each punch he threw. Lou was massive and intimidating, but also slow. Belton, on the other hand, had taken a free public housing martial arts class as a kid and had honed his fighting skills whenever his temper flared. Soon, he was laughing and playing to his audience, landing a blow, then an insult. "You all afraid of him? He's a big coward."

Most people blamed Charles Locke for what happened next. Lou had grabbed Belton, and Belton's man, December, had stepped in to break up the fight. He'd pushed himself between them and commanded Lou to let go. Locke, once again wielding a .357, raised the weapon, aimed, and fired, so close he couldn't miss. The bullet ripped through December's thigh.

That shot was the signal Belton's men had been waiting for. Bullets flew from multiple directions. Bystanders who'd been enjoying the spectacle sprinted for their lives and dove behind cars. Belton took cover behind his Cadillac, drew his .45 automatic, rose enough to see Big Lou, and emptied his gun. The shooting continued, popping and echoing off the buildings that lined Hollywood Boulevard. Inside apartments, mothers dialed 911 and ordered children away from doors and windows. The battle may have lasted thirty seconds or five minutes, but afterward, people said it felt like a lifetime. As the gunfire ebbed, there were screams and cries for help. Belton executed a barrel roll over the hood of his car, ran to December, grabbed him under his arms, and dragged his wounded friend behind the Cadillac. For a moment, he worried that he'd popped his surgery stitches. Big Lou, who'd been lying in the street, heaved himself upright and ran into an apartment.

A few blocks away, Nancy Webb was starting the three-to-midnight shift at the *Charlotte Observer*. Webb, twenty-six, was the newspaper's junior police reporter, relegated to nights and weekends. She had just parked the Ford Taurus staff car across the street from the station, where she planned to check with the duty captain and thumb through reports. But then a call came over the car's police scanner: shots fired at Piedmont Courts. Webb knew that shots often got fired at Piedmont Courts, considered the city's most dangerous public housing project. This time, however, the urgency in the dispatcher's voice told her she needed to move.

She pulled from the lot, drove to the project less than a mile away, and parked on Seigle Avenue. As she looked toward the dense layout of apartments, she heard panicky shouting. She saw people running and spotted one man crouched behind a car. What she didn't see were cops. She'd been so near the crime scene that she'd beaten most police, maybe all of them.

A moment later, sirens wailed. Squad cars, fire trucks, and ambulances pulled into the complex, clogging narrow streets that weren't built to handle large vehicles. Webb grabbed her reporter's notebook and began looking for anyone who'd talk. Gradually, she gleaned tidbits about drug dealers and gang involvement and pieced together a sketchy narrative. She returned to the office and banged out 775 words with the most detailed lead she could write: "Seven persons were injured in a shooting spree that followed a fight Saturday at Piedmont Courts, a public housing project in Charlotte. The scuffle reportedly involved rival drug gangs, but police would not comment Saturday on the reason for the fight."[3]

Webb got her best quote from a Charlotte Fire Department captain: "Most of the people were in a panic . . . blood was everywhere and people were fallen. We had one victim inside of a car, and we had another victim, a female, she was hobbling around and she had been shot in the kneecap. We had another man who was walking down the alleyway. He had been shot four times. There were a bunch of bullet holes. There was a Cadillac that had, we counted eight bullets in the side—plus the windshield had been shot out."[4]

In coming days, the events of this afternoon would alert the city that it had a problem. The problem would be identified as cocaine. It could just as easily be viewed as entrepreneurship born of poverty.

3

CARRIE PLATT AND THE AMERICAN DREAM

Carrie Lee Johnson Platt went into labor on a hot, sticky day in September 1963. Charlotte's September weather was unpredictable—a hint of autumn one minute, midsummer humidity the next. The high hit eighty-six on this day, and people across the city marveled over new blooms on dogwoods, azaleas, and apple trees that shouldn't have been flowering until the spring.[1] Carrie sweated as she headed to Charlotte Memorial Hospital in the passenger's seat of her father's station wagon, but she felt grateful for a reliable dad with reliable transportation. Her husband, Alphonso Platt, didn't own a car, and she wouldn't have counted on him anyway. Carrie herself refused to get behind a wheel. Driving was one of the few things that frightened her.

This baby would be Carrie's third in five years, but the first born at Memorial. In 1959, she had delivered her oldest, Alphonso Jr., at an underresourced hospital for Charlotte's black citizens called Good Samaritan. In 1960, she had given birth to Donna at Mercy, the city's first white hospital to accept black patients, sharing a room with other laboring black women.[2]

Because she was African American, Carrie's choice of hospitals, like many decisions, had been dictated by racial segregation, a practice masterfully lampooned by Charlotte's Harry Golden, a writer known for fighting bigotry with humor. "The white and Negro stand at the same grocery and supermarket counters; deposit money at the same bank teller's window; pay phone and light bills to the same clerk; walk through the same dime and department stores, and stand at the same drugstore counters," he wrote in a 1958 piece he called the "Golden Vertical Negro Plan." His conclusion: A vertical Negro posed no problem for southern whites. Problems arose only when people sat down. Golden's solution? Integrate the schools by removing all chairs, adding taller desks, requiring everyone to stand.[3]

In 1963, if Charlotte Memorial's leaders had thought the Golden Vertical Negro Plan would have solved their dilemma, they might have given it a try. They faced growing protests from civil rights activists. But they also feared that if they integrated completely, they'd run off the insured white patrons who kept the institution solvent.[4] As a public hospital, Memorial, near downtown between two of the city's first suburbs, Dilworth and Myers Park, took in indigent whites and anyone suffering trauma injuries, including gunshot and stab wounds. Higher-class citizens tended to avoid the hospital, even when it was all white. Many preferred Presbyterian, a private hospital with a columned entrance that suggested a southern country club and a policy that excluded black people.[5] Carrie had always suspected Presbyterian would shoo her away if she got too close.

When Carrie chose Memorial, it remained in a semi-integrated limbo, accepting some black patients, but keeping them mostly segregated from whites. But it had integrated its maternity department to comply with a directive from the U.S. Department of Health, Education, and Welfare.[6] Carrie, who favored both integration and competent care, assumed Memorial would be a good place, if only because it was still basically a hospital for white people.

At twenty-seven, Carrie had known segregation all her life, yet she refused to know her place. Barely five-foot-two, she stood out in almost any crowd, puffing on a Benson & Hedges, delivering opinions with a forceful certainty. "Getting on people's nerves, both black and white," as she liked to say. She had attended meetings of the National Association for the Advancement of Colored People, knocked on doors during President Kennedy's campaign, and marched for voting rights. She also had questioned Rev. Martin Luther King Jr.'s insistence on nonviolence, given the Ku Klux Klan's history of stringing up black people. "I thought he was crazy—with everything being done to black folks," she recalled decades later. When he announced plans to speak in Charlotte, "I thought, 'I got to see this nut.' I know that sounds sort of bad."

She did see King in Charlotte, and though she didn't remember details a half century later, she most likely heard his speech to North Carolina NAACP branches on September 25, 1960. That talk, titled "The Negro and the American Dream," foreshadowed his 1963 "I Have a Dream" speech, describing a future in which "men of all races, colors and creeds will live together as brothers." But in the Charlotte address, King included an ominous warning: "The price that America must pay for the continued oppression of the Negro is the price of its own destruction."[7]

Less than a month after King's "I Have a Dream" speech, Carrie arrived at Charlotte Memorial. In the delivery room, an injection sent her into twilight sleep, wiping out pain along with any memory of the birth, which occurred about sunrise, 6:45 a.m., on September 10.

He was a healthy boy, light skinned with a head of dark hair. She intended to name him Lamont. She had read that it meant strong and industrious, and she had a feeling it would fit this child. Her father, James Johnson, suggested that she also name the boy after her Uncle Belton, who'd given Carrie her first bed and tricycle. They settled on the name Belton Lamont, but agreed he'd be called by his middle name. On the birth certificate, she directed the nurse to write it like a French word: *Lá mont*. In time, the boy would drop the accent, the space, and, many years later, the name itself.

Carrie was smitten with her new son, but the timing of this pregnancy could hardly have been worse. It had thwarted any thoughts she had of leaving Alphonso, who had physically abused her since before their marriage. It also had sidelined Carrie during the most exciting political year of her life. Stuck at home, pregnant and caring for two toddlers, what Carrie had wanted was to march on Washington and to join activists making civil rights history in Charlotte. In May, while she was pregnant with Belton, her friend Dr. Reginald Hawkins had led a downtown protest of local hotels, theaters, and so-called white-tablecloth restaurants that barred African Americans. Hawkins, branded by whites as a militant, had been organizing protests since the Supreme Court shot down the notion of "separate but equal" in its 1954 *Brown v. Board of Education* decision. "Any day might be D-Day," Hawkins warned, standing outside Charlotte's courthouse. "They can either make this an open and democratic city or there is going to be a long siege. They can choose which way it's going to be."[8]

Carrie loved how Hawkins stood up to power, never flinching when whites condemned him as a radical who refused to work within the system. The spectacle of Birmingham turning police dogs and fire hoses onto unarmed protesters was fresh in the minds of Charlotte leaders when Hawkins led that May 20 protest. Mere days after his warning—*any day could be D-Day*—dominoes of change fell one upon another. Charlotte's chamber of commerce asked businesses to voluntarily open their doors "to all customers without regard to race, creed, or color." The Charlotte City Council ordered the city codes stricken of any references to segregation. Then, at the suggestion of a young, white restaurateur, the city turned the sit-in tradition on its head: White leaders and black professionals paired up to lunch together at local eateries. On May 29, the mayor announced that they'd continue lunching in coming days in top dining rooms across town.[9] It was a clever solution, having the restaurants integrate together. Just like Charlotte Memorial, none had wanted to integrate alone for fear of losing white clientele.

Charlotte's actions won favorable mentions in the *New York Times* and helped cement its reputation as a progressive city in the South's most progressive state.[10] Even Rev. King had been impressed. When he visited at the end of May 1963 to speak to graduates of black high schools, he spent the night in the newly integrated Manger Motor Inn and praised Charlotte's progress as "very significant and meaningful."[11]

This is not to say, however, that Charlotte's white and black citizens had become one happy family. Schools and neighborhoods remained almost entirely segregated, and racial animosity simmered below the surface. The week of Belton's birth, a *Charlotte News* poll found that local support for civil rights legislation proposed by President Kennedy was running about 70 percent against. Maybe the polling was faulty, but that 70 percent opposition equaled the percentage of white people in Charlotte.[12]

Yet Charlotte's passion for growth pushed integration forward. The population had jumped by 50 percent from 1950 to 1960, to just over 200,000, and city leaders sought to maintain momentum, to attract new business, new industry. The last thing they wanted was bad publicity. Belton was born as the chamber of commerce prepared to launch an advertising campaign ("Charlotte, the Action City") in the *Wall Street Journal*. "We must show Charlotte as a smart, modern, dynamic and moving city," a businessman heading the campaign told colleagues. The campaign would show illustrations of the city's "many modern facilities," a *Charlotte News* story explained, such as the public library, YMCA, Charlotte Coliseum—and Charlotte Memorial Hospital.[13]

The hospital had pledged to treat more African Americans as soon as it finished building a new wing with an entire floor reserved for blacks.[14] But that wasn't enough for Hawkins, who had charged that Memorial was breaking nondiscrimination rules required by the federal Hill-Burton Act, through which the hospital had received millions for new construction. In August 1963, officials with the U.S. Public Health Service had visited the hospital's board of managers to discuss Hawkins's charges.[15]

A month later, just hours after Belton's birth on the maternity floor, the Charlotte Memorial Board of Managers met in the staff dining room. Board members discussed a state sales tax refund, noted a trend of increased emergency-room visits, and agreed to raise the price of

anesthesia from $15 to $17.50. Then they moved to a piece of business that would change their history. The U.S. Public Health Service
had been unequivocal. Charlotte Memorial could no longer limit the
number of black patients it accepted. It also couldn't keep them segregated, not if the hospital wanted federal building funds.

One white man made a motion. Another white man seconded it.

"Now, therefore be it resolved, the Board of Managers, Charlotte
Memorial Hospital at its regular meeting on September 10, 1963 does
by unanimous vote adopt the policy that the same admission policies
of the hospital shall apply to persons of all races and that the total
facilities and services of Charlotte Memorial Hospital will be available
to all persons of all races on the same basis."[16]

As Carrie enjoyed her soft pillow and crisp white sheets, she had
no idea that racial discrimination was being outlawed a few floors
below her. Every few hours, a white nurse wearing a little white cap
tucked a thermometer under Carrie's tongue and lay fingers on her
wrist, counting her heartbeats. Another would arrive with a swaddled
Belton and a bottle of warmed formula. Carrie's half-hearted breast-
feeding attempt hadn't lasted much longer than it took to say *Hand me
that bottle*. As a modern woman, she believed formula was fine. That's
what she'd given Al and Donna, and they'd been the healthiest babies
in the world.

She never learned about the board's resolution during or after her
stay. News of the action didn't appear in the next day's newspapers,
and maybe that was intentional. Just as hospital officials had feared, as
they admitted more black patients, it became harder to attract paying
white patients. Presbyterian, which didn't integrate until 1965, became
the hospital of choice for white people with money.[17]

But perhaps local newspapers overlooked the hospital's decision
that week because other news was grabbing headlines. In Alabama,
hundreds of shouting, Confederate flag–waving white students were
boycotting newly integrated public school classrooms.[18] In Louisburg,
North Carolina, black students boycotted segregated classrooms.[19]
The University of South Carolina enrolled its first three black students

since Reconstruction and reporters described the event as peaceful.[20] Then came the biggest headline, five days after Belton's birth: four black girls, dead, in a Birmingham church bombing.

Belton's first home was an orange-brick rental that could have been designed by a child with a crayon—seven hundred square feet with a triangle of a roof and single windows to the left and right of the front door. Built in 1962, the house and two identical homes flanking it on Cummings Avenue represented the downscale segment of a construction boom that was throwing up new neighborhoods around Charlotte—ranches, split-levels, and tri-levels that advertised fireplaces and paneled family rooms, plus intangibles such as "incomparable charm" and "the grace of antebellum days."

Much of this construction was on the city's east and south sides, both white parts of town. Those Cummings Avenue rentals were in the town's northwest section, off Beatties Ford Road. Northwest Charlotte's destiny as the black part of town had been set in the nineteenth century, when a college for freed slaves that would become Johnson C. Smith University established its campus there. Northwest Charlotte had been one of the few areas where new housing hadn't come with deeds specifying that the property be owned and occupied only "by members of the Caucasian race, domestic servants in the employ of the occupants excepted."[21] Even after the U.S. Supreme Court ruled race covenants unenforceable in 1948, color lines persisted. In the early 1960s, everyone knew that if you were black and wanted new housing, you moved to the northwest part of town.

Though the Platts' house was short on both charm and antebellum grace, Carrie's knack for finding attic sale bargains—a perfectly good lamp or almost-new table linen—gave it a homey atmosphere. Her father's generosity helped her buy some big-ticket items—a washer and dryer, a stereo, and her favorite living-room chair, upholstered in white leather with mahogany arms and legs. Belton slept in a bassinette in his parents' bedroom; his siblings, Donna and Al, shared the second bedroom. To an outsider, the house at 1902 Cummings

Avenue was a peaceful tableau of working-class domesticity. But appearances deceived. By the time Belton was born, Carrie saw her marriage more as hostage situation than blessed union.

She and Alphonso Platt had wed, against her parents' wishes, in a quick civil ceremony in 1956. She had just turned twenty, and was, by her own description, a "hot-in-the-pants fast-ass girl," so eager to walk on the wild side that she settled for a man who would nearly kill her.

More than a half century later, Carrie understood why abused women stayed in bad relationships, but she still found it difficult to describe why she'd married an abuser in the first place. Her family had been full of take-charge women; she wasn't repeating a cycle of family violence. As far as she could see, the only explanation was destiny: "The only thing I can understand about why I run away and marry that man is because I was supposed to have five kids."

Carrie had grown up just south of downtown in Cherry, a black neighborhood carved out of a cotton farm that had been tended by slaves and named for cherry trees that blossomed on a hillside. When she was born in 1936, it was a neighborhood of modest cottages populated by maids and gardeners and nannies, black people who spent their working lives serving white families. Many of those whites lived nearby, in gracious mansions along the tree-lined boulevards of Myers Park, a neighborhood where black hired help—a man and a cook, at least—was considered a necessity.[22]

Many of her peers would have envied her childhood. On winter mornings, she lay under the quilt her mother had sewn, waking to smells of sausage, biscuits, eggs, and grits. Her father, who loved cooking, rose before dawn to make breakfast for his wife and five children, then headed to work in his black chauffeur uniform and cap. His boss, a state legislator who owned a construction company, called him Shorty. He called his boss Mr. Blythe. But James Johnson, with just a second-grade education, wasn't afraid to speak his mind to white people. Years later, Carrie remembered her father's reaction the one time the landlord, looking for rent money, entered the house uninvited. Landlords often did that, walking right into black people's houses. "They made folks feel inferior," she said. "They held the key to a person having a place to live or being out in the street." But James Johnson wouldn't have it. He picked up a kitchen chair, confronted the man, and warned him never to do that again.

Outside her home, however, Carrie couldn't escape limitations her city imposed because of skin color. Race governed the type of work people did, the relationships they had, even the places they could go. This realization came gradually, puzzled together as she observed interactions of whites and blacks and listened to her parents at the kitchen table. It crystallized when older cousins visiting from South Carolina headed one Saturday to the air-conditioned Visulite Theater in Elizabeth, a white neighborhood.

"Can I go along?" Carrie asked.

No, her cousins told her. She wasn't white.

They weren't white either, but there had been a white great-grandfather on her mother's side, according to family stories. In 1920, the U.S. Census had identified both her grandfather and mother as "mulatto," or mixed race. Her cousins had gotten enough of that light pigment to pass. Carrie hadn't.

Carrie's ancestors had come from slavery, and they included share-croppers who'd moved north to Charlotte in the early twentieth century from rural Lancaster County, South Carolina, an alternative to the Great Migration that saw millions of African Americans leaving the South for points north and west.

Her mother had a gentle temperament, but Carrie took after her sharp-tongued father, and by her teen years, in the early 1950s, she was often outraged at anything she saw as hypocritical, confining, or simply racist. She loathed her straightened hair, for instance, which her mother would force into a white-girl ponytail with the help of a hot iron and Royal Crown Hair Pomade. She hated hearing her father saying *yes, sir* and *no, sir* to younger white men who didn't give him the same courtesy. She even hated her middle name, Lee, which re-minded her of the general who fought for slavery. When a white girl called her *nigger* one day, she went after her with scissors and snipped a chunk of her blond hair. And when a drugstore waitress ordered her little brother out of a booth, where he had perched while waiting for hot dog takeout orders, she had an instant retort: "If you can take our money, then he can sit in that booth."

Carrie also chafed at her parents' rules. She snuck Lucky Strike cigarettes, flirted with boys, and climbed from her bedroom window at night to meet a young man, buying her sisters' silence by letting them listen to her prized radio, tuned to rhythm and blues on Nashville's WLAC.

"Don't tell Mama and Daddy I went out," she would instruct them. "And don't lock the window."

Carrie dropped out of eleventh grade and left home at seventeen, unable to abide her parents' rules any longer. She didn't run far, just across town to the Greenville neighborhood, where she moved in with her friend Joan. Now, finally, she felt like an adult, unconcerned with curfews or an overprotective daddy who tended to show up in his station wagon while she was making time with a boy. She was standing on Joan's front porch the day Alphonso Platt called out from his mother's back stoop.

Hey, what's your name?

"Who, me?" Carrie asked.

He was handsome—six feet tall, wearing a white T-shirt that showed off muscular arms. When they began going out, Carrie enjoyed having such a sharp escort, with his neat trousers, sport coat, and two-toned shoes. She was less enamored of the dates themselves, often spent at liquor houses, where she sat through long evenings, watching as he pulled a wad of money from his pocket, peeling off one bill for a bourbon and another for a poker game, drinking and gambling until the sun rose.

Liquor houses flourished in certain parts of black Charlotte, private homes serving up fried chicken and fish and providing havens for gambling and illegal liquor sales, along with shootings and knife fights that sometimes followed drunken arguments. Police raids were common, and that's how Carrie found herself cowering behind a door one night as officers shoved their way in, searching unsuccessfully for evidence of gambling. Carrie came to hate liquor houses. They brought out the worst in Alphonso—his propensity to gamble like an addict, and, even worse, to get "pissy drunk," as she called it, swaying and cussing and eventually taking his rage out on her with his fists. Often, he went for her face, blacking her eye, busting her lip, accusing her of fooling around with any man who happened to speak to her.

Afterward, however, he told her that he loved her and promised it wouldn't happen again. Then he bought her a gift, a nice pair of sunglasses to cover her swollen eyes. She figured a man wouldn't hit you if he didn't care about you. And surely, he would change. She moved in with him and his mother.

Alphonso had grown up in Charlotte, left school after ninth grade, married a woman named Mildred at age nineteen, and had a daughter six months later. They hadn't been married three years before Mildred divorced him, but they had two more daughters after the breakup, including one born the day after he married Carrie.

Like Carrie's chauffeur father, Alphonso worked in service of white men. In the morning, after Carrie fed him breakfast, he took a bus across town to the Modern Barber Shop in Park Road Shopping Center. There, from his shoeshine chair in the front of the shop, he donned a blue apron and attended to businessmen and city leaders, applying the polish, pulling his brush across the shoe, buffing the leather until it shone. Alphonso excelled at the craft, because he realized it was about more than rubbing Kiwi into leather. A good shoeshine man knew how to laugh at his customers' jokes and acknowledge the astuteness of their political observations. He also knew when to keep quiet. Generous tips made it a decent living, but with his gambling and drinking, Carrie never saw much money.

Carrie had grown up in a family that paid bills on time, shared with neighbors in need, and enjoyed occasional splurges, like prime cuts of meat her father bought when he chauffeured his boss to Reid's, a Myers Park grocery. She'd left home in search of a different life, and she got her wish, but it was a life of late-rent notices, welfare checks, and visits to the charity food pantry.

She came to dread Fridays, when Alphonso started drinking. Her parents often took her children for weekend visits, so she was alone Friday nights when Alphonso showed up, stinking of booze and ready to pick a fight. Jekyll and Hyde, she called him, charming sober, a monster drunk. Carrie tried various defenses—cowering, hitting back, pleading. Her preferred strategy was to hightail it to a neighbor's house. By the time she gave birth to Alphonso Jr. in 1959, she'd had four miscarriages, which she blamed on her husband's beatings. She thought Al's birth might soften his father. She continued hoping when Donna was born. By the time Belton came along, her hope was gone.

Carrie never understood the source of her husband's anger. Perhaps he felt inferior to his sharp-witted wife, or he inherited his temper from his father, who'd left his family when Alphonso was young. Perhaps he aimed his rage at Carrie because he didn't dare direct it at white people. She hung on, believing in *for better or for worse*, for one thing, and also suspecting her husband might kill her if she tried to leave. She wore long sleeves to hide bruises, or she stayed home, avoiding her parents. Her efforts didn't fool her father. He called Alphonso *that no-good asshole SOB*.

In 1964, fifteen months after Belton was born, Carrie had her fourth child, Gordon Ivan Platt. Gordon was barely sleeping through the night when Carrie realized she was pregnant again. She couldn't believe it. The Pill had hit the market in 1960, but Carrie was clueless about contraception. The women she knew didn't plan their families. In Carrie's world, women discovered pregnancies, like you discover your wallet has been stolen or your front left tire has gone completely flat. Once the situation presented itself, there was nothing to do but deal with it.

Carrie hated this new pregnancy so much she contemplated getting rid of it. She knew one girl who'd gotten an illegal abortion, and she'd heard you could coax your body into aborting by drinking quinine. Or you could use a clothes hanger, but you had to be ready to go to the emergency room if you bled a lot. Carrie didn't know where to get quinine, and anyway, she was scared. In the end, she was too scared.

It was a Sunday afternoon in 1965 during that pregnancy when she finally snapped. The four children were with their grandparents. She'd been preparing for the week, washing dishes and cleaning out the refrigerator, figuring her father would be bringing groceries, as he often did, when he returned with the children. She was folding the laundry when her drunken husband arrived and headed to their bedroom, where he turned on the TV, deposited himself on the bed, and yelled for her to fix him something to eat.

She usually obliged. But this afternoon, something came over her, something akin to the ferocity that once prompted her to snip a white girl's blond hair. *I ain't gonna fix you nothing*, she thought.

She spooned beef stew into a bowl, carried it through the living room, and arrived at the bedroom door.

"Here you go," she said, and winged the stew bowl at him.

He sprang up, lunging toward her: I'm gonna kill you!

That's when Carrie, five-foot-two, pregnant, maybe 135 pounds, lifted the white leather chair—the nice one with mahogany arms—flung it, and knocked the hell out of him. Alphonso toppled.

She fled to the neighbors' house around the corner, where she called her father. Except for one quick visit to collect the children's clothes, she never returned to 1902 Cummings Avenue.

Carla Adair Platt arrived on Thanksgiving Day 1965, several weeks early. In Charlotte Memorial, Carrie dined on turkey and fixings, courtesy of her parents, and stashed an empty Pepsi-Cola bottle at her bedside for protection, in case Alphonso decided to visit.

Early in the new year, she returned to the hospital for a hysterectomy after setting straight a doctor—"This is *my* body"—who initially insisted she needed her husband's consent. There would be no more babies, and the marriage should have ended, but it didn't. Carrie and the children moved a couple blocks from her parents to a rental at 338 Cherry Street, a white house that seemed dark inside, even with open blinds. It wasn't long before she took Alphonso back.

For a while, his behavior was better, perhaps because he knew his father-in-law, now just around the corner, owned a shotgun and would use it. Carrie got a waitress job downtown at the restaurant in the Charlotte Union Bus Terminal. She loved meeting the colorful clientele, which included the first man she understood to be gay, a handsome white fellow who complimented her bright pink earrings, then confided he wouldn't mind borrowing them.

Belton and his siblings often spent time with their grandparents, and on Sundays, Carrie took them to St. Paul Baptist, the church she had attended with her family as a child. She also taught all her children to cook, and by age eight, Donna could fry a chicken. Donna was the oldest girl, ever the responsible one, taking on the role of a second mother.

Belton, on the other hand, was the sickly child, allergic to almost everything—grass, chocolate, strawberries, seafood—and prone to asthma attacks that landed him in the emergency room. He also had a speech impediment—not just a lisp or trouble saying his Rs, but broader difficulties that made him hard for people to understand. Speech therapy eventually cured him, but in his early years, he didn't talk much, especially not to strangers. His asthma often kept him home from school and forced him to watch from a window while siblings played. And yet Belton delighted his mother with his antics. When President Lyndon Johnson's War on Poverty brought the Head Start preschool program to Charlotte, Carrie enrolled him and began volunteering. One day, as a visiting school supply salesman extolled the virtues of a line of indestructible crayons, he handed one to Belton. *Snap* went the crayon.

Carrie also immersed herself in local politics, taking on the vice presidency of the Cherry Community Organization and serving on the board of the nonprofit that administered Head Start and other anti-poverty programs. More black leaders were moving into professional and political roles in Charlotte. In 1965, Frederick Douglas Alexander, the son of a funeral home owner, became the first black man elected to Charlotte's city council in the twentieth century. Alexander succeeded in removing one of Charlotte's most ludicrous examples of segregation—a fence that separated dead white people from dead black people in the city's Elmwood and Pinewood cemeteries.[23]

But many activists, including Carrie, wanted to challenge the status quo in bigger ways, to break the lock that white businessmen had on the city's power structure by replacing at-large elections with district representation. As city council elections approached in spring 1969, five candidates from a new group called the Black Political Organization placed their names alongside Alexander's on the ballot. Carrie Lee Platt was one of them.

Carrie had no campaign funds—none of the BPO candidates did. But she eagerly attended political forums and even crashed her opponents' fancy campaign breakfasts, offering her spiel to anyone who would listen. By then, she'd adopted a Black Power look that included an Angela Davis–style Afro and African-print dresses.

Alphonso disapproved of his wife's political career, as he did most any activity that took her out of the house. Carrie suspected he felt threatened by her new friends, a better class of people who weren't part of the world Alphonso knew. Sometimes she grabbed her jacket and purse and sprinted out the door to a friend's waiting car. She knew she'd face Alphonso's wrath when she returned. She didn't care.

The week before the election, the *Charlotte News* published a photo of Carrie along with a short profile. In the photo, her eyes were downcast, and even with her Afro and hoop earrings, she looked more like a demure mother than a radical. But her message was bold. A proposal to consolidate city-county government was "a racist trick to keep inner-city residents bottled up and powerless," she declared. "If Charlotte and the county are consolidated, Charlotte will be a poor, black city run by white county suburbanites." She continued: "The city government must function for the people, poor as well as rich. Black submission is dead. Black people in Charlotte are now ready to govern themselves."[24]

She lost, coming in eighteenth out of twenty candidates in the primary. Fred Alexander was reelected, but no Black Political

Organization member placed high enough to make the general election. That didn't bother Carrie. As she saw it, she and the BPO paved the way for more black candidates. They proved that black politicians didn't have to be middle-class bourgeoisie to run for office.

As Carrie's public profile rose, Alphonso often disappeared for days or weeks at a time, then reappeared, full of drunken accusations that she was cheating on him. She finally quit her waitress job after he repeatedly showed up intoxicated and belligerent at the restaurant.

He was no better with his children. He gave Gordon a gun and laughed when he shot up his bedroom, and when Belton whined for a gumball in the drugstore, he slapped the child across the face. One day when Carrie was gone, he slapped Donna with a force that snapped her head back. Fearing he would strike three-year-old Carla next, Donna grabbed her little sister's hand and pulled her outside. Alphonso chased them down the sidewalk, but was so impaired he couldn't keep up.

Carrie found that anything could set off Alphonso Platt, even the color of his sons' skin. Donna and Belton had been light as infants, their skin gradually darkening to the same caramel color as Carrie's. But Alphonso complained that Al and Gordon had darker skin than he did, and one day, as they played with cowboy pistols in their room, he burst in and slung them both against the wall, ranting that they were little black bastards, too dark to be his children.

Carrie couldn't see a way out. It would be years before Charlotte opened a battered women's shelter or offered support groups, years before Carrie understood how abusive men controlled women by destroying their self-esteem. Unless a serious injury or murder was involved, domestic violence in the 1960s was a private family problem, not a criminal act. Judicial protective orders that required an abusive spouse to stay away wouldn't become part of North Carolina's statutes for another decade. A woman took a risk if she filed for divorce or swore out a warrant against a violent man. Even if she won a conviction, the sentence was more likely to be days or weeks than years.

Once, when Carrie sought help from a police officer, he propositioned her. Another advised her to give her husband what he wanted, which she took to mean sex. But by 1969, Carrie had begun reporting her beatings, even though Alphonso was never jailed for long. She knew she should get free of her husband because he could injure or kill any one of her children. His actions were damaging them psychologically, too, every time they witnessed him choking her with a belt or landing blows to her head while she staggered from living room to kitchen. Donna, who'd witnessed her dad stab her mom, included a plea in her nightly prayers to let her brothers and sister forget the bad things they'd seen. Every so often, Belton announced, to no one in particular, "When I get older, I'm gonna kill my daddy."

On June 13, 1969, a lovely late spring day, Carrie, wearing pedal pushers, was inside, struggling to plait Carla's hair, a skill she'd never quite mastered. Gordon and Belton were on the porch steps, when Belton, five years old, spotted his father walking up the street toward the house.

"Daddy's coming!" he called out.

"Shut up, boy," Carrie called back. "That's not your daddy."

Carrie figured it couldn't be him, because she'd sworn out a warrant after his latest attack and he'd been jailed. But when she joined her children on the porch, she realized her son was right. Alphonso was approaching. He looked drunk, and she knew he'd be furious.

Her first thought was to get the money in the house before he found it. She jumped up and ran to the bedroom for her purse. As Alphonso climbed the steps, Belton raised his arms to his dad. Alphonso stepped over him and opened the screen door. He headed to the kitchen, pulled at a drawer, and found a butcher knife.

Moments later, Carrie's panicky voice rose from inside the house.

"Stop. Stop it. I'll get the warrant lifted."

Belton ran toward his parents' bedroom and froze in the doorway. His father was on top of his mother on the bed, trying to pin her arms with his knees, stabbing at her as she shouted and struggled.

He aimed for her face, to fuck her up, he told her. When she tried to shield herself, he struck her arms and hands. He aimed lower, going for Carrie's belly.

I'm gonna kill you, he growled.

Carrie twisted, pushed at his arm, and kept pleading. She would go right down to the police station. She would tell them not to lock him up. He finally relented and released her. She slipped off the bed and headed toward the front door.

"Run," she yelled to her children.

She made it to a neighbor's house. Alphonso disappeared. Minutes later, an ambulance arrived. Belton was in the yard now, watching as emergency workers carried a stretcher into the neighbor's house, then reemerged with his mother, blood on her arms, a dark stain blossoming on her blouse, more blood than he had ever seen. The men slid the stretcher into the ambulance. The boy watched, sobbing, as they drove away.

4

CANDY KINGPIN

In the early 1970s, in the hall outside his Myers Park Elementary classroom, ten-year-old Belton handed out candy and collected coins—a Blow Pop for a dime, Now & Laters for a quarter. On good days, he sold out by the time the morning bell rang. He purchased his stock—five taffy packs at ten cents each, ten bubble gum–filled Blow Pops for a nickel each—from a rundown grocery near his Dalton Village apartment. He paid with the dollar he received from his parents, who didn't know he got a free school lunch, then he stowed the candy in his bedroom until it was time to board the school bus for the five-mile ride to Myers Park. For every dollar outlay, Belton earned $2.25. At day's end, his pants pockets jingled.

Among his classmates, Belton stood out for his candy business, and also because he was a black boy from the projects at an affluent, formerly all-white school. His presence at Myers Park Elementary was a quirk of history, the product of Charlotte's imperfect attempt to rectify centuries of racial discrimination. The legal challenge that prompted it had come in 1965, when a brilliant African American civil rights attorney named Julius Chambers filed a lawsuit, *Swann v. Charlotte-Mecklenburg Board of Education*, on behalf of ten black families. Chambers had arrived in Charlotte in 1964 to find a city with "blacks on one side of the track and whites on the other; blacks realizing they

Belton Platt, in an undated photo from his late elementary-school years. Courtesy of
Carrie Graves.

were not able to be employed as clerks, or tellers in banks, so they
didn't apply. People sort of accepted that situation in 1964."[1] Schools,
too, remained largely segregated, with nearly 90 percent of black students attending all-black schools in the mid-1960s. This was despite
the U.S. Supreme Court's 1954 *Brown v. Board of Education* ruling that
"separate but equal" schools were inherently unequal, and despite the
fact that Charlotte schools no longer had a formal segregation policy.
Schools were segregated because neighborhoods were.[2]

Swann changed everything. Chambers's central argument was
that the Supreme Court in *Brown* had called for governments to do
more than simply forbid segregation. Charlotte's black and white
neighborhoods hadn't formed by chance. Discriminatory govern-
mental policies—redlining, zoning ordinances, urban renewal—had

created them, so the government was obligated to employ new policies to end the segregation it had caused. In 1969, the white federal judge hearing the lawsuit agreed. James McMillan ordered the Charlotte-Mecklenburg school board to mix black and white students in all public schools. "Buses for many years were used to operate segregated schools," he wrote. "There is no reason except emotion (and I confess to having felt my own share of emotion on this subject in all the years before I studied the facts) why school buses can not be used by the Board to provide the flexibility and economy necessary to desegregate the schools."[3]

By the time Charlotte had implemented, revised, and re-revised its busing plan in the early 1970s, Chambers's home and office had been bombed, an anti-busing group called the Concerned Parents Association had gained tens of thousands of followers, and student fights had repeatedly closed high schools. In spite of all that, Charlotte crafted a system that, for a time, worked well. After the U.S. Supreme Court unanimously affirmed *Swann* in 1971, the decision reverberated beyond Charlotte, setting a national precedent. Charlotte became the nation's largest integrated school system. When Belton reached sixth grade in 1974, the city had actually begun taking pride in making busing work.

For Belton's candy business, busing meant booming sales. He never questioned why he was being bused to a neighborhood full of white people. But he knew he could count on a cadre of regular customers with ready pocket change, classmates such as Adam Gilbert, an affable kid with black-framed glasses and a fondness for Now & Laters. Adam became Belton's first white friend. Belton loved afternoons at Adam's house, an oak-shaded two-story Tudor across the street from the school. There, he played in a backyard fort on an expansive lawn and ate brand-name snacks in a well-stocked kitchen overseen by the hired help—two black women wearing uniforms of black dresses with white aprons. Belton learned that Adam's dad owned several dozen auto parts stores and that the Gilbert family traced its ancestry to Sir Walter Raleigh, the English explorer for whom the capital of North

Carrie Graves in 1975, speaking at a meeting of the Charlotte-Mecklenburg Commission on the Status of Women. Photo by Jim Wilson, courtesy of the *Charlotte Observer*.

Carolina was named. After school, Belton helped himself to cookies and milk and settled with Adam in a pine-paneled den to watch cartoons on a big color television. When dinnertime approached, Adam's mother drove Belton home in her station wagon.

It never occurred to Belton to envy the Gilbert family's wealth. Myers Park was another world, and he was just visiting. "I probably compared myself more to my peers in the projects," he said. "I was more focused on how blessed we were in the projects compared to others. In our own little world, we were like the rich people. We had a nice apartment with new furniture and when we needed stuff, we got it. We were one of the top families in Dalton Village."

The family had moved in 1970 from the Cherry neighborhood to Dalton Village, a new west side public housing project. Their apartment had four bedrooms and all-electric appliances. Most important, it didn't have Alphonso. Carrie's stabbing, which had required several dozen stitches, convinced her to leave him for good. Attorney James Ferguson II filed her divorce complaint. Ferguson, Julius Chambers's

Columbia University–educated law partner, was among the state's leading civil rights attorneys. He knew Carrie through her community activism, and though his civil rights firm normally didn't do divorces, it did hers for free. The complaint described Alphonso's "cruel and barbarous" treatment that included the stabbing, a threat to blow Carrie's brains out, and a beating delivered on Mother's Day. Alphonso didn't show up at the 1971 hearing, but the judge took one look at the medical records cataloguing Carrie's injuries and granted the divorce.

One frigid day the next winter, Carrie and a friend, Mary Ann, were waiting for a bus on West Boulevard when an eighteen-wheeler pulled up. Carrie's friend Marvin was in the back seat, having hitched a ride; when he spotted Carrie and Mary Ann, he'd urged the driver to pull over. While Mary Ann climbed in beside Marvin, Carrie, clutching a pack of panty hose she was planning to return to Woolworth's, perched on the lap of a handsome man in the passenger seat. Later, that man, Lonnie Graves, showed up at her apartment holding the hosiery she'd left behind.

"Did you give my panty hose to your woman?" she teased.

No, Lonnie told her. He didn't have a woman.

"Rainy Night in Georgia" was playing on the stereo. Belton's younger brother, Gordon, descended the stairs and looked Lonnie up and down. "You gonna be my daddy?" he asked.

Carrie and Lonnie married in July 1972. Lonnie, a janitor at the public library, was twenty, sixteen years younger than Carrie. Friends teased she was robbing the cradle. Her retort: "I didn't either. He walked in on his own."

Lonnie Graves was the most mature twenty-year-old Carrie had ever met. He'd grown up outside Pensacola, Florida, one of three boys fathered by three men they never knew. His mother was in and out of mental institutions, so his grandmother raised Lonnie and his brothers. She kept them in line with smacks to the head and relied on welfare checks and hand-me-downs from her house-cleaning customers to feed and clothe them. At fourteen, Lonnie was already working on a fishing boat.

Carrie never forgot her father's response when he learned she was becoming Mrs. Lonnie Graves. Pumping Lonnie's hand, James Johnson announced that he was happy to know the man taking on his five grandchildren. Lonnie must love those kids, he said. Either that, or he was crazy as hell.

Belton's asthma gradually improved. It had been so severe when they moved to Dalton Village that Carrie gave him his own room, where he slept to the hum of a humidifier on homemade hypoallergenic pillows stuffed with cedar shavings. On nights when he awoke gasping for breath, he sought his older sister's help. At least twice, they almost lost him. "He would come get me and say, 'You need to wake them up so they can take me to the hospital,'" Donna Brown recalled. Carrie figured Belton simply outgrew his affliction. But perhaps he also improved because life had a new structure and stability. Alphonso wasn't terrorizing the family anymore.

Lonnie, too, thrived in his new role. He joined the family for church services at St. Paul Baptist and Sunday dinners at his in-laws' house. At Christmas, he donned a red suit and white beard. On his birthday, he blew out candles at the first party he'd ever had. The Graveses might have been the only people in Dalton Village to hold educational movie nights. Lonnie would borrow black history films from the library and project them on the wall, while the kids watched cross-legged on the living-room floor. By the mid-1970s, he and a business partner had launched a janitorial service that cleaned offices and institutions.

Carrie, meanwhile, became an advocate for fellow tenants, always willing to alert the Charlotte Housing Authority when she spotted a problem. Dalton Village had many. By 1974, more than one thousand of its thirteen hundred residents were children and teenagers, and yet the development hadn't been designed with children in mind. Its thirty-five-mile-per-hour streets lacked speed bumps or crosswalks, and its single play area was little more than swings and a basketball court.[4] When a driver struck and killed a three-year-old girl on one of its streets in 1975, Carrie led protests. "We lost one of our babies and if they don't do something we're going to block the damn street and not let anyone in until something is done," she told the *Charlotte News*.[5] Residents did just that, dragging tree limbs and boards into the street to stop traffic, then painting five makeshift crosswalks.[6] Carrie and her neighbors eventually prevailed. The housing authority installed stop signs and speed bumps in Dalton Village and other developments as well.

Other problems remained intractable. Poverty announced itself with the smell of urine, a mattress on the floor, an unemployed boyfriend sprawling on a sagging sofa. Truancy was rampant, and crime so pervasive that Charlotte's police chief called for eleven additional officers to patrol the development.[7] Gunfire in those years was rare, though men carried box cutters or knives, and there were plenty of fistfights. For any child who loved compatriots, however, the neighborhood was full of playmates. Football, basketball, and hide-and-go-seek games sprang up at a moment's notice. The lone asphalt basketball court set in the dust of Dalton Village's central yard became Belton's second home. In middle school, he played before the bus came, charging up and down the blacktop, sweating up his good clothes, launching the ball at hoops that lacked nets. He played during recess at Piedmont Junior High, then again after school, and also evenings if he'd finished helping with supper dishes and daylight lingered. He also joined the Dalton Village basketball team, competing against kids from the city's other public housing projects. Even before he reached his adult height of five-foot-eight, he could pass, drive to the basket, and shoot all day long.

This was how he met Lisa Williams. One evening, as Dalton Village's boys' and girls' basketball teams finished a practice, Belton climbed onto the bus to head home and eyed the empty space beside a pretty girl with a curly Afro.

"Can I sit there?" he asked.

Lisa recognized him. In Dalton Village, Belton was known for his good looks—the soulful brown eyes, the winning smile, the six-inch-tall Afro—as well as his generosity. He had a habit of giving things away—a checkerboard, a football, a pair of shoes. If his mother wasn't paying attention, even the groceries she'd just purchased. Girls, especially, were drawn to him. They'd show up at his back screen door and call out: *Is Lamont home?*

When he plopped down beside Lisa, however, he found her unimpressed. "I remember all the girls was wanting him," she said years later, "but not me."

Lisa's disinterest made her more desirable. He asked her to a movie and got a no. Lisa was the youngest of eight. Her father had died when she was twelve, and her mother ran a strict household. She thought her daughter was too young to be dating. Undeterred, Belton headed to his kitchen with a plan to win her over. Later, he appeared at the Williams' apartment with a cake he'd baked from scratch. Soon, he and Lisa were going steady.

Belton kept busy during junior high school. In addition to dating Lisa and practicing basketball, he'd become an enthusiastic Boy Scout. Both he and his brother Gordon had joined when Lonnie took the helm of an all-black troop that met at St. Paul Baptist. Gordon dropped out following a tick bite and high fever, but Belton thrived. Holed up in his room with a Boy Scout handbook, he practiced knot tying, memorized first aid for sprains and cuts, worked toward several badges simultaneously, and focused on becoming the youngest black Eagle Scout in county history. Belton had been slow to read, partly because asthma had kept him out of school in his early years. He'd once grown so frustrated trying to decipher a children's Bible story about King Solomon that he dropped to his knees and pleaded to God for wisdom. His learning deficits were still apparent in 1976 and 1977, at ages twelve and thirteen, as he recorded much of his Scout work in spiral notebooks. For his physical fitness badge, he explained that "nickoteam" in your lungs shortens your life. He critiqued alcohol and drugs ("When you take drugs it will might make you have night mares or you will get scared or think strange like you can fly or some might cause liver or brain damage").

For a cooking badge, he defined a balanced menu: "when you eat something from all 4 basic food groups in *one* meal." For a badge focused on community citizenship, he described various community organizations, including basketball teams, which existed, he explained, "to keep the boys off the streets." His favorite badges sent him outdoors—pioneering, hiking, learning to spot poisonous plants, lighting a fire without a match, navigating with a compass. He loved camping, and the freedom he felt when he lay beneath a sky dome of stars in the Blue Ridge foothills.

High-minded Boy Scout law wasn't the only influence shaping Belton in those years, however. When he enrolled at Piedmont Junior High, he learned Alphonso lived just down the street, at apartment 87, Piedmont Courts. Belton hadn't forgotten his childhood pledge to kill Alphonso, but he also hadn't stopped craving his father's love. Despite Lonnie's paternal efforts, Belton judged his stepfather harsh and unaffectionate. More than five years had passed since he'd watched his father stab his mother. Alphonso had spent several months in prison. Perhaps he'd changed. Belton knocked one day, the door opened, and there was Alphonso, six feet tall, slim. A woman stood behind him.

This is my son, he told her. He appeared pleased Belton had come calling.

To an adolescent boy, Alphonso's life seemed exciting. He drove a 1969 Cadillac, spoke with swagger, and ran Big Al's, a smoky, dark poolroom across the street from Piedmont Courts. Belton began dropping in with his cousin to play eight ball, unintimidated by the grown men around him because his father was in charge. Alphonso did dote on his son, in his way. He'd slip him a few dollars. He once presented Belton with a new pair of Converses. These acts, trivial compared to the damage Alphonso had caused, still impressed. Belton had a vague awareness that his father had a hand in another business venture, which he thought involved alcohol. He didn't know his dad sold marijuana and heroin. He did know enough not to mention his pool hall visits to his mother. Alphonso again exited Belton's life in 1977, heading to prison after pleading guilty to dealing heroin and marijuana. An officer had caught him stashing a bag of marijuana in a car tire's wheel well.

Belton's stepfather, Lonnie Graves, at lower left, led his Boy Scout troop. Belton is pictured in the top middle. Photo by Tom Franklin, courtesy of the *Charlotte Observer*.

When Belton was fourteen, in 1978, he had his first brush with notoriety, as he and six members of his Boy Scout troop prepared for a three-week camping expedition in New Mexico. To raise nearly $3,000 for the trip, mothers helped their sons hold bake sales, and St. Paul Baptist pitched in $450. The Mecklenburg County Council of Boy Scouts of America came through with a little more. For the rest, Lonnie wrote dozens of letters soliciting civic and business leaders. When Charlotte's two daily newspapers got wind of the story, each wrote a feel-good feature portraying Lonnie as a hardworking black father helping to make scouting dreams come true. The boys remained short of money until the day before it was due, when a local businessman's donation put them over the top. "I couldn't believe it," Lonnie told the *Charlotte News*. "I thought I was going to have a heart attack right there."[8] Belton's picture made the newspaper. His Scout kerchief was neatly tied around his neck. His smiling gaze was fixed on his stepfather.

Like many upbeat newspaper stories, however, this one left out some complications, never hinting at the troubling undercurrents tugging at the family. One was Belton's temper, which flared whenever he believed he or someone else was being wronged. As Belton saw it, he delivered only righteous payback, at a community center dance, for instance, when he went to fetch punch and returned to find that a young man named Gerald had taken his chair and begun conversing with Lisa, his girlfriend.

"That's my seat," Belton said.

Gerald ignored him and continued to flirt. Before Belton lunged, he handed Lisa the punch cups. A chaperone broke up the fight and ejected the boys, but they started back up in the parking lot, grappling until they were in the street, Belton atop Gerald. When a station wagon pulled up, its bumper nearly touching him, Belton jumped off his opponent and looked up. There was Lonnie.

Get in this car, he commanded.

The truth about Belton's stepfather was also complicated. Lonnie—the troop leader, the stand-up guy raising another man's five children—should have been Belton's savior. In fact, Belton saw Lonnie as the family drill sergeant, quick to discipline with shouts and whippings. Present, but never showing affection. As Belton and his brothers grew into teenagers, Lonnie's parenting became more ineffectual. His relationship with Carrie also frayed, and though she always said Lonnie never hit her, Belton could hear them fighting, angry shouts carrying beyond their bedroom door. Belton appreciated Lonnie as a provider, but he didn't love him and never completely trusted him.

Still, Lonnie made that New Mexico trip happen. In June 1978, the summer after Belton graduated from Piedmont Junior High, he boarded a bus bound for Philmont Scout Ranch in New Mexico. The camping expedition put Belton into yet another white world. All Charlotte troop leaders making the trip were white men who led white troops, and years later, Jim Diedrich, a Charlotte salesman who was Belton's troop leader on the trip, confessed that he initially worried that Belton and another black Scout in his charge would need close supervision. He had felt out of place visiting the Graves's Dalton

Village apartment in his dress shirt and tie. He'd had no experience interacting with African American teenagers.

But Belton, who'd become accustomed in elementary school to being the minority kid, had a grand time. He savored one new experience after another: a naval air station south of New Orleans, a YMCA in Houston, a church in Carlsbad, New Mexico. As it turned out, it wasn't the black Scouts who caused Diedrich worry. It was the group's youngest member, a thirteen-year-old nicknamed P.Q., who collapsed with abdominal pain during a demanding wilderness hike in New Mexico's Sangre de Cristo Mountains. Several Scouts hacked down saplings to make a stretcher. Belton and an older Eagle Scout hiked out of the canyon to flag down help along the nearest highway. By the time emergency workers got P.Q. to a hospital in Taos, his appendix had ruptured, but quick action was credited with saving his life. Diedrich recalled that those three weeks deepened his understanding of other races. He remembered Belton as funny, bright, "never a moment's problem."

When Belton returned home that summer, he and Lisa continued their courtship. Their relationship was now documented with a ninth-grade prom photo that showed two grinning teenagers, arms around waists. They made an intimate yet wholesome couple in their blinding white attire—a tux for Belton and a short-sleeved, turtleneck frock for Lisa that was modest enough to satisfy her mother. She wasn't allowed to show her neck, she recalled.

Not long after the New Mexico trip, Belton dropped out of scouting, settling for being a Life Scout, one rank below Eagle. Lonnie was crushed. But Belton's desire for badges had been eclipsed by his passion for basketball—and Lisa.

He would start tenth grade at West Charlotte High School in the fall. While his academic career had been unimpressive, his ninth-grade standardized achievement test suggested untapped potential. He scored at a 12.3-grade level in language and a tenth-grade level overall. He'd begun telling people he wanted to be a lawyer. No one had suggested the profession to him, and he couldn't explain why it drew him. But for a black teenager growing up in Charlotte in the 1960s and '70s, a lawyer was a fine thing to be, almost like a superhero, giving voice to the voiceless, demanding justice for all.

Belton shared his dreams with Lisa, often by telephone, stretching the cord into a closet or bathroom so he had some privacy. He told her he loved her. He told her he would one day have a business and a nice house. One day, he told her, he would be rich.

West Charlotte High in the late 1970s was a rare institution in America, integrated not by black students, but by whites. Founded in 1938, it had long been the pride of the African American community, considered superior to Second Ward High, the city's oldest black high school, which officials opted in 1969 to close rather than integrate. But next to white schools, West Charlotte had been the neglected stepchild. Even school colors were hand-me-downs: maroon and gold because those were Harding High's colors, and West Charlotte for years made do with the white school's used athletic uniforms.[9]

That was before the arrival of hundreds of white students, many from moneyed Myers Park and Eastover neighborhoods. The transition was initially rough—fights in halls, parents vowing to boycott. But a cadre of high-profile white parents—families that could have easily chosen private schools—gave West Charlotte both their children and their support. Enrollment doubled, to more than two thousand students, and before long, the school had a refurbished interior, more tennis courts, and paving for the gravel parking lot.[10] School officials also went to terrific lengths to achieve parity, even providing for black and white co-presidents of the student body.[11] The school became such a success that its students hosted peers from racially divided Boston to explain how to make school integration work. For national reporters writing about busing, West Charlotte's campus, tucked in a middle-class neighborhood off Beatties Ford Road, was a required stop.

Kids from Dalton Village usually went to Olympic High, formerly an all-white school. But Belton was eligible for West Charlotte because he'd attended Piedmont Junior High, a magnet that fed into the high school. Carrie preferred West Charlotte, figuring that the city's only remaining historically black high school would instill an appreciation for black history. In fall 1978, his first semester, Belton made a sartorial impression, showing up for picture day with his Afro, polyester shirt, and white vest, looking like he'd walked off the set of *Soul Train*. He had been buying his own clothes for a while, combing thrift stores with money earned from janitorial jobs with Lonnie. Some days, he wore a thin tie and suit with baggy pants that suggested a film-noir character. He liked when classmates commented on his sharp look. He earned B's and C's in classes, and at Lonnie's urging, he took Junior ROTC. That's where he met Rhonda.*

Many who attended West Charlotte during Belton's era came to speak of their alma mater reverentially, describing a spirit of togetherness and diversity that shaped their lives for the better. "It was a sliver of time when it was kind of utopian," one African American member of Belton's class told me. Belton also enjoyed his classmates, but he barely recalled his teachers and couldn't remember a class that sparked his interest. At home, no one checked his grades or nagged him to buckle down if he wanted to go to college. The course of his life was altered in high school, but not by classes or teachers, or the many clubs he could have joined, or the historic diversity of West Charlotte High.

His life changed when he met Rhonda. He and Rhonda disagree about how they became a couple. He said he enjoyed bantering, "picking at her," as he called it, in seventh-period ROTC class. Though she was pretty, he wasn't eyeing her as a potential girlfriend. His recollection is that Rhonda one day announced to him it was her birthday and asked what he was going to give her. He grinned and blurted the first thing that popped into his mind: "Me."

Days later, he noticed her seated on a bench, crying as friends tried to console her. When he asked what was wrong, one young woman explained that he had pledged to date Rhonda but hadn't spent any time with her. Belton had no idea she had interpreted his playful remark as

---

* Rhonda's name has been changed at her request.

a romantic declaration. But he didn't want to see her upset. He agreed to date her, even though he was still seeing Lisa, who attended Olympic High.

Rhonda told me Belton's recollection was wrong. "Lord have mercy, no. I doubt that was it," she said. "I don't think I would ask him that. I'm not a talker. I was shy and quiet in high school." They did meet in ROTC class, she said, and simply started dating.

What is undisputed is that Belton two-timed Rhonda and Lisa for months without the other knowing. He saw Rhonda at school, sometimes skipping class so they could sit and talk in a nearby park. After school, Rhonda and her teenaged siblings worked for her father, who had a janitorial company similar to Lonnie Graves's cleaning business. The siblings would clean an office building from about five to nine, then hit several Hardee's restaurants, where they might work until two in the morning, even on school nights.

Despite Rhonda's work schedule, she and Belton managed to steal enough time together that they lost their virginity one afternoon at a friend's house.

At home in Dalton Village, meanwhile, there was Lisa, who would cheer Belton from the stands during public housing basketball games at the community recreation center. That's where she was one Saturday when the team's center pulled Belton aside during a break and nodded toward the bleachers.

Rhonda is here, he said.

Belton watched, feeling as if he were in a nightmare, as Rhonda descended the bleacher steps and took a seat.

The game resumed, but his head was no longer in it. Opposing team members stole the ball from him once, then twice. His coach pulled him out.

When the final buzzer blared, both young women approached.

Belton was caught. He turned to Rhonda and looked at her blankly. "Who are you?" he asked.

Years later, Rhonda said she didn't remember this incident, either. "It could have been. I don't know."

But Lisa said she did. "I left with him," she said.

He took her hand and pledged his love on the walk home.

Later, he telephoned Rhonda and patched things up.

He continued seeing them both. "I knew it was wrong," he said. "But when my heart got connected to somebody, it was just connected."

Belton also began having sex with Lisa. Once, Lisa hid in Belton's room while Carrie and Lonnie were home. And on a rare night when Lisa's mother was away, she stashed Belton in her bedroom closet until her older brothers were asleep. As a precaution, she pushed her dresser against the door before they climbed into bed.

By junior year, Belton no longer talked about college or law school. That fall, he signed up for Industrial Cooperative Training, which gave class credit for having a job. He'd begun working for Rhonda's dad instead of his own stepfather so he could spend more time with Rhonda. When they finished cleaning Hardee's restaurants in the wee hours of the morning, he had an excuse to stay the night at her house.

He flunked every class except ROTC that semester. He had stopped doing homework, then stopped going to school. Instead, he worked and squirreled away money, enough to buy a used AMC Hornet, light blue, priced at $500 because the driver's seat was detached from the rusted floorboard. He also began building a business of his own. When Rhonda's dad ceased cleaning the Hardee's on Eastway Drive, Belton asked Rhonda to get the area supervisor's number from her father. He called, interviewed, and landed the job.

Second semester junior year, early 1980, Lisa found out she was pregnant. It was almost inevitable. She'd been clueless about birth control, and her mother's idea of a sex talk, a warning not to "mess with no weenies," had only perplexed her. Belton didn't like the way condoms felt and never worried about unprotected sex. He reacted to the pregnancy with the nonchalance of a sixteen-year-old boy who'd observed that fatherhood carried minimal responsibilities. Carrie recalled years later how he broke the news: "What would you say if I told you you were going to be a grandma?"

He made an attempt to be responsible, forging Carrie's name on a transfer request to Olympic High so he could attend school with Lisa. But then someone told him he could shortcut two years of high school with a GED. At age sixteen, he dropped out of Olympic.

Belton had ceased considering college when he realized he had zero chance of getting a basketball scholarship. Neither of his parents had finished high school, and as far as he knew, a GED was as good as a diploma. He was already making money, and since his goal was to get rich, school, rather than a path to success, seemed a hindrance.

When Lisa gave birth to their daughter, Kim, in September 1980, he wasn't present. By then, he was living with Rhonda and her parents and often working seven days a week to build his own business. After Kim was born, Lisa confronted him: "You want me and your daughter?"

The upshot was that he didn't. "I walked off and left," Lisa recalled. "I gave up on him."

Decades later, Belton said he wasn't sure of his motivations, but he suspected he stayed with Rhonda because she was the first woman with whom he'd had sex, and he couldn't stand the thought of her with another man. Rhonda announced *her* pregnancy soon after baby Kim was born. Belton was landing more cleaning jobs—eventually five Hardee's restaurants—so he and Rhonda were able to get an apartment and replace his Hornet with a used brown Chevette. Often, Rhonda worked alongside him. They cleaned from ten or eleven at night until dawn, ferrying supplies from store to store, scrubbing grease-laden grills and sticky milkshake machines. Belton earned about $750 a week after paying family members and Dalton Village friends he'd hired to help out.

They didn't marry in haste. Their son, Belton Lamont Davis, arrived in June 1981. It was nearly two years later, on April 21, 1983, that they drove south on Interstate 77, about thirty miles, into South Carolina. People in Charlotte found it handy to cross the state line for certain commodities, such as fireworks, which were legal, and marriage licenses, which involved less red tape than North Carolina imposed. Belton said it was Rhonda who had pushed to marry. He agreed after waking one morning to find her crying. He agreed, he said, because he wanted her to be happy, and, if he was being honest, he wanted her to stop bringing it up.

Rhonda recalled that she wore a white skirt and suit jacket. Bolton recalled that he wore a sweatsuit—a nice one. Once they signed the papers, they drove home. There was no celebration, no honeymoon. It was a Thursday. That night, like every night, five Hardee's restaurants waited to be cleaned.

5

THE DEALER'S MOTHER

Carrie Graves had been resting Saturday evening, November 30, 1985, stretched out on her living-room sofa when her phone rang. It was a friend of Belton's, calling to tell her that people had been shot in Piedmont Courts. Not her sons; they were okay. But all three—Al, Belton, and Gordon—had been arrested. They'd probably be released on bond. As she listened, the telephone receiver shook in Carrie's hand.

Carrie hung up, then lifted the receiver again, dialing one person after another as she tried to find out more. Finally, she turned on the television news, where the top story was the shootout at Piedmont Courts. More than a hundred shots had been fired, and seven people had been hit, most of them bystanders. One was a fourteen-year-old girl, eight months pregnant, struck in the arm and leg.

Carrie's thoughts swirled from the wounded victims to the charges her sons might face to the lawyers they would need. She found herself focusing on Belton. She had seen him on Thanksgiving, two days earlier. Lacking a dining room for a sit-down meal, she instead had organized a short-order feast—ham and turkey, macaroni salad, collards, yams—which she dished up one plate at a time whenever family members dropped in. Belton had moved gingerly that day. He'd just had a tumor removed; stitches held together his backside. He was supposed to be home resting. Why was he at Piedmont Courts?

Even as she asked herself that question, she knew the answer. She knew her son was selling cocaine, though she hadn't discussed it, not even with Lonnie. If she didn't actually say the words—*drug dealer*—it was easier to pretend otherwise.

She hadn't suspected at first. Of her sons, Belton had caused Carrie the least worry. She'd been disappointed when he dropped out of high school and surprised when he'd become a father and married Rhonda so young, but she'd believed he was mature enough to handle the responsibility. He'd never been in trouble with police, unlike Al and Gordon, who already had felony convictions—Al for larceny, Gordon for stealing cars. Also, he had never used drugs.

She'd tried at first to assure herself that his sudden prosperity was legitimate. He worked all the time with his janitorial business, and he'd been a moneymaking whiz since childhood, never begging her for cash because he earned his own. But not long after his 1983 marriage, she'd noticed that he was hanging out with some new young men. They occasionally dropped by her Dalton Village apartment with him, carrying little beeper things on their belts. Belton had one too.

"What you need that for?" she'd asked him.

He didn't answer.

The evolution of his cars had been the giveaway. First came his junky AMC Hornet, then the brown Chevette, neither of which was a drug-dealer car. After the Chevette, however, he bought a two-toned Lincoln Continental Mark V, and then the green Cadillac, which practically announced his new profession.

"You know," Carrie told him one day, "you was not raised like this."

That was not exactly true. Nineteen-year-old Belton had reconnected with his father when Alphonso returned to Charlotte in 1982 after serving five years in prison for dealing marijuana and heroin. Undeterred, Alphonso was dealing again—cocaine this time. What Carrie didn't know was that her ex-husband had encouraged her son to get into the business.

An undated photo of Alphonso Platt, Belton's father. Courtesy of Belton Platt.

It had unfolded almost unintentionally. Rhonda had applied for public housing before she and Belton married in 1983, but by the time she received the letter offering the subsidized apartment, they had wed. Belton told her to forget it. His son wasn't growing up in public housing. When he relayed this story to his father, however, Alphonso perked up, pointing out that a unit in Piedmont Courts provided the perfect operations base for a lucrative business.

Keep the apartment, he counseled. You'll be a millionaire in a year.

Everything about his father's life should have warned Belton away. By 1983, after spending hundreds of nights scrubbing smashed French fries and ketchup drips off sticky fast-food floors, he was proud that he owned a business. He wasn't looking for a new gig. He'd never even seen coke. After witnessing his father's alcoholic rages as a child, he'd scrupulously avoided drugs, cigarettes, and alcohol. He refused to sip champagne on New Year's Eve and had once applied, unsuccessfully, to work in a program aimed at keeping young people off drugs. But the idea of becoming a millionaire, even by means of illegal drugs, that was an intoxicating prospect.

Alphonso was right about the profit potential. Demand for cocaine had crossed race, class, and income lines. Rich people snorted it at parties. Poor people smoked it in bedrooms. A gram sold for $100. The markup was huge.

Belton decided to give it a try. He handed over $150, and Alphonso bought half an eight ball, 1.75 grams. He took his son to the kitchen of one of his Piedmont Courts customers. Seated at the table, Belton watched as his father emptied the white powder into a strainer, then used a spoon to push it through. He did this several times, first with the cocaine, then with a second white powder, mannitol, a plant-derived sugar alcohol often added to cocaine to stretch it. A quarter gram for every gram of cocaine, Alphonso advised. Use more and you risked a reputation for selling mostly cut.

Once both powders were smooth and free of hard nuggets, Alphonso used a playing card to mix the two on the table, then applied a rolling pin to blend them some more. Belton watched closely. Cocaine was more work than he had imagined. And Alphonso still wasn't done. With the card, he scraped up the product, dumped it back into the strainer, and again pushed it through with the spoon. Finally, after straining the mixture several more times, Alphonso bagged his product, using a card to deposit bits of powder into cut-off corners of sandwich bags, then securing them with twist ties. He pointed to each: You charge ten dollars for this one, and twenty-five for that one.

Belton examined the tiny amounts. "Nobody's going to pay twenty-five dollars for that little bit of stuff."

Alphonso looked his son in the eye. They'll buy it, he said.

As business grew, Belton replenished his supply with larger amounts—a quarter ounce, an ounce, a half kilo. He found a source—a white car salesman who stashed cocaine in vehicles on the lot—willing to front him product whenever he needed it.

He told his mom as little as possible for her own good. For a woman who lived in public housing, Carrie was unusually connected and powerful. Charlotte's mayor and city council members knew her by name. She'd met many famous people, including baseball great Hank Aaron, who relaxed in her living-room rocking chair while in town to register voters. The *Charlotte Observer* profiled her in 1975 as the "Voice of the Welfare Mother" and quoted her often.[1] In 1980, for instance, after riots killed fifteen people in Miami following the acquittal of white officers charged in the beating death of a black man, the newspaper had asked whether such a thing could happen in Charlotte. Yes, she said. Police harassment of blacks was the root of the problem. "Black youth are afraid of the police," she said. "When you see one, it means you run because they are after you."[2]

Her activism had taken her around the globe. In 1977, she joined First Lady Rosalynn Carter and twenty thousand other women at the National Women's Conference in Houston,[3] and later attended an international women's conference in Prague. When a cousin worried for her safety around all those Communists, Carrie laughed. She'd grown up in the South with the Ku Klux Klan. Communists were the least of her worries.

Some people considered Carrie a mouthy troublemaker. But others, including Arthur Griffin, saw her as an inspiration. Griffin, who led the Charlotte-Mecklenburg school board in the 1990s, had been a young legal aid worker when he met the short woman sporting an Afro who reminded him of Angela Davis. "I thought she was fabulous, to be a public housing tenant, to stand up for herself and her neighborhood," he said. "I think everything she was asking for, you and I would want for our family."

In the days after her sons' arrests, Carrie realized the Piedmont Courts shootout wouldn't be forgotten, like most public housing crimes, once it dropped off the news pages. Charlotte's police chief, assistant city manager, and about a half dozen other city officials toured the apartment complex on Monday, two days after the melee, and announced a crackdown on lawlessness. They were adding eight patrol officers to the one or two usually assigned to the development. "We are not going to tolerate this foolishness," the assistant city manager told reporters.[4] It was an odd word choice—*foolishness*—as if the gunmen had been pranking each other.

Carrie could almost feel the heat of neighbors' gossip. The irony was rich: Carrie Graves, long an advocate for public housing anti-crime programs, was the mother of the biggest dealer in Piedmont Courts. At the time, she was directing the Pan-African Culture and Resource Center, a shoestring operation that provided meeting and event space for several local civil rights groups. But after her sons' arrests, she was so humiliated she found it hard to leave her apartment. Her relationship with Lonnie, which had been deteriorating for years, was also falling apart. Not long after the shootout, he moved out.

She could have disowned Belton, barring him and his drug-dealing friends from her house. She knew mothers who had done that. She'd also seen mothers turn in their children. Carrie couldn't imagine shunning her own flesh and blood. She remained certain Belton wasn't to blame for the shootout. And no one had died. Even Big Lou was fine, out of the hospital after a couple of days despite taking shots to the side of his nose, his left temple, his leg, and back.

When Carrie considered the taxonomy of illegal activities, she assured herself that selling cocaine wasn't the worst kind of crime. It was a hustle, really—buying low, selling high—and she'd grown up in a world where people relied on hustles to pay rent. Her grandfather had cooked buck, a moonshine he brewed from corn and other vegetables, and operated an unlicensed barbershop in his backyard in Cherry, giving his customers the opportunity to sip bootleg liquor while waiting in line for haircuts. Her chauffeur father spent his days driving for a wealthy white construction company owner. But after work, he ran a lucrative side hustle—a butter-and-egg lottery, so named because the winning number, a stock quote in the morning newspaper, might be chosen from the butter- and egg-trading listings. "All we knew 'til we got up big was that my daddy's buddies came to see him every evening," she said. Carrie's mother, Sybil Lee, had disapproved of any illegal activity, including her husband's lottery business. She regarded its profits as dirty money. Carrie sided with her father. "He would say, 'Sybil Lee, if you don't want to spend it, you don't have to. I'm pretty sure the children won't mind.' He loved spending his money on us."

How does a person simultaneously oppose and benefit from crime? Carrie accepted this contradiction. Belton helped a lot of people, including her. Even before he began dealing, he gave her money, tens and twenties from the janitorial business, and now he was giving her more. She would never say she approved of his work, but she spent his money, and she didn't regret it. Dirty money, she believed, could do many good things. "A lot of folk in Charlotte benefited. Regardless of how dirty the money was, they benefited from his money."

6

WHAT WENT WRONG WITH
PIEDMONT COURTS?

Three months after the shootout, Charlotte mayor Harvey Gantt did what officials often do when trying to solve problems that defy answers: He formed a task force. He put the police chief and district attorney on it and charged the group with finding ways to make Piedmont Courts safer. As spring turned to summer, residents showed up at meetings to vent pent-up complaints: The housing authority didn't care about them. Police didn't arrive when called. Their own neighbors aided and abetted the drug dealers. Task force members heard about overflowing dumpsters and aging refrigerators and a bad project design that squeezed too many people into too small a space.[1] While the city prepared to relieve crowding by demolishing ten of Piedmont Courts' forty buildings, the task force investigated job opportunities for residents. But no one got to the essence of the problem, the question so deeply embedded in the situation it was nearly invisible: Why did troubled, drug-ridden Piedmont Courts exist in such a prosperous city?

The answer was complex, largely forgotten or misremembered. And ultimately, it was rooted in race discrimination that began with slavery. In 1865, when the Civil War ended, Charlotte wasn't much—not even three thousand people, most of whom lived in the four wards that comprised the present-day downtown. Newly freed African Americans made up about 40 percent of the population and, contrary to common assumptions, the city was integrated.

Urban historian Tom Hanchett, author of *Sorting Out the New South City: Race, Class, and Urban Development in Charlotte, 1875–1975*, documented this integration with the help of old city directories, which listed residents and businesses by address and noted African Americans with a "c" for "colored" beside their names. Guided by an 1875 directory, Hanchett used pushpins to plot a map of citizens in the First Ward neighborhood by address and race—yellow pins for black residents, green and brown pushpins for middle- and working-class whites, blue pins for business owners. The result: a mix of colors on every street—blacks and whites living side by side. Hanchett initially attributed this intermingling to African Americans who remained in former slave quarters beside white homes. But that didn't explain everything. In some cases, blacks owned their homes. Also, after the Civil War, African Americans built First United Presbyterian Church right next to white-owned homes and businesses. He concluded that in the late nineteenth century, most of Charlotte's real estate wasn't segregated.

That changed around the turn of the century with the rise of the North Carolina Democratic Party's White Supremacy Campaign, a movement with vast repercussions. By convincing working-class whites to break alliances with black voters—in effect, voting against their interests—the campaign sparked a bloody government coup that murdered dozens of blacks in the coastal city of Wilmington, inspired similar violence elsewhere, and launched the Age of Jim Crow in North Carolina. Newspapers, including the *Charlotte Observer*, fanned the flames of fear and hatred with race-baiting stories and editorials. In 1898, Raleigh's *News & Observer* published a front-page cartoon titled "The Vampire That Hovers over North Carolina." It depicted a marauding African American bat-winged vampire grabbing at white people as they flee in terror. On his wings are the words: "Negro Rule." Like other southern states, North Carolina codified this new era of discrimination with an amended constitution. Ratified in 1900, it required voters to pay a poll tax and pass a literacy test. Voter participation, black and white, plummeted. Blacks who'd won political office in the previous century now faced impossible odds, while new Jim Crow laws barred African Americans from public accommodations and relegated them to the backs of buses and trolleys. "The one that really gets me," Hanchett said, "you know you swear on a Bible in court? In 1901, there were separate white and colored Bibles in the courthouse here in Charlotte."

When Hanchett mapped First Ward again, this time with a directory from 1911, the results of the White Supremacy Campaign became clear. Yellow pins—black residents—filled all but the outermost streets. The city had sorted itself by color. Starting around 1901, segregation became formalized, with deeds on new houses specifying that only Caucasians occupy the properties. It was the dawning of institutionalized segregation.

Things soon got worse for African Americans. In the middle of the Great Depression in the 1930s, the mortgage market froze, much as it did when the American economy tanked in 2008. To convince nervous bankers to loan money, federal officials mapped cities by credit risk, identifying neighborhoods that were good bets and areas they deemed too sketchy for loans. In 1935, the government produced a map dividing Charlotte into sections—red, green, blue, and yellow. Wealthier white people lived in the green neighborhoods. They were considered the best investments. Yellow and blue were in between. And the red neighborhoods were populated by what the feds called "undesirable social or economic groups," which included blacks. This redlining, as it came to be called, persisted for decades, strangling investment in black neighborhoods and perpetuating segregation by favoring homogeneous neighborhoods. As part of redlining, the Federal Housing Administration used race and ethnicity to judge creditworthiness. One economist ranked various groups from one to ten, putting English, German, Scotch, Irish, and Scandinavian in the number-one slot. Negroes ranked ninth; Mexicans, tenth.[2]

These policies help explain how African Americans were excluded from the greatest accumulation of wealth in the nation's history, and why, thanks to compounding interest and housing appreciation, a typical white household in 2015 had sixteen times the wealth of a typical black household.[3] When Hanchett gives talks on how Charlotte got segregated, he points out that his own white European roots helped his parents get an FHA-insured loan, which gave them a lower down payment and lower interest rate and ultimately helped them save enough to give him a down payment when he bought his home. "If my dad had been a black person," he has said, "I probably wouldn't own my own home."

This history repudiates what most of us have been taught—that America's march is always toward progress. In fact, even when the federal government began enacting laws banning race discrimination in housing, education, and employment, a countervailing government program blunted their effects. Officially, it was known as urban renewal. Black people called it Negro removal.

The American Housing Act of 1949 was created with a worthy aim—to give slum dwellers better housing. With the federal government's help, municipalities would buy neighborhoods of dank tenements and drafty shacks, then sell at reduced prices to private developers who would replace the slums with sound, affordable homes. But that goal shifted in 1954, with legislation that emphasized replacing slums with commercial development, a new policy direction that appeased conservatives.[4] In Charlotte, as in most cities, the worst slums occupied property in or adjacent to downtown. City fathers decided it was a waste to use such valuable land to house the poor. Instead, they used eminent domain to take land for nonresidential development and highways. In cities across the nation, black neighborhoods near downtowns got demolished.

In Pittsburgh, it was the Hill District. In Richmond, it was Navy Hill. In Charlotte, it was Second Ward, the heart of black Charlotte, also known as Brooklyn. This lost neighborhood had businesses and restaurants, a library, hotel, and theater, with fine houses existing near ramshackle rentals. It was the kind of mixed-used neighborhood now favored by urban planners. But newspaper accounts from the late 1950s and early '60s gave a different portrayal. In 1958, the city's planning director characterized planning board members as "horrified" after touring Brooklyn.[5] An *Observer* editorial the next day noted the area's "narrow streets and darkened alleyways, open ditches and polluted streams," but failed to mention that the city's own neglect had created the lousy infrastructure. Stories often implied that relocating poor people would somehow eradicate poverty. Urban renewal would "mean the end of the vermin-infested tinderboxes," wrote *Charlotte News* reporter Charles Kuralt, who later achieved national fame at CBS News.[6] Over eleven years, Charlotte tore down 1,480 structures in Brooklyn, including restaurants, small businesses, and churches. It replaced them with sterile government buildings, a hotel, an urban park. The park featured a man-made lake, lots of concrete, and a statue of Dr. Martin Luther King Jr., erected years later without irony. After razing a dozen black churches in Brooklyn, the city sold acreage to First Baptist Church so its white congregation could expand. In all, this renewal displaced 1,007 Brooklyn families.[7]

The White Supremacy Campaign, Jim Crow, redlining, urban renewal—all of this had shaped Piedmont Courts. It started as public housing for whites only, while Fairview Homes, a similar project for blacks, opened across town. When the first white tenants moved into Piedmont Courts' furnished brick townhouses on January 2, 1941, a newspaper story recounted their excitement, describing one woman passing "her thin young hand lovingly over the smooth white combination sink and laundry tub." An exaggerated description, perhaps, but the point—that residents were grateful—seems accurate. White Piedmont Courts blossomed into a tight community that included many families of World War II draftees. Residents tended lawns, planted gardens, pinned laundered sheets on clotheslines. They also abided by strict rules: married couples only, regular housekeeping inspections.[8] In the Charlotte Housing Authority's 1947 annual report, the development sounds like a utopia: "It's no wonder that living in

Piedmont Courts has made adults healthier and happier and the children more rosy-cheeked and able to do better in school."

As a boy in the 1950s, Arthur Griffin, the former school board chairman, admired those apartments from across a creek, on the playground of Alexander Street School, an elementary school for black children. "Ask anybody who went to Alexander Street what they thought of Piedmont Courts," he said. "They thought it was for rich people." It was a logical conclusion, because black women, including Griffin's mother, worked as domestics for Piedmont Courts residents, who were poor by white standards but still able to afford black help.

By then, Charlotte bore little resemblance to the 1875 black-white, rich-poor patchwork Hanchett had documented. The city in the mid-twentieth century was divided into racial and economic wedges, with blacks mostly in the west and northwest, whites in the east and southeast.[9] In the 1960s, as Charlotte leveled Brooklyn and other "urban renewal" areas, black residents who had owned homes there moved to west Charlotte, where some built in new neighborhoods off Beatties Ford Road, not far from all-black West Charlotte High and Johnson C. Smith University. But Brooklyn's poorest residents had few options. City officials were supposed to find housing for those displaced, but they rejected black leaders' pleas to build new low-income housing, bowing to arguments from real estate interests that existing rentals could absorb the flood of urban renewal displacements. That proved a mistake. Many properties the city chose were too costly. Former Brooklyn residents moved in, only to be evicted months later after falling behind in rent.[10] Many also applied for public housing. Days after the Civil Rights Act of 1964 became law, the Charlotte Housing Authority heeded pressure to integrate. Black residents moved into Piedmont Courts. Almost immediately, white residents began to flee.

And that is how Piedmont Courts went from white to black, hastened by Brooklyn's destruction, bolstered by America's rigid construct of black inferiority. For most whites, the housing project became foreign territory, just as white neighborhoods remained unexplored terrain for public housing residents. The immensity of this gulf hit me when a Charlotte native told me how her Baptist youth group in the 1960s provided Piedmont Courts kids with vacation Bible school. She had braces on her teeth and blond hair, both of which the children found exotic. By 1970, Charlotte had become the country's fifth most racially segregated city.[11]

Piedmont Courts didn't acquire its big-city drug-gang reputation until the 1980s, when cocaine became the hot commodity. Buyers were both black and white. As demand grew and the product became more valuable, sellers armed themselves for protection. Cocaine was cited as the culprit that explained Piedmont Courts' woes, even though it was more symptom than cause. Jobs had moved to the suburbs. Most elderly residents, who'd served as an important stabilizing influence, had departed for new senior apartments. This left a thousand women and children, plus countless men who weren't on leases but lived with girlfriends, mothers, cousins, sisters. The development, like public housing across the country, had relaxed its rules. No one kicked out the boyfriends. No one inspected the housekeeping.[12] This shift, which occurred across the nation, can be traced to the real estate industry. After postwar housing shortages eased, the industry lobbied success- fully to change income guidelines to admit the poorest families only. By excluding slightly better-off families, public housing lost a con- stituency that could lobby for upkeep and amenities, and the federal government ceased providing adequate subsidies to make the housing a decent place to live. "As a result, the condition and then the reputa- tion of public housing collapsed," Richard Rothstein explains in *The Color of Law: A Forgotten History of How Our Government Segregated America*.[13] In Piedmont Courts, bare dirt and garbage replaced what had once been tidy yards. By 1985, the playground was so littered with broken glass and hypodermic needles that vigilant parents kept their children away. Gunfire, especially at night, became commonplace. Po- lice warned white church volunteers to stay away. All the while, Belton Platt fostered goodwill with his generosity. "When opportunities are closed for people in one direction, they turn to another direction," said John Hayes, a sociologist who worked for the Charlotte Housing Authority in those years.

The year before Mayor Gantt formed his task force, the housing authority, sensing a brewing crisis, had already appointed one committee to address social problems and increase residents' community involvement. Writing about Piedmont Courts' troubles in 1984, the *Charlotte News* quoted a member of that first task force, a resident named Annie Cassells. The development, she said, was turning into Cocaine City.[14]

When I met Annie Cassells, in 2012, she was Annie Fiadjigbe (pronounced *fajabay*), a fifty-seven-year-old teacher in an after-school program. She lived with her husband, who was from Togo, in a Habitat for Humanity–built home not far from where Piedmont Courts had stood. As we talked, I could see why a minister once described Fiadjigbe as having "an inner steel."[15] She'd moved with her two young children into Piedmont Courts in 1975, a single mother who'd grown up near Rock Hill, South Carolina, one of fourteen children from a family of cotton sharecroppers. She'd earned a GED and an associate's degree while juggling children and work. (She first met Belton during her 5 a.m. shift at Hardee's. When she arrived at the fast-food restaurant before dawn to make biscuits, Belton would be finishing work, emptying his mop bucket and packing his supplies.)

"To me, Piedmont Courts was an opportunity, a stepping stone," she told me. "I took advantage of it. You had to really be strong to make it." She credited her Christian faith and her church, Seigle Avenue Presbyterian, for giving her that strength. The church, across the street from Piedmont Courts, was then a rare institution in Charlotte—an integrated, historically white church that focused its mission on its black neighbors.

Out of everything I'd heard about Piedmont Courts, Fiadjigbe's perspective was particularly insightful. She'd been elected president of the Piedmont Courts Residents Association when she was only twenty-one, and residents had come to trust and confide in her. Some of these women were illiterate and many more she judged to be depressed, stuck in miserable lives they felt powerless to escape. "I worked with so many women, I'd knock on doors, give opportunities to them," she said. She'd describe community college classes and offer to help them enroll. A few took her up on the offer, but most declined. "It was like a demonic spirit over that neighborhood," she said. "Women were cursed and didn't know it. You're depressed and you don't have what it takes to get out."

America's welfare system, she said, made it near impossible to get ahead. If you landed a job, your rent went up, and you had to pay someone to keep your children, and you might lose your food stamps or Medicaid. If you married your boyfriend, your rent went up, and you could get evicted. "To do one thing, you had five things working against you."

Selling drugs and consorting with dealers might have been unwise responses to the situation, but Fiadjigbe understood them. "When you lose hope, you do anything you have to do to fix the problem you're going through. That's why you had the seller and that's why you had a buyer."

She knew this from experience. Despite her own hard work, despite the care doled out by church volunteers, her son, Tyrone, got caught stealing cars as a young teenager. When he began working for one of the neighborhood's up-and-coming cocaine dealers, Fiadjigbe had issued an ultimatum. "I told him I was a community leader and he had a choice—to do the right thing, or leave. And he chose to leave." He chose to make his fortune with Money Rock.

On the afternoon of the 1985 shootout, fifteen-year-old Tyrone was elsewhere, but Fiadjigbe was in her apartment. She heard the pops of gunfire and telephoned police. A few months later, she agreed to serve on Mayor Gantt's task force.

In the end, the task force found that standards at Piedmont Courts were lower than at other public housing developments. "When the physical appearance of the complex began to deteriorate, appropriate measures were not taken to upgrade the neighborhood, fostering the perception that the Housing Authority and, ultimately, the City had no real interest in the project nor the residents," its report said. "The apathy, whether real or perceived, engendered in the residents the feeling that it was pointless for them to take an active interest in their community so they, in turn, became passive." [16]

The task force called for measures to defeat this passivity—full-time police, job programs, and apartment management more assertive than the past manager, who was reportedly afraid to walk around the complex. The goal was to empower Piedmont Courts residents "to take charge of their own lives and the future of their community." [17]

The measure of the city's success is debatable. Crime did decline, and a 1990 *Charlotte Observer* story described "the remarkable transformation" of the place, citing new programs aimed at helping residents learn skills, save money for home down payments, and eventually leave public housing. [18] The drop in crime was at least partly due to the population decline after the city relocated residents and demolished more than 120 apartments. And while the city offered to hire remaining residents to work on the renovation project, Fiadjigbe recalled that when she tried to cajole neighbors to take part, there was often some obstacle—no transportation to job training, no money to buy steel-toed boots required for the renovation work. "A lot of stuff was put in place, but it was put in place to help people be failures," she said.

Piedmont Courts finally died in 2006, demolished and replaced with a federally funded Hope VI mixed-income development called Seigle Point, stylish three-story townhomes where yellow jessamine bloomed on balconies. Smooth tennis courts had replaced the park's broken merry-go-round. Residents drove on streets named Skyline View Way and Greenway Crescent Lane. Hollywood Boulevard was no more. Charlotte leaders had learned that concentrations of poor people in public housing—housing often neglected and deprived of adequate resources—exacerbated crime. They could promote stability by mixing low-income tenants with higher-income renters and homeowners—people who had a financial stake in their neighborhood's success. The trend was the total reverse of the Federal

Housing Administration's discredited emphasis on homogeneous neighborhoods, and it had generally proved successful. But replacing old-fashioned public housing projects with mixed-income development nearly always has a major downside: It destroys more affordable units than it creates. As Charlotte grew, so did its affordable housing deficit.

7

STATE OF NORTH CAROLINA
VERSUS MONEY ROCK

On her first visit to Piedmont Courts, Shirley Fulton wanted to appear approachable, but she also wanted to avoid being shot. She compromised: She wore blue jeans and tennis shoes, but kept a uniformed police officer by her side as she knocked on apartment doors, trying to gather potential testimony against Money Rock, Big Lou, and the seven other men charged with shooting up the housing project. When she introduced herself—*Shirley Fulton, Mecklenburg County District Attorney's office*—she often got plenty of nothing— residents who claimed they'd seen nothing, individuals who answered their doors and listened to her introduction, then denied being the tenants she sought. *It's like a murder in a liquor house*, Fulton thought. *A room full of people, and nobody saw a thing.*

Fulton knew from the outset that this would be her highest-profile trial in three years as a prosecutor. It wasn't just the violence that made the crime headline-grabbing. Charlotte had seen worse shootings, including the July Fourth Massacre of 1979, the murder of five Outlaws motorcycle gang members in their own clubhouse. That incident, however, had been a private affair, with perpetrators attacking the Outlaws on their own turf, in an isolated area of north Charlotte.[1] Piedmont Courts, on the other hand, was midafternoon gunfire in a

public space, blocks from police headquarters. The brazen quality of
the crime had rattled even Fulton. She understood why people sold
drugs in poor neighborhoods, but dealers firing into a crowd of innocent people showed a reckless disregard for human life. It crossed
a line.

The district attorney's office had randomly assigned the case to Fulton, but it was a fortuitous match. She was the county's only African
American prosecutor. Though she'd occasionally found herself under-
estimated and misidentified—once, a white defense lawyer looking
for the district attorney spoke to nearly everyone in the courtroom
before approaching her—Fulton found her race could also be an asset.
It allowed her to communicate with black defendants in ways white
colleagues could not. She could threaten to inform defendants' mothers of their misdeeds and chide them for embarrassing their community. *Boy, you better get yourself straight*, she could say. And she could
get away with it.

She also understood the reticence she was encountering. The
thirty-three-year-old prosecutor had grown up in an insular community, Kingstree, South Carolina, on her family's cotton and tobacco
farm, where she'd spent summers working through brutal heat to har-
vest tobacco leaves and pull cotton from prickly brown pods. In this
majority-black town, natives spoke a Geechie dialect, passed down
from African slaves, and they regarded outsiders warily, knowing
from experience they couldn't rely on police protection or the rule
of law.

In Piedmont Courts, there was a similar insularity, a belief that you
looked out for your own people, even if that meant withholding information. Numerous residents were friends or relatives of defendants.
Dealers built loyalty by doling out financial support. And anyone who
snitched risked retribution. So law-abiding tenants learned to live
with dealers. "If you don't bother them," one resident explained to a
reporter, "they won't bother you."[2]

Fulton had come far. She'd attended a two-room black elementary
school in a South Carolina county that required potential voters to

prove they could read. She'd been shy but so smart that she'd skipped grades. Early on, she'd understood that race discrimination permeated her community, extending even into her segregated high school, where a light-skinned counselor ignored darker-skinned students like Fulton. But she found a mentor, a local funeral director who made sure she enrolled in North Carolina A&T State University in Greensboro by driving her there himself. Fulton, who'd never attended school with white students, felt less intimidated by NC A&T, a black college that offered familiarity and camaraderie. She was only sixteen when she enrolled, "book smart, but otherwise like a deer in the headlights," she recalled. She dropped out junior year, eloping with a man ten years older. Soon, she had a son, Kevin, and a job in the register of deeds office. There, she encountered the first lawyers she'd ever met. They intrigued her with their briefcases, full of important papers that might change a client's life. She liked that. She could see herself with a briefcase, and, as months passed, she saw herself as a lawyer.

By 1977, on the day her son started kindergarten, Fulton attended her first law school class at NC Central, a historically black university in Durham. Fulton, then twenty-five years old, had divorced, finished her bachelor's degree, and earned a law school scholarship. A year later, at a professor's urging, she transferred across town to Duke University, more prestigious and mostly white. Soon after graduating, she got a call from Charlotte's district attorney, Peter Gilchrist. Initially, she was reluctant to join a criminal justice system that seemed so often stacked against African Americans. But a talk with a black prosecutor changed her mind. He helped her see she could wield power that extended beyond punishment. Prosecutors could dismiss a case or defer prosecution. Working inside the system, she would have opportunities to address inequities.

Fulton began with misdemeanors, gradually working her way up to serious felonies. She wasn't a natural orator. The first time she argued before the U.S. Fourth Circuit Court of Appeals, her voice had trembled. But by the time she was assigned to the Piedmont Courts shooting several years later, she'd developed a calm, solid courtroom persona. She'd long since scrubbed Geechie from her speech, mastering the art of what family members referred to as "speaking proper." People hearing her dignified cadence sometimes thought she was from the North, or even Jamaica. They never guessed she was the daughter of South Carolina tobacco farmers.

In every way, Fulton personified the extraordinary gains many African Americans had made over the past quarter century. And yet this shootout case and, in particular, the hopelessness she sensed among Piedmont Courts residents, suggested that something had gone awry in those same years. When she was growing up, almost everyone worked, even if they were poor. Most Piedmont Courts residents she met lacked jobs and, it seemed, any optimism about a different future. The children they were raising often dropped out of school and had babies while still children themselves. If the civil rights era had improved the lives of these people, it was hard to tell.

Gradually, as she continued her witness interviews, Fulton cracked the code of silence. She got some of her best information from the youngest shooting victim, Sabrina White, fourteen years old and eight months pregnant when she'd taken bullets in the arm and leg. The day that Fulton interviewed the pregnant teenager at a dining table, several adults in the apartment pointedly avoided them. She'd expected Sabrina's mother to appear and introduce herself. She never did. Nor did any other adult. Sabrina struck Fulton as street smart, a child who'd grown up too fast. She said goodbye to the teenager feeling sadness.

Though Sabrina couldn't say who shot her, she placed several defendants at the scene. Sabrina's seventeen-year-old brother, Andre, also proved helpful. He'd seen two defendants—one shooting from the window of an apartment, the other firing out of the door—though he couldn't say if either had hit anyone.[3]

Even with eyewitness testimony from Sabrina, Andre, and several others, Fulton wasn't sure exactly what had transpired at Piedmont Courts. She knew she was dealing with rival dealers and that residents viewed Louis Samuels as a dangerous bully. One wounded bystander,

Veronica Streeter, had complained that Lou, though awash in cash, refused to support the two children she'd had by him.[4] Money Rock, however, was a mystery. He had no criminal record, and she didn't know that he'd instigated the confrontation by bringing armed men into Piedmont Courts.

While she built her case, Fulton tried to calm community fears. One evening, she attended a public meeting at Seigle Avenue Presbyterian Church, across the street from Piedmont Courts, to reassure attendees that the city was taking serious action. The church—the same one Annie Fiadjigbe attended—was an unusual mix of congregants—blacks who lived in or near Piedmont Courts, whites from all around Charlotte. It had begun as a white church in a white neighborhood, but when urban renewal pushed blacks into the neighborhood, whites fled. Instead of packing up and fleeing with them, the congregation's response had been to embrace its new neighbors, providing free or low-cost after-school care, preschool, and summer field trips for neighborhood children. That social-justice mission attracted like-minded people from around Charlotte. During the church meeting, Fulton noticed that some of the people most upset about crime lived outside the community. For many residents she'd interviewed, the dangers of random violence and drug dealing had become an unfortunate fact of life, as inevitable as a thunderstorm. But the outsiders—people who didn't deal with the violence on a daily basis—still had hope. They believed citizens working together could change Piedmont Courts. Fulton believed that too.

The nine defendants each faced the same charges—felony riot, plus five counts of assault with a deadly weapon with intent to kill, inflicting serious injury. Fulton decided to prosecute them in two groups, partly to keep the trials manageable, but also to minimize conflicting testimony from witnesses representing the two warring camps. She'd get to Big Lou and his gang later. First, she was prosecuting Money Rock's crew.

When jury selection began on Monday, April 14, 1986, Belton Platt arrived dressed to impress, wearing a tight suit jacket that emphasized

Belton Platt outside the Mecklenburg County courtroom during his 1986 Piedmont Courts shootout trial. Photo by Jeep Hunter, courtesy of the *Charlotte Observer*.

his extra poundage. His accessories—pocket handkerchief, narrow tie, diamond ring, diamond ear stud—did nothing to help his case.[5] If Belton Platt's attire said gangster, Fulton's straight-skirted suit and businesslike pumps signaled status-quo professionalism. Her Afro years behind her, now she straightened and curled her hair.

The case presented Fulton with an array of complications. Her primary task was to convince jurors that Money Rock and Big Lou got into a childish argument, which escalated into a barrage of gunfire as the dealers and their men emptied their guns on the public housing project's main street. But she couldn't answer one basic question: Who shot whom? Police never found the weapons that had fired the bullets, and without those, she couldn't know for sure. But she could use a legal concept called "acting in concert," which says a person who's

Louis Samuels heading into the Mecklenburg County courthouse for his trial in 1986.
Photo by Candace Freeland, courtesy of the *Charlotte Observer*.

acting with others to commit a crime can be guilty without committing all elements of that crime. She would rely heavily on circumstan-
tial evidence, mostly testimony from victims and bystanders. Even so,
she believed she could marshal a solid prosecution.

Fulton kicked off testimony by calling several shooting victims, including Sabrina White. Sabrina, wearing jeans and white tennis shoes,
looked like a child as she settled herself on the stand. In the four
months since the shootout, she had turned fifteen and given birth to
a son.[6] She spoke softly, telling jurors that she had been sitting on her
porch when bullets struck her arm and leg. She was too busy diving
for cover to see who shot her.[7]

Sabrina's brother, Andre, came next. He testified that he'd been close
enough to hear part of the argument between Big Lou and Money

Rock that had preceded the shootout. "They was arguing about who had the most stuff—money, cars, whatever else," he told jurors.[8]

By the time Judge Joseph Pachnowski recessed that afternoon, Fulton had made a good start. But outside the courtroom, new problems were brewing. Witnesses yet to be called complained they didn't want to testify and didn't intend to return the next day. A prosecutor assisting Fulton had the task of corralling them, making sure they showed up in the morning and returned after lunch break. When one man announced that he wouldn't be back, Fulton hauled him before the judge, who threatened arrest if he didn't return the next morning.

Fulton understood that witnesses' lives might be entwined with those of the defendants, but she hadn't appreciated how entwined until she looked out the courthouse window after court recessed. There, two stories below, she saw Money Rock. He was free on bond, a bond Fulton considered ridiculously low. He was climbing into his large car and leaving for the day. But she did a double take when she saw his female passenger—one of the shooting victims. From what Fulton could tell, her main defendant was giving one of his victims a ride home.

On Wednesday, the second day of testimony, Fulton called a young man who was potentially her best witness, or her worst. Ideally, lawyers interview witnesses ahead of time, asking every question they intend to ask at trial so they're prepared for the testimony they'll hear. But Fulton hadn't been able to find Willie Townsend. After the shootout, he'd given police a written statement saying he had watched Money Rock fire a gun and shoot Big Lou. He was the only person who'd said he saw someone shoot someone else. She could only hope he'd say it again.

Townsend placed his hand on a Bible, swore to tell the truth, and immediately began backtracking, explaining he'd changed his mind about seeing Money Rock shoot Big Lou. "It was just talk going on in the street," he told the jury. "I didn't see anything because I started running."[9]

Fulton tried again. She asked Townsend to read the statement he'd given police. He refused. "It's not the truth," he said.[10]

At an impasse, Fulton asked the judge to admit Townsend's prior statement as evidence. At least the jury would understand that her witness had changed his story.

Fulton's prosecution would have been easier if she'd had two things—drugs and guns. But experienced dealers almost never carried drugs on them. They delegated that job to underlings. And though police had found nineteen guns in Big Lou's house a couple of days after the shootout, none matched bullets at the scene. Fulton suspected she knew what had happened to Money Rock's guns. Townsend, in the statement he'd now recanted, had said he'd watched Al Platt, Money Rock's brother, place guns in the trunk of a Toyota. The car had sped away before police arrived.[11]

But Fulton had one sort of physical evidence: cash. When police opened the trunk of Money Rock's Cadillac Seville after the shootout, they found six diamond rings, plus a garbage bag and purse filled with $12,983. Nothing illegal, of course, about carrying thousands of dollars and diamond rings in a car trunk, but the evidence spoke volumes. Surely, she thought, it would help convince jurors that Money Rock was a big-time cocaine dealer.[12]

On Thursday, the third and final day of testimony, Fulton put a crime lab chemist on the stand, hoping to drive home the connection between Money Rock's cash and his illegal profession. The chemist testified that he'd found traces of cocaine on the money in Belton's Cadillac trunk. This sounded damning until Jim Carson, the veteran defense lawyer representing Belton, conducted his cross-examination. Given that cocaine had become so widely used, he asked, wouldn't you find tiny amounts on most paper money in circulation? Wouldn't any large amount of money show small traces of cocaine?

I don't know, the chemist admitted.[13]

Carson also introduced an explanation for the cash in the trunk. It belonged not to Belton, but to his mother, community activist Carrie Graves. She had raised it for the Pan-African Culture and Resource

Center, a community center she had founded. In January, three months before the trial, mother and son had gone to court and successfully demanded that police return the money. A judge had agreed there was no evidence tying the cash to a crime.[14]

Fulton rested her case soon after the chemist's testimony. It surely wasn't airtight. None of the five victims could identify their assailants. Willie Townsend had recanted the best evidence against Money Rock. Another witness had claimed that the detective investigating the case had tried to bribe him, offering a thousand dollars a head if he'd help convict Money Rock and Big Lou.[15] Money Rock appeared to be providing transportation for his victims, and Fulton knew that many in Piedmont Courts didn't appreciate her tireless efforts to bring criminals to justice. But she had no regrets. She'd done the best she could.

Once she rested her case, the defendants' lawyers all moved to dismiss charges because the prosecution failed to prove the cases against their clients. These motions are standard, and judges usually don't grant them. But in this case, Pachnowski agreed to drop charges against two men—Gordon Platt, Money Rock's younger brother, and William "December" Hamilton, the man who was shot when he tried to break up the fight between Money Rock and Big Lou. Pachnowski ruled the state had failed to show that either had been engaged in a riot.[16]

Fulton knew the evidence against those two had been flimsy; she could live with the dismissals. Her goal was to get Money Rock.

Carson, Belton's attorney, presented no defense. He wasn't about to let Belton take the stand. But Carson had tried to poke holes in Fulton's case during cross-examinations. He'd also tried to explain away the fact that several witnesses had identified his client with the drug-dealer moniker "Money Rock," suggesting through his questions that they'd somehow misheard the name. Repeatedly, Carson insisted his client's nickname was "Monty Rock," based on his middle name, Lamont. Fulton listened, trying not to roll her eyes. What Carson said was technically true. "Monty Rock" had once been Belton's nickname. But that was another time, another life.

Closing arguments came next. Fulton, in hers, emphasized that the trial was about something larger than shootings—the basic right of people to feel safe in their own community. "Acquit these men," she told jurors, "and you might as well say to Sabrina White, this is your life. Cocaine and street fighting are something you'll have to learn to deal with." Acquit them, she said, and the defendants will get their guns and cocaine and return to Piedmont Courts. Acquit them, and it will be business as usual.[17]

8

CONVICTIONS

Money Rock's jury took only a few hours to return the verdict: guilty on all charges.

On one side of the courtroom, Fulton took a breath, relieved.

On the other side, Belton sat in shock. The shootout and his arrest had momentarily chastened him, but he'd made bond without spending a single night in jail. As months passed, he no longer felt panicked recalling the shootout scene, and his hubris had returned. During the trial, he assured himself that his attorney was sharp, the government's case was weak, and not a single witness had testified that he shot a gun. He didn't imagine that jurors could convict him of attempted murder.

At the sentencing hearing the next week, lawyer Jim Carson presented a portrait of Belton as Boy Scout and lifelong do-gooder—a young man who'd registered voters, worked with children, volunteered on political campaigns. Carson introduced letters from both a county commissioner and the president of the Charlotte Housing Authority Residents' Association attesting to Belton's virtues. By the time Carson finished, Money Rock sounded like he deserved a citizenship award.[1]

Fulton figured Belton's mother, Carrie Graves, had lined up these glowing endorsements. She knew that Carrie's work with African American candidates and Democratic causes gave her connections. People owed her, and she was calling in favors. Though Fulton had

sensed Carrie's hostile stares during the trial, she respected her reputation as an activist who, under different circumstances, Fulton would
have enjoyed knowing. She also didn't discount the praise she was
hearing. Succumbing to the lure of drug dealing made Belton a law
breaker. It didn't necessarily make him evil.

Still, she wanted this case to send a message. What would Charlotte
become, Fulton thought, if drug dealers felt emboldened to solve dis-
putes with public shootings? In the four days between verdict and sentencing hearing, she decided she needed someone to testify about how
the shootout had damaged the community. She telephoned the mayor.

Harvey Gantt, a forty-three-year-old architect, was a rising star in
the Democratic Party and a popular figure in Charlotte. The son of a
shipyard worker in Charleston, South Carolina, he'd lived as a child in
segregated public housing not all that different than Piedmont Courts
in its better days, then gained fame when he integrated South Carolina's Clemson University in 1963, the year Belton was born. After
serving on Charlotte's city council and losing in his first mayoral run,
he was elected on his second try in 1983, the first African American
mayor in a city that was 70 percent white. In the process, he became
a symbol, embodying the aspirations of a place eager to forget its past
and become a progressive city in the New South.

Gantt took the stand, placed his hand on a Bible, swore to tell the
truth. Yes, he said, the city had increased police patrols in Piedmont
Courts following the shootout. But you couldn't solve this problem
in the long term by turning the public housing project into an armed
camp. A better answer, he told the judge, was swift and sure punishment of those who violated the law.[2]

Years later, Gantt recalled little about this testimony, though he said
he realized even then that swift and sure punishment wouldn't make
Piedmont Courts' problems disappear. An illegal economy would
always prosper when poverty forced people to find ingenious ways to
survive. Some enterprising young man would step into Money Rock's
place as soon as he was gone. Gantt also admitted that Charlotte had

different priorities in 1986, and fixing impoverished inner-city neighborhoods didn't top the list. The city was starting to take off economi-
cally as local banks began expanding into other states. "That probably
was more of our focus, unfortunately, than dealing with the crime in
low-income neighborhoods or the bigger drug problems in the city,"
he said.

Belton, twenty-two years old, had no prior convictions. Judge
Pachnowski weighed character witnesses' glowing testimony and the
mayor's request for swift, sure punishment, then announced a thirty-
five-year sentence. State prison sentences were rarely as long as advertised. With time deducted for good behavior and a solid work record,
thirty-five years might end up closer to fifteen. Still, this was a real
punishment—more time than Fulton had expected.

Again, Belton was stunned, but didn't give up. He returned to Pachnowski's courtroom the next day to ask for bond while he appealed.
Standing in leg chains before the judge, he explained somewhat
vaguely that he was helping to create a drug and alcohol rehabilitation
center, so it would be useful if he could be free during the appeal. Even
a high bond would be acceptable. "I feel like the Lord knows we're not
guilty," he said, "and he'll make a way for us to make a high bond. I'm
not somebody who would hurt anybody. I'd help them before I'd hurt
them."[3]

Fulton suppressed a smile. Pachnowski denied the bond request.
"You may believe in your innocence," the judge told Belton, "but
twelve people didn't."[4]

Pachnowski was right. Belton believed in his innocence. He felt bad
about the blood spilled on Hollywood Boulevard, but blamed Big Lou,
not himself, for the debacle. He viewed himself as an entrepreneur—a
job creator who gave generously to his community. He would have
loved building a drug rehab center. "Drugs are poison," he'd told the
judge, straight-faced.[5]

Belton wasn't deceiving anyone in the courtroom, but he'd become
adept at deceiving himself. He was known to duck out of the room

when a user—his brother Al, for instance—smoked cocaine. He couldn't see the dotted line connecting the white powder he sold and the misery he witnessed in Piedmont Courts.

Several diversions kept his mind off this contradiction. One was sex, often not with his wife. It relaxed him. Another was his side business—the Money Rock Express, a hole-in-the-wall nightclub with about a dozen tables, a dance floor, a pool table on Astroturf. He'd hired a manager to run it and stopped in regularly, sometimes spinning records from the DJ booth. The club was located in a shopping center on West Boulevard near Dalton Village, the housing project where he grew up. It wasn't much, but he saw it as a step into legitimate businesses and out of illegal dealings.

As he awaited trial, Belton had found an even bigger diversion—religion. He'd been at the nightclub one day when Carrie had dropped in, eager to tell him about her new church, a nondenominational start-up that met in a school gym. Since the shootout, Carrie had been desperate for spiritual consolation. Lonnie had moved out. They would soon divorce, and the man who'd tried hardest to be a father to Belton would disappear from his life.

Normally, Carrie would have attended St. Paul Baptist, a mainline black church near Piedmont Courts. This had been her family's church since childhood, when it was still in Brooklyn, before urban renewal forced it to relocate. But St. Paul was a mostly middle-class congregation—Carrie referred to members as *the bourgeoisie*—and she'd come to feel she didn't belong. Class differences in Charlotte's African American community were nothing new. They'd existed since at least the 1880s, when emerging black leaders began referring to themselves as "the better class."[6] But urban renewal had magnified class distinctions, destroying socioeconomically mixed black neighborhoods. Public housing became home to the poorest black citizens. Many better-off blacks, including Reginald Hawkins, the dentist and fiery civil rights activist who helped integrate Charlotte's public facilities, took pains to separate themselves from that group. "When I was a child, we had public housing, but people had pride," he told the *Observer* in 1986, after the shootout. "I think you've got a whole different breed of blacks living in these projects."[7]

Feeling estranged from St. Paul, Carrie had sought a church where she could be sure people empathized with her problems. She'd tried out several, including the Seventh-Day Adventists, but crossed that church off her list when she learned she'd have to stop wearing jewelry and button her dress to her neck. Even in her lowest moments, Carrie had style.

She'd first heard the pastor of Jesus Christ Outreach Ministries on a radio broadcast, where he described his former life as a drug dealer. His church turned out to be a perfect fit. She explained to Belton that its members didn't care what you wore, or if you'd served time, or even if you showed up inebriated. She told him she'd been tithing the money he'd been giving her. She urged him to join her for a worship service.

Belton had inherited his mother's concern for the poor and had grown up attending St. Paul Baptist, but he had little use for Christianity. As a child, he contemplated God only occasionally, usually after breaking some rule and worrying he might go to hell. By the time he began selling cocaine, he saw Christians as soft and weak. He didn't trust preachers. He especially distrusted this man taking his mother's money. Ever since his father stabbed his mother, he'd felt bound to make sure no one else took advantage. The more he thought about this new preacher, the more Belton resolved to teach him a lesson. One Sunday soon after Carrie had invited him to church, he woke early and put on his suit. He called and offered to drive her to church. Before heading out the door, he tucked a pistol inside his suit jacket.

Carrie, with no clue her son was plotting a confrontation, thought Jesus had finally touched Belton's heart. She slid into his passenger's seat, praising the Lord for this turn of events.

"Mama," Belton told her, "don't start."

They pulled into the parking lot and found seats midway back in the school gym. Then the preacher stepped out, and Belton realized he knew the guy. For a time, Andrew "Butch" Lockhart had dated one of Belton's half sisters, Alphonso's daughter by his first marriage. But the last time Belton had seen Lockhart, the man was a drug dealer and cocaine user, a fellow who wore a mink coat and drove a convertible Cadillac. He nudged his mom and informed her of this.

"Honey," she replied, "that's what he used to be."

Belton listened, awed by the preacher's authority, not so much what he said, but the way that he said it. Belton sensed God's presence, a feeling he'd never had before.

When Lockhart invited worshippers forward for the laying on of hands, Belton made his way to the front. He waited in line, feeling guilty about the gun in his jacket.

"Butch," Belton asked, "when did this happen to you?"

The Lord called me, Lockhart told him, and I had to surrender.

"Man," Belton said, "that's all right."

Lockhart's hands went to Belton's head, as he beseeched God to break Satan's power over his life. The gun remained inside Belton's jacket. As he awaited trial, he became a regular at the church, so enthusiastic about Lockhart's preaching that he wanted his men to experience it too. He made quite an entrance, attired in a suit and gold jewelry, accompanied by his drug-dealing entourage.

The jailhouse conversion is a phenomenon well known to criminal defense lawyers. With the chips down, a defendant discovers religion, only to lose it once his fortunes improve. Belton would insist that this turn to Christianity had been sincere, even though it came after he'd been charged in the shootout. Lockhart agreed—a season of planting, he called it, when the results were still invisible. Belton kept selling cocaine, but years later, he pinpointed that Sunday with his mother as the day his eyes were opened to the sins he was committing. Then came the conviction, and everything in his life—church services, nightclub visits, his affairs—came to an abrupt halt.

Two months after Belton's conviction, I covered Lou's trial. From what I'd seen, Big Lou was the heavy in this drama, the bad actor who'd been charged with more than thirty crimes yet somehow avoided prison time. Belton had seemed tame by comparison, fairly new to crime, no previous felony convictions. Some Piedmont Courts

Belton Platt during a 1986 interview with the author in Raleigh's Central Prison. Photo by Candace Freeland, courtesy of the *Charlotte Observer*.

residents liked him. One shootout victim, a bystander caught in the crossfire, described him to me as "a nice young person."

Lou's prosecution had the same difficulties as Belton's—no guns, no physical evidence. Fulton won a felony riot conviction, but a jury acquitted Samuels on five charges of assault with a deadly weapon with intent to kill. He got a five-year sentence.

Belton, meanwhile, was praying for a miracle. He'd landed in Raleigh's Central Prison, about three hours east of Charlotte. That's where I first interviewed him. Then the state transferred him farther east to Caledonia Correctional Institution, a prison built on what was once a slave plantation. He got a job folding laundry and met an inmate who gave him a slim book by Kenneth Hagin titled *The Believer's Authority*. Hagin, father of the international Word of Faith movement, preached a message of empowerment that often resonated with people who felt shut out of the American dream. Much of Hagin's teachings stemmed historically from Pentecostalism—a belief in prophecies and faith healing, for instance, and a belief that God spoke regularly to individual followers. Hagin also taught that Christians have the power to transform their own lives, to achieve wealth and health, if only they use the authority Christ has given them. His teachings, also known as the prosperity gospel, offered a very different message from those of mainline Christian denominations, where believers learned that suffering in this life eventually was rewarded in heaven. Hagin's message seemed very American—this idea that you could change your station, that you could control your destiny.

Belton found it a revelation. Incarceration had robbed him of control. But as he studied and prayed, he came to believe that he could exercise God's authority to change his life. His focus wasn't on wealth. He just wanted God to overturn his conviction. Soon, he came to see the Holy Spirit all around him, even in the human form of an inmate he knew only as Bishop. One day, as Belton was headed toward his dorm, Bishop approached him.

"Hey, Bishop," Belton said.

Bishop responded, not with a greeting, but by swiping his hand across the top of Belton's head.

Receive the Holy Ghost, Bishop said. The inmate continued on his way, but Belton halted, frozen. He felt struck by lightning, infused with a power that flowed through his body. This near intoxication persisted as he made his way back to his dorm. Soon after their encounter, Bishop disappeared from the prison. Belton asked, but never found where he'd gone.

After only months in Caledonia, Belton was transferred again, this time to Harnett County Correctional Institution, where he made $2.50 a week counting and boxing the blue soap that inmates manufactured for use throughout the prison system. In early 1987, as he labored over soap bars, three North Carolina Court of Appeals justices convened in Raleigh. Their task, to decide whether to overturn or uphold his conviction, would determine his future.

The appeals discussion centered on Willie Townsend, that one reluctant prosecution witness. Townsend had been the only person who told police he'd seen Money Rock shoot Big Lou, but recanted on the witness stand, claiming he was only repeating gossip on the street. When testimony ended and jurors began deliberating, Judge Pachnowski had allowed them to examine Townsend's recanted witness statement. This action, the appeals justices ruled, had been an error. And it was an error serious enough to warrant a new trial.

Belton didn't know it yet, but his prayers had been answered.

9

HEAVY IN THE WEIGHT

Belton had been praying to find a nice home for his family, and when he spotted the classified ad in the newspaper, it practically glowed on the page. The three-bedroom ranch was a foreclosure in Mint Hill, a suburb ten miles east of downtown, safely distant from inner-city black neighborhoods. It was nestled in a neighborhood of cul-de-sacs and curved streets, their names apparently plucked by some developer from a map of the United Kingdom—Heathersgate Lane, Cairnsmore Place, Lancashire Drive. The house on Ravenglass Lane, named for a coastal village in Britain's Lake District, was what real estate agents call a starter home—a first step toward the American dream that, by definition, wouldn't be the last. He bought it for $60,000 in December 1988. The house had a brick façade, a small porch with five steps, and a living-room fireplace. He put a chain-link fence around the backyard and a basketball hoop in the driveway for seven-year-old Lamont. In the bedroom closet, he installed a safe. He got a mortgage to avoid attracting attention, though he could have paid cash.

At that point, he'd been out of prison eighteen months, since May 20, 1987. Instead of thirty-five years, he'd served one, a stunning fortune reversal that the Mecklenburg County District Attorney's office blamed on a lack of evidence and that Belton credited to God. The state could have prosecuted him again after the NC Court of Appeals overturned his conviction, but with no proof that he'd fired a gun and no witnesses testifying who shot whom, prosecutors knew the case was weak. Shirley Fulton and colleagues concluded that another trial would likely be a costly waste of time.

Belton had returned home vowing to make the most of this second chance. No more cocaine dealing. No more adultery. Rhonda, pregnant when he was convicted, had given birth to their second son during his prison stint. They'd named the child Stephen after the Biblical Stephen, pronouncing it "STEF-en." In the Book of Acts, Stephen, described as full of faith and the Holy Spirit, is killed by stoning after testifying for Jesus before his fellow Jews. In the Bible, Stephen dies a martyr. Stephen had his first birthday not long after Belton returned. Big Lamont, his oldest son, turned six.

At first, Belton resumed his old line of work—a janitorial business. His Cadillac was gone. Now he hauled squeegees, mops, and buckets in a used Ford Escort. He serviced a doctor's office and several Burger King restaurants and won a contract to clean construction dust and debris from brand-new apartments, leaving each unit ready for its first tenant. He was supporting his family, paying the bills, again attending Pastor Lockhart's church. But his marriage was a mess. Rhonda had admitted to an affair while he was in prison. He'd been devastated, though his own extramarital liaisons had already produced seven children. Some of these offspring Rhonda had always known about—Lisa's daughter, Kim, who was born before Rhonda and Belton married, and a son and daughter he'd had with Janie Robinson, who he'd gotten to know because she lived in Cherry, his grandmother's neighborhood. Rhonda and Janie had made peace for the children's sake. Rhonda even took Janie Christmas shopping, footing the bill for clothing and toys.

But there were other children Rhonda discovered only belatedly. She said she hadn't known about Derrick and Demario until she spotted the two of them in a store. The curly-haired brothers so resembled Belton that she knew the truth immediately. And then there was the day that Belton's pager buzzed insistently while he slept. Rhonda finally responded by telephoning the number. A woman answered.

Who's this? the woman asked.

"This is his wife," Rhonda replied.

You need to tell your husband, the woman said, that he needs to bring his baby some Pampers.

That's how Rhonda discovered the son named Antonio.

Despite Belton's serial infidelities, he felt powerfully wronged by hers. She'd sworn she'd broken off her affair, but he took to quizzing her about her whereabouts, even searching the car for incriminating evidence. Rhonda didn't trust him, either. She suspected his visits to his other children were excuses to see their mothers. Their arguments grew frequent and sometimes violent. Once, he punched Rhonda in the mouth, busting her lip. Another time, he grabbed her around the throat, choking her until his mother stepped in and knocked his hands away.

After one fight, Belton left their house in tears, furious and trying to keep himself from attacking her. He headed out to see Janie, a good listener, someone he could confide in. As they sat on the sofa, he told Janie he was determined to keep his marriage together, and yet he and Rhonda were making each other miserable. He recalled to me years later that Janie consoled him, hugging him and wiping his face. She assured him his marriage would survive. And then, minutes later, the two had sex.

Janie didn't remember these exact details when I shared them with her, but she did recall Belton visiting once after a bad fight with Rhonda. She also recalled having relations with him. "People do stuff out of madness and hurt," she said.

After the sex, Belton felt worse, convinced he had failed God and his wife. It was in this defeated state, he recalled, that he decided to sell cocaine again—just a little on the side, extra income to ease financial worries while he continued his cleaning business.

He got an ounce from his old supplier, the car dealer, who'd been surprised to see him after having recently heard him witness about his newfound faith. Belton divided it into bags, sold them, and soon bought more. One day, he met up with his old friend Bernard Torrence.

He opened his briefcase, pulled out a bag of powder, and suggested they try to turn it. "It was a dry run, nine ounces," Bernard recalled. "See if he could make some money, but stay low key."

This was early 1988, and the list of celebrities and athletes busted with, addicted to, or dying from cocaine had grown long. Comedian Richard Pryor set himself on fire in 1980 after attempting freebasing—dissolving coke in ether, then heating the mixture and smoking it. The FBI nabbed automaker John DeLorean in 1982 for putting up $1.8 million for 220 pounds of cocaine that he'd hoped to sell for $24 million. In 1986, University of Maryland basketball star Len Bias, newly signed by the Boston Celtics, had dropped dead after snorting cocaine. In Miami, New York, and other big cities, rival dealers gunned each other down in public.

To understand America's reaction to this growing problem, it's instructive to know what happened the first time the drug became popular in America—around the turn of the twentieth century, before any laws prohibited it. Cocaine, processed from the leaves of the coca plant in South America, was initially hailed as an effective treatment for assorted maladies—sinusitis, allergies, even opium addiction. The Hay Fever Association endorsed it as an official remedy. It gave aptly named Coca-Cola its special zip.[1] Employers doled out cocaine to laborers who toiled at punishing jobs—unloading ship cargo, picking cotton, building levees and railroads—hoping to get more work out of these men, most of whom were black.[2] By the early twentieth century, stories spread, mostly in the South, of coke-hyped black men transformed into violent monsters. Even the *New York Times* published dubious tales, with a 1914 column headlined "Negro Cocaine 'Fiends' Are a New Southern Menace." Its author, a physician named Edward Huntington Williams, offered one anecdote from a North Carolina police chief who claimed that a black attacker remained unfazed after being shot by a revolver at point-blank range "over the negro's heart."[3] This Negro-as-cocaine-fiend narrative became useful to justify attacks on African Americans—white-led race riots, lynchings, new Jim Crow laws that wove racial inequality into the nation's fabric.

Cocaine nearly disappeared after the Harrison Narcotics Act criminalized it in 1914. When it reemerged more than a half century later, in the late 1970s and '80s, many equated its rise with America's prevailing mood. The narcissistic excess of the times aligned nicely with the sense of invincibility that came with a coke high. While the nation's zeitgeist may have helped fuel the cocaine boom, several policy decisions also played a role by unintentionally boosting the coke market. When the New York–based World Bank financed construction of a stretch of the Pan-American Highway through the high jungles of Peru, for instance, the new paved road eased shipping difficulties for many products, including coca previously transported by mule pack. With this infrastructure, South American cocaine dealers could ramp up production. Meanwhile, America clamped down on other popular highs, reducing production of amphetamine-type drugs, getting tougher on sales of abused sedatives such as quaaludes.[4] Marijuana took a hit too, with enforcement efforts intercepting smugglers in the Atlantic and destroying crops with herbicide. As a result, many dealers simply switched product lines. Cocaine was easier to pirate into the country than bulky, fragrant bales of pot. Also, it commanded bigger profits.[5]

As America's new cocaine culture blossomed under presidents Ford and Carter, Charlotte remained a cultural backwater, full of barbecue joints and fried-seafood restaurants known as fish camps, a town where it remained illegal for restaurateurs to sell cocktails. Anti-liquor forces, particularly the influential Southern Baptist *Biblical Recorder* newspaper, had long fought legalization of mixed-drink sales, forcing highball lovers to endure the peculiar custom of brown-bagging. Those wishing to drink had to bring their own liquor, sheathed in bags, while restaurants provided mixers. Business leaders finally convinced voters to approve a liquor-by-the-drink referendum in 1978 by using the same arguments they'd employed to push integration: Mixed drinks, essential to attracting restaurants, tourists, and national conferences, were key to Charlotte's big-city dreams. The referendum won in a landslide; victors celebrated by burning brown paper bags. The first drink served was a bloody Mary. Local press gathered at a restaurant called Benedictine's to cover the event.[6]

Cocaine already had a foothold in this Bible Belt town when that first legal vodka and tomato juice was poured. It had become a staple at certain clubs—nightspots such as the Odyssey, the Roxy, the futuristically named 2001—where dancers pulsed to Donna Summer and Andy Gibb, a sea of sweaty flesh in tight pants, platform shoes, big-collared polyester shirts that hugged chests like shrink-wrap. At regular intervals, users visited restrooms. Friends squeezed into a stall and shared a few lines tapped out onto a mirror. They'd Hoover the powder up through a rolled-up bill or scoop with a miniature spoon that delivered drug to nostril. Inhale into one side, then the other. Feel a telltale acrid drip down the back of the throat, harbinger of that rush of euphoria. Everybody loved the drip.

Then came the 1980s. Users started dying, and the pendulum of public perception lurched from tolerance to condemnation. As Belton eased back into business in early 1988, he didn't know that the Anti-Drug Abuse Act of 1986 had already established mandatory minimum drug sentences, or that a public opinion poll had ranked drugs ahead of nuclear war as the country's most pressing problem, or that President Ronald Reagan and his vice president, George Bush, had had their own urine tested for evidence of cocaine, marijuana, and heroin use.[7] He was aware, however, that the local cocaine landscape was changing. When he was dealing in Piedmont Courts, he'd known the big players—the guys moving weight. Now, dealers were more numerous. Some had come from Jamaica and the Dominican Republic. But the biggest change was in the product itself. Crack had joined Charlotte's retail market.

It's impossible to say who invented crack. Likely multiple people at different times, because the chemistry of crack isn't rocket science. Years before it was sold on the streets, many users, including Belton's oldest brother, cooked it at home. Al Platt recalled that he learned to make crack because he didn't want to risk an explosion that could come with freebasing using flammable ether. Instead of ether, crack used baking soda. He'd put the coke in a test tube with baking soda, add a few drops of water, then hold the tube with a metal clamp while boiling it over a burning cotton ball soaked in rubbing alcohol. By the late '80s, dealers microwaved crack in Pyrex dishes for retail sale. Whatever the method, the process left hard yellowish chunks of coke alkaloid that ignited at a lower temperature than powder cocaine. Small nuggets went for $5 or $10 each. A user heated the nugget in a pipe, inhaled the vapor, and got an intense high. As a retail product, crack became the fast food of cocaine—affordable, ready when you were. Like the high-octane liquor that bootleggers distilled during Prohibition, it delivered a cheap high to the masses.

Belton, however, was a powder man. Powder was what he knew, what he continued to sell. When he restarted his business out of a cousin's apartment in Dalton Village, his immediate family no longer lived there. Lonnie Graves, Belton's stepfather, had divorced Belton's mother, and Carrie, now by herself, had relocated to Savanna Woods, a new development known as "scattered site" public housing, nestled in a white middle-class area instead of in a poor black part of town.

Belton's initial plan to keep the business low key didn't last long. Soon, he had employees again. He also sold wholesale, peddling quarter and half and whole kilos to dealers who cut and resold the coke, or cooked it into crack. He fronted smaller amounts to his own men, who worked in specific neighborhoods. These partnerships resembled franchise operations in that Belton demanded identical product quality across locations. He forbade cutting the cocaine any further. Before long, Money Rock's product was in public housing developments and low-income areas around the city. These neighborhoods— Grier Heights, Clanton Park, Dalton Village, Frazier Avenue, Fairview Homes, Southside Homes—were where many of Charlotte's poorest black people lived. The areas had never been prosperous, but they had become even poorer following urban renewal projects in the 1960s and '70s that demolished blighted neighborhoods and forced uprooted residents into remaining low-income areas. Unemployment and poverty got even worse as unskilled labor jobs dried up and businesses migrated to the white suburbs. In 1960, residents in Grier Heights, just southeast of downtown, earned about half of the city's median income. By 1990, they earned only a third. The story was the same at Fairview Homes, the city's oldest public housing project. In 1960, its residents earned 56 percent of Charlotte's median income. In 1990, they were earning less than a third. In this environment, where single mothers survived on public assistance, Belton had no trouble finding residents who let dealers work out of their apartments in exchange for a couple thousand dollars a month.

Key to success was a new supplier. Like any product, cocaine jumped in price each time it went through another person's hands. Wholesale cocaine was sold by the kilo, 2.2 pounds of powder, a tight brick wrapped in plastic and duct tape, the size of a small bag of flour. Belton, still relying on credit, paid nearly $30,000 a kilo when he dove back into dealing in 1988. Once he'd saved enough, he and his dad went together to buy their first kilo outright. They paid $28,000 in twenties, fifties, and hundreds that they packed into a brown grocery bag and handed to a businessman-dealer named Ace Rivers in the parking lot of the grocery store he owned near Piedmont Courts.

But then Belton got a big break, connecting with a Miami-based Haitian he'd met through a friend of a friend, a dealer who'd sell him uncut kilos for $12,500. He could add half a kilo of mannitol, then sell three half kilos at $14,000 each. His profit: about $30,000 per kilo. He moved multiple kilos per week.

This was pre-internet, of course. Belton had no handbooks, no online message boards that taught the art of the drug deal. Like most dealers in those days, he relied on trial and error. To avoid detection, he varied locales where he prepared the coke, often paying people for use of their dining-room or kitchen tables. A quick glimpse of the operation would suggest a culinary endeavor. Biscuit making, perhaps. Armed with the basics his father taught him, he and his men broke up the cocaine bricks with rolling pins and crushed them into powder. After that, they added mannitol, then shook the mix through sifters to incorporate the cut into the cocaine. Then they rolled some more and sifted again. Belton insisted on repeating the tedious process three or four times. He was a perfectionist, a cocaine artisan. When a junkie dissolved cocaine in water before injecting it, the cut usually left a residue. Belton bragged that his product was so well mixed you couldn't detect it.

Still, he didn't always know what he was doing. He didn't realize you needed masks and plastic gloves when you worked with large amounts of coke to keep it from seeping into pores and nasal membranes. He learned the hard way—when he got jazzed and paranoid after inhaling particles floating in the air.

Belton stayed paranoid even without the drug. But he viewed caution, even paranoia, as prudent, considering he regularly held tens of thousands of dollars in cash or product. Until he could sell the coke, he stashed it at several apartments and houses. He didn't divulge these locations and never kept his money with his product. For a time, he would drive to Miami to buy kilos from his supplier. But he became such a good customer that his supplier agreed to deliver—a duffle bag full of bricks. Even then, somebody in his organization traveled to Florida to place orders. Belton refused to risk a tapped phone line.

Across the nation, smart, ambitious dealers like Belton were creating similar protocols. In 1997, Biggie Smalls, aka the Notorious B.I.G., released the rap hit "Ten Crack Commandments," a top-ten list of rules for drug dealers. "I been in this game for years, it made me an animal," Smalls begins. "It's rules to this shit, I wrote me a manual." The inspiration for the song: a 1994 article "A Crack Dealer's Ten Commandments," published in a hip-hop magazine called *The Source*. The author, journalist Khary Turner, wrote the piece as a sidebar accompanying an article about crack in Detroit, crafting the commandments from his interviews with dealers. These were their basic rules:

1. Never let anyone know how much money you have.
2. Don't let anyone know your next move.
3. Trust no one.
4. Never use what you sell.
5. Never give credit.
6. Never sell out of your home.
7. Keep family and business separate.
8. Never park your stash on your person.
9. Don't be seen communicating with the police.
10. Don't take drugs on consignment—if you can't pay your sup-
    plier up front, don't take the product.[8]

Years before they entered American pop culture via Biggie Smalls, Belton followed these commandments instinctively—most of them, anyway. Buying the Ravenglass Lane house on Charlotte's outskirts kept business and family separate. For good measure, he installed a home alarm system with a nightstand panic button that could trigger the burglar alarm and dial 911. He went to bed with an AK-47 assault rifle in the corner of his bedroom and stashed his .45-caliber pistol under his pillow.

One day, he got word of plans to rob him at an apartment where he had a sales operation. This happened occasionally, but he'd been lucky—he would say blessed—that he'd thwarted robberies after receiving early word, thanks to reliable informants. This time, when the stickup man, known as Chilly, showed up at the apartment complex on Frazier Avenue, Belton was waiting, standing behind his car, holding his AK-47 low and out of view. His men, meanwhile, were hiding, poised to ambush Chilly's driver as soon as Belton handled Chilly.

Chilly approached. Belton raised his weapon and aimed at the man's head. His men, guns drawn, surrounded Chilly's driver, who wet his pants. Belton took Chilly's pistol, marched him into one of the apartments, and ordered him to empty his pockets. By now, the man was begging for his life. Chilly was a dealer, same as Belton, but he'd become addicted to crack. He was getting high on his own supply.

As Belton emptied the bullets from Chilly's pistol, he told him he respected him as a hustler; he would spare him, but if he tried anything again, he'd kill him. Then, so that Chilly could get back on his feet, Belton also violated a commandment, offering to front Chilly some product. As Biggie Smalls warned, *You think a crackhead paying you back, shit, forget it!* But Belton, aware that Chilly had once been successful, sized him up and saw not just a thief, but a potentially good customer. Belton extended a lot of credit.

He also tithed his income, donating 10 percent to good works. He gave his mom hundreds in cash to drop into the offering basket at Pastor Lockhart's growing church. Lockhart had rejected Belton's first donation, sending it back home with Carrie, but Belton kept insisting, arguing that the money was a gift to God, not Lockhart. The pastor relented, reasoning that ministers often don't know how church members come by their offerings. They might be profits from sales of alcohol or cigarettes. He didn't see ministers objecting to those donations. Like Carrie, he saw that you could do good things with dirty money.

In some parts of Charlotte, Belton became known for generosity. Once, when his daughter Kim told a man that Money Rock was her daddy, the man dropped to his knees and bowed to her. "They acted like my daddy was a god," she told me. Belton liked the acclaim and cultivated his image. Occasionally, he and his men would meet up with rival dealers on the basketball court. When they did, it was easy to pick out the women on the sidelines who were part of his crew. They were the ones with the T-shirts that said "Money Rock's crew."

He had both a white and a charcoal-gray Mercedes. The front vanity plate on the gray one said "ROCK." He ordered custom pieces from a local jeweler and dropped $30,000 for a Presidential Rolex, its face encircled by diamonds. He wore diamond rings, a gold cross necklace studded with rubies, a signature gold chain that said "Money Rock."

All this flash seems imprudent if you aim for a low profile. When I asked Belton decades later why he practically advertised his illegal business with his vanity-plated Mercedes and lavish jewelry, he shook his head, regretting wasting so much on that Rolex. "I could have started a business with that," he said. But he'd never considered that his flashy image might have made him a target; he knew many people in those days with similar style. He couldn't explain why he coveted the bling. "I just liked it," he told me.

What it appeared to be was the sort of conspicuous consumption people displayed when they came into fortunes. Robber barons built hundred-room mansions. Donald Trump decked out his penthouse with gold and marble in the style of Louis XIV. In Charlotte, industrialist James B. Duke built the once-legendary Wonder Fountain in the early twentieth century. With water pumped from the Catawba River, miles away, the fountain at Duke's Myers Park mansion drew visitors who watched it spray 150 feet into the air. These men were all making a statement. Money Rock, whose bracelet spelled out "Rock" in diamonds and rubies, was making a similar point.

By early 1989, he was buying cars every few weeks. He might see tens of thousands of dollars over a few days. But narrow escapes, attempted holdups, close calls—these also occurred with alarming regularity. One night, while finishing business at a Frazier Avenue apartment, he was sitting in the kitchen, facing one of his men, who sat with a loaded pump shotgun, his finger on the trigger. A young woman came in, plopped herself onto the man's lap, and sent the gun upward. As it rose, the man's trigger finger flinched, enough to squeeze off a shot. The .357 bullet headed for Belton's head. By the time he'd thrown up his hands and exclaimed: "Oh Lord!" it had grazed his hairline and embedded itself in the wall.

There was a phrase, *heavy in the weight*, that Belton used to describe dealers moving as much coke as he did. Weight referred to kilos, but in Belton's case, the phrase worked as metaphor. He'd put on weight when he began selling cocaine in Piedmont Courts, becoming bloated and moon-faced at age twenty-two. In state prison, he exercised and dropped fifty pounds. But in 1988, after a few months on the streets, Belton was gaining again. His erratic schedule played havoc with his health. When a shipment arrived, he might stay up two or three days straight until it was all cut, packaged, and sold. He ate ribs, steaks, barbecue, and macaroni and cheese to relieve stress. He found solace in banana pudding. By early 1989, he weighed 270 pounds. And there was another weight he felt—a cloak of weariness that pressed down when he stopped hustling long enough to contemplate what he had become.

He still professed his faith. He even witnessed to customers, describing Jesus's love and plan for their lives. His twin desires—to help people and to make big money—created absurd contradictions. When he encountered a customer in particularly bad shape, he sometimes refused to sell. A woman prostituting herself to feed her habit might find Money Rock moving her into an apartment, helping her back on her feet instead of selling her coke. One day, he gave money to a man newly released from prison so he could get new clothes. Later, when he learned the cash had gone for drugs, he confessed his disappointment to his mother. Carrie looked at her son and thought to herself that he was the strangest drug dealer she'd ever seen.

Belton was often gone days at a time from Ravenglass Lane, and Carrie had moved in, helping Rhonda with the children. Carrie had come to accept Belton's profession, and she sometimes performed a ritual to ease her worry for his safety. If he telephoned to say he'd be dropping by for dinner and bringing friends, she'd fetch olive oil from the kitchen, a special bottle she'd prayed over. She dabbed it on her finger. She touched the doorknob that the men would touch and the chairs where they would sit, anointing them with the sign of the cross.

As the grits bubbled on the stove and the eggs cooked in the skillet, she anointed them too, sprinkling in a bit of oil. Then she prayed over them, asking a blessing for the men, some of whom she knew only by street names—Hawk, Diamond, Rabbit. *Lord, keep them safe.* She continued discreetly after they arrived, anointing the jackets they'd shrugged off or the Filas they left on the floor. A dab of olive oil, and then a prayer. *Lord, let them go to sleep. Don't let them go back out tonight.* Night was the worst. After a certain hour, the telephone's ring could only mean tragedy. "When the phone ring, when I heard a siren, it was like something in me collapsed," she recalled. "It was a living hell."

Pastor Lockhart wanted Belton safe too. As a former dealer, he knew it was hard to walk away from easy money. Belton would be shutting down a business that supported employees, fed family members, paid for girlfriends' apartments. "That was part of what made it difficult for him to make the changes," Lockhart recalled. "He had so many people to support." But Lockhart disclosed something Belton found hard to ignore. Lockhart believed he was able to see the future, that he possessed the gift of prophecy. Looking into the future, he saw that if Belton kept dealing, he wouldn't survive.

10

GOING DOWN

One day, early in April 1989, Belton's beeper flashed with a phone number he didn't recognize. When he called the number, the man who answered, LaMorris Watson, reminded him they had met before. Watson, a twenty-five-year-old hustler from Gaston County, just west of Charlotte, said he wanted to do some business. By business, he meant a drug buy. They agreed to meet, though as Belton hung up, something didn't feel right. He turned to Sheila, his latest girlfriend. "That guy's trying to set me up," he told her.

Belton thought more about it, though, and decided he must be wrong. He and Watson had met through a mutual friend, a Charlotte businessman he respected. Belton trusted his friends, and that meant LaMorris Watson must be okay.

He should have had nothing to sell. Some weeks earlier, he'd resolved to leave the game, and had even told his men to find other arrangements. Those bags of cash he tithed were no longer enough to justify the addiction he saw. He felt weary, even after a night's sleep. Pastor Lockhart's dark prophecy rattled in his brain.

But then he'd received a call from a cousin who'd been busted for cocaine in Rock Hill, South Carolina. It had been a sting, with officers posing as high-level drug dealers. His cousin was desperate for money to hire an attorney. He told Belton he had $8,000; all he needed was a half kilo, a little more than a pound. If Belton would buy it, the cousin would sell it and use the profits to pay an attorney.

On that first ask, Belton turned him down, but when his cousin called again, pleading for a favor, he relented. Belton found it difficult to say no when someone needed his help, especially family. Boredom had also eroded his resolve. Though he'd begun searching for a legitimate business, he found himself with too much free time, too little structure. He told his cousin he'd buy the coke for him. He decided to increase the order since he was already buying. If you're going to take a chance on one key, he figured, you might as well buy twenty. He swore to himself that this buy would be the last.

By the time Watson got in touch, Belton had already received and sold most of the shipment. His cousin's plan to sell his share himself had fallen apart when a judge revoked his bond. So with that half kilo left to unload, the timing of Watson's call was perfect.

They met up on a Monday evening, April 10, 1989, at an apartment in Villa Court, a low-income complex in the Grier Heights neighborhood. Belton arrived first, wearing a track suit, driving a Mercedes. The car was charcoal gray; the track suit, powder blue.

Watson also arrived in a Mercedes and also came attired in a track suit—leather, Adidas brand. Inside, Belton introduced Watson to his brother, Gordon, who happened to be riding with him that day. Belton told Watson he'd sell the half kilo, a little over a pound of powder, for $11,500, but he didn't have the product on him. He needed to pick it up. Watson and the Platt brothers left in separate cars, planning to rendezvous across town, near an apartment off West Boulevard, about seven miles away.

As Belton drove, he noticed that funny feeling again, the sense that something was wrong. As a precaution, after retrieving the cocaine, he dropped it and Gordon on West Boulevard, a short walk from the meeting place. He would cruise by to scope out the scene. It was dark, about 9:30 p.m. As he passed a parked sedan, he spotted two men sitting inside. He kept driving. The sedan began following, tailing him around a curve. Blue lights flashed in his mirrors. As Belton pulled to the curb, a second unmarked car zipped past on his left, swung around, and halted in front of him.

In a moment, agents had pistols and a pump shotgun trained on him.

Agent Steven Holland approached and patted him down, unclipped the beeper from the waistband of his pants, and extracted Belton's walking-around money, $989, from his right pocket. Holland continued patting. Belton assured him he had no gun.

To prove it, he pulled up his jacket, then stretched the elastic on his pants away from his body. As Belton stood with FBI guns pointed at him, it was clear his suspicions had been correct. Watson had set him up. Watson was a snitch.

Months earlier, Watson had been charged with trafficking cocaine and faced a long sentence. In deciding to cooperate with law enforcement, he had plenty of company. By 1989, tougher drug laws and mandatory minimums were convincing many young men that cooperating was preferable to decades in prison.

Holland continued his search for drugs, scouring the Mercedes's interior. Nothing. Then he tried to unlock the trunk. After several failed attempts, he commanded Belton to do it.

"You got a search warrant?" Belton asked.

Eventually, the trunk was opened, revealing a wallet and brown paper bag. Inside each, the agents found several thousand in cash, plus Belton's diamond-studded Presidential Rolex, the ID bracelet that spelled "ROCK" in diamonds and rubies, and eleven more gold rings, bracelets, and necklaces. Belton had worn them to a birthday party the previous night, then stashed them in his trunk for safekeeping.

Absent from the trunk, however, was the slightest trace of cocaine.

After Holland searched Belton's Mercedes, he asked Belton to sit with him in his car so he could ask some questions.

"What's your name?" Holland asked.

"Greg," Belton Platt said.

"What's your last name?" Holland asked.

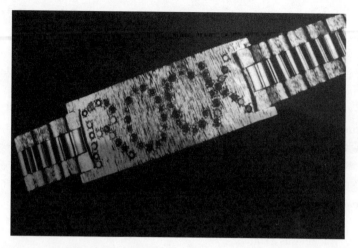

Belton's diamond and ruby bracelet. Photo from U.S. Attorney's Office records.

"Williams," Belton said. The name just came to him. Belton didn't even know a Greg Williams. So far, he wasn't too worried. The FBI had nothing.

"Where do you live?" Holland asked.

"Up the street," Belton said.

"Could you be more specific?"

"Across town."

"You just told me that you lived up the street."

"Well, I live up the street across town."

Belton clammed up when Holland asked for his date of birth. No more questions without an attorney, he said.

He waited as the agents conferred. This they hadn't anticipated. They had equipped Watson with a sophisticated tape recorder with suction-cup microphones, taping it to his torso. They had given him $2,300 in government money, what they called a "flash roll," that he could show Belton. They had coached him about what to say and sent him to carry out the sting. Now they had nabbed Money Rock. And he was clean.

Holland told Belton he wasn't under arrest, but they were seizing his possessions as ill-gotten gains, the proceeds of drug crimes. Three agents returned to the two FBI cars. The fourth agent took Belton's key, climbed into the Mercedes, and cranked the engine. Then they drove off, with cash, jewelry, and car. Belton, his track suit pockets empty, stood alone by the side of the road. He remembered Gordon, who would be meeting up with Watson. Gordon didn't know Watson was a snitch. Now Belton began to worry.

The FBI agents had stopped Belton because Watson had called them on his cellular phone, explaining that Belton would be picking up the cocaine, then heading back to their meeting place off West Boulevard. But it was Gordon who had the cocaine, stashed in a paper bag concealed under his jacket. Belton needed to stop his brother from making the sale. He ran into a nearby convenience store, where he spotted a woman he knew and convinced her to give him a ride.

Gordon was sitting with Watson in Watson's Mercedes when the car pulled up and Belton jumped from the passenger's seat.

"It's a setup!" he yelled to his brother. "Something ain't right." He warned that FBI agents were nearby and instructed Gordon to get out of the car and run.

Watson also got out, and as he did, Belton grabbed the arm of his jacket and led him across West Boulevard. His thought was to maneuver Watson into a secluded area and use Gordon's gun to put a bullet through his head. Gordon joined them in a parking lot behind apartments, but he'd ditched both gun and cocaine, hiding them following his brother's warning.

Belton suspected the FBI might return, so he approached a man in a car and asked for a ride, ordering Watson to pay the man one hundred dollars out of his cash roll. Belton was pushing Watson toward the man's car when he felt a solid object on Watson's back, under his jacket.

"Wait a minute," Belton said. "Wait a minute."

Watson tried to run. Belton threw him down and yelled to Gordon: "He's wired. Get the wire."

The two brothers ripped off the adhesive tape that had secured the recorder to Watson's back. They punched him a few times, made sure they had the recorder, then got into the car with the man they'd paid and zoomed away. Now, it was LaMorris Watson, disheveled and frightened, who was left standing alone.

In June, about two months later, a federal grand jury indicted Belton and Gordon on charges of conspiracy to traffic cocaine and theft of government property—the tape recorder. Belton, ever an optimist, wasn't overly concerned. Did the government have cocaine? No. Did it have a recording of the sting operation? No. All the government had was LaMorris Watson, a convicted drug dealer trying to snitch himself out of a jam. Still, the charges scared him enough to carry out his retirement plans. He made bond, using his Ravenglass Lane house as collateral, and launched his new business endeavor. A few weeks after the FBI had pulled him over in April, he'd rented a restaurant, already equipped and ready for customers, on Twenty-Fourth Street, in an industrial area just outside downtown Charlotte.

He named the place for his mom—"Carrie's Kitchen," displayed in big black letters across the building's plateglass window. It was a casual diner, with a linoleum floor and mustard and ketchup bottles on the tables, and it offered his mother's soul food—fried chicken, ribs, collards, macaroni and cheese, butter beans, biscuits and cornbread, cobblers, sweet potato pie, banana pudding—the beloved fare of generations of southerners. For Carrie, who had done catering work and always wanted her own place, this restaurant was a long-held dream. She liked to say she cooked with love, and the food tasted better that way.

Carrie's Kitchen opened at six to serve the early breakfast crowd. Carrie took a cab so she could arrive by four or four-thirty to prep the day's food. Belton's big sister Donna baked pound cakes. His little sister Carla made cobblers. Carrie had taught all her children to cook, figuring that if you eat, you should be able to prepare your own food. She gave away meals to needy people who stopped in, especially on

weekends. Belton put in long hours, handling the business arrangements. At times, he'd dabble in food preparation while Carrie groused
that he got in her way. This was to be Belton's way out of the game—a
new start, a clean slate. Not that he was a completely new man, however. He was still cheating on his wife, and sometimes he even two-
timed one girlfriend with another.

That was what he was doing—cheating on both wife and girlfriend—
on September 1, 1989, the Friday before Labor Day, the last long weekend of summer. At 7 a.m., with the sun just rising, he awoke to the
sound of the doorbell ringing and someone knocking.

Had Belton been home, lying next to his wife in his house on Ravenglass Lane, he would already have encountered Doug Childers, a deputy U.S. marshal. Childers and other law enforcement officers had
arrived there before dawn to deliver a warrant seizing the property,
alleging it was purchased with drug money. Rhonda had answered the
door, accepted the papers, and told the men she didn't know where her
husband was. Before they left, a county police investigator canvassed
the house, recording video of each room, finding Belton and Rhonda's
three children asleep in the bedrooms.

From there, the officers drove about five miles to a ranch house in
east Charlotte that Belton had purchased for about $50,000 in June,
after his cocaine trafficking indictment. They knew they'd come to the
right place: Belton's white 1986 Mercedes-Benz, the Mercedes the government hadn't seized, was in the driveway. Childers rang the doorbell, then knocked, then knocked again, announcing he was a U.S.
marshal with a warrant.

Belton knew he was in trouble when he approached the front door
and heard crackling walkie-talkie voices. He did an about-face for the
back door, but officers stood in his backyard too. They had him. He
opened the front door and saw a man with a video camera. It was
that camera—not the armed men converging on his house—that most
alarmed him. In the back bedroom, a young woman lay beneath the
covers. The last thing Belton wanted was footage of the two of them on
the evening news for his wife and girlfriend to see. In fact, Belton had

misunderstood. The government had assigned a police officer to film the house's interior to document its condition. Belton had assumed the man was a television reporter. His first thought: Get the woman out of there as quickly as possible.

The agents relented when he asked for a minute so he could wake his friend. She dressed and left the house to wait in the driveway. Belton told the agents he'd been house-sitting, keeping an eye on the place while his renters were out of town. Because he was free on bond, it was crucial that Belton obey all laws in order to maintain his freedom. So he should have known not to do what he did next. When the cameraman finished filming the house, the agents served their papers, and the group drove away, Belton climbed into his Mercedes and headed out of the neighborhood. He hadn't gone far when an officer who'd followed him from the house pulled him over. Belton was driving with a revoked license.

Later that same day—and it had been a very long day—Magistrate Paul Taylor presided over a bond revocation hearing at Charlotte's Corinthian-columned federal courthouse. Assistant U.S. Attorney Robert Conrad argued that Belton had violated two conditions of his pretrial release: He'd broken a law—by driving with a revoked license—and he wasn't living with his wife. Also, since the government had seized his house, he could no longer use it as bond collateral.

Belton did his best to explain his way out of this latest predicament, assuring the magistrate that he and his wife were happily married and living together, that he'd recently paid off traffic tickets and assumed it was okay to drive. He explained he'd been working at Carrie's Kitchen, which he described as his mother's restaurant. "I got my life together and me and my wife, you know, we're serving the Lord and he's just rehabilitating me on the inside," Belton said.

What Belton didn't know was that Carrie's Kitchen was now gone too. While federal agents had been seizing his two houses, a second group had been at the diner. The government alleged he'd bought the place with drug money and was selling drugs out of the business.

Carrie had been there, prepping for breakfast, when she saw the faces of several men staring in the window from the predawn darkness.

Once inside, one officer went to Carrie's cash register and scooped up eighteen dollars in singles and change.

"Why you stealing my money?" she'd asked him.[1]

At the bond revocation hearing, Belton's description of his rehabilitation failed to impress Taylor, the federal magistrate. He also chafed at Belton's professions of Christian faith. "You say your trust is in God," Taylor told him. "Well, so is mine and I don't think anybody around here has a monopoly on having trust in God. In fact, I'm getting sick of hearing people say that."

Belton would stay in jail until his lawyer, who was out of town, could represent him at a full hearing. At that hearing, a week later, Assistant U.S. Attorney Conrad presented the magistrate with many arguments—a veritable evidence buffet—to prove that Belton Platt should not be on the streets. A Charlotte police investigator reiterated Belton's role in the four-year-old Piedmont Courts shootout. A special agent for the Bureau of Alcohol, Tobacco, and Firearms described how Belton and a woman had purchased two rifles, two shotguns, and fourteen boxes of ammunition at a Service Merchandise store in February. He'd pulled a wad of money from his pocket and paid the $1,000 bill in cash.

Local law enforcement officers, it turns out, had been on Belton's trail, working to build a case with tips from confidential informants even before LaMorris Watson had offered the FBI his services. Alcohol, Tobacco, and Firearms agents, working with Charlotte vice officers, were tracking weapons he bought that they believed, correctly, he used to protect his drug operation.

The most surprising news was that Watson, the government's key witness, had fled. Agents had arrested him in California in May, but he was fighting extradition, claiming that Belton Platt had a $50,000 contract out on his life.

This statement was hearsay. Watson claimed his girlfriend and wife had received threatening phone calls. Watson's girlfriend told an FBI agent that someone was calling her phone and hanging up, and then she began getting calls in which someone was making threats. The content of those alleged threats was a mystery. FBI agents hadn't managed to locate Watson's wife or reach the girlfriend after an initial interview.

Belton's attorney, Jim Carson, argued that Watson more likely had absconded because he was facing sentencing on cocaine trafficking. "It's just grasping at straws to say LaMorris Watson fears for his life," Carson told the magistrate.

But Taylor's mind was made up. Perhaps the only reason Belton hadn't fled, the magistrate said, was because he was "secure that La-Morris Watson will never be able to testify against him. In fact, if anything happens to LaMorris Watson, this whole case will collapse."

He ordered Belton to be held without bond until trial.

After the hearing, a *Charlotte Observer* photographer snapped a photo as a U.S. marshal led Belton to a van that would take him to the county jail. He looked uncharacteristically sloppy. His short-sleeved plaid shirt, unbuttoned at the neck, showed his undershirt. His pants were too long, perhaps because he required such a large-sized waist. His beach-ball stomach strained under his shirt. His legs were shackled, his hands clasped in front of him, handcuffed, secured with a chain around his waist. Most striking was the expression on his face—sadness, confusion. A realization that the jig was up. That life as he knew it was over.

11

UNITED STATES VERSUS
MONEY ROCK

B elton waited seven months in the Mecklenburg County Jail for his case to come to trial. With nothing but time, he studied the Bible, prayed, and quizzed fellow inmates about Robert Potter, the U.S. District Court judge who would preside over his case. What he learned should have alarmed him. Potter, a law-and-order conservative, won his judicial appointment in 1981 after managing Ronald Reagan's first presidential campaign in the county. As a Mecklenburg County commissioner in the 1960s, he opposed anti-poverty programs, once accusing their supporters of trying to buy off militants who favored socialism and violent revolution.[1] He also opposed busing children to desegregate Charlotte's public schools.[2]

In the courtroom, the stern, white-haired judge was known as a polite southern gentleman with draconian leanings. While Belton was in jail contemplating Potter's record, the judge was presiding in the trial of his most famous defendant, television evangelist Jim Bakker, founder of the PTL Club (PTL for "Praise the Lord"), on fraud and conspiracy charges. A jury convicted Bakker of bilking his followers out of $158 million, money that had funded Rolls-Royces, gold bathroom fixtures, and a heated doghouse. During sentencing, Potter, a Catholic, stated: "Those of us who do have religion are sick of being saps for money-grubbing preachers and priests."[3] He gave Bakker forty-five years, a sentence that shocked even Bakker's detractors.[4]

Sentences like that had earned Potter the nickname "Maximum Bob." His prison sentences in 1986 had been about one and a half times longer than those of other federal judges. A bank robber who'd appealed another judge's twenty-year sentence and won a new trial ended up with fifty years from Potter. He'd also sentenced two marijuana smugglers from Wilkes County, in the foothills of the Blue Ridge Mountains, to seventy-five years without parole.[5]

Belton understood the general outlines of Potter's judicial history, but remained so sure of his own persuasive powers that in November 1989, about the time Potter was sentencing Bakker, he spent fourteen single-spaced handwritten pages trying to convince the judge he was innocent and should be free on bond. "While setting here in this jail," he wrote to Potter, "I have heard several rumors about you, such as 'he burn anybody that comes to his courtroom,' 'he's crazy,' 'he's prejudice,' 'he hates anybody that is charged with drugs whether they're guilty or not,' 'he has got a quota for the year of 89 to send an X amount of people to prison. . . . '"

Belton went on to invoke God, quote the Bible, and inform Potter that no matter what anyone else said, he'd concluded after reviewing Potter's record "That you are a Just and Fair, Judge of these United States of America."

Belton never received a response.

And yet he remained confident, even as he sat behind bars dressed in jailhouse orange. Confidence was one of the first attributes Larry Hewitt noticed about his new client. Belton had claimed he couldn't afford a lawyer and had been appointed Hewitt, a seasoned, well-regarded attorney. Hewitt found Belton likable and easy to work with, but he knew an acquittal was unlikely. Federal prosecutors won more than nine of every ten cases that went to trial. With the drug war in full swing, they had plenty of resources to go after dealers. In Belton's case, for instance, the FBI sent a photographer up in an airplane so jurors had aerial photos of the area where the sting operation occurred.

Hewitt, on the other hand, found little to build a strong defense. He went with the obvious option—convincing the jury that LaMorris Watson was an unreliable witness. "That was the only way to attack it," he recalled.

The government had decided to try Belton and Gordon together. Their trial began on Monday, April 16, 1990. The thirty-one-year-old prosecutor, Assistant U.S. Attorney Robert Conrad, was a year into the job and still better known as a former star point guard at Clemson University. He began his case with Watson, calling him to the stand, then launching a line of questions that put his star witness's motivations squarely on the table.

"Mr. Watson," Conrad asked, "did there come a time when you began cooperating with the government?"

"Yes, sir," Watson responded.

"And why did you do that, sir?"

"Well, I guess drugs is wrong and I was caught up and I was just trying to do what I could."

That wasn't the answer Conrad sought. He tried again, more to the point.

"You were cooperating with them because you were hoping to get some consideration of that when you were sentenced, is that correct?"

"Yes, sir."

Watson pointed out Belton for the jury—the man at the defense table in the blue suit and tie. He knew the defendant as Money Rock. He'd seen him sell coke twice before, at a park and a nightclub. He described how he set up a buy from Belton, and how the sting operation went awry. They'd planned to reconnect after Belton picked up the cocaine, but only Gordon was waiting at their meeting place. When he saw the bulge in Gordon's jacket, he realized Belton didn't have the cocaine. Then Belton arrived and discovered Watson's wire. Once his cover was blown, the Platt brothers ripped the recorder off his back, punched him in the stomach, and paid a man to drive them away.

After they sped off, he pulled out his cellular phone and called the FBI office again. "I said, 'Y'all going to get me killed. Y'all going to get me killed.' And my stomach was hurting real bad and I told them I think I might need to go to the hospital."

During cross-examination, Hewitt depicted Watson as a man trying to save his own skin. "You're going to tell anything you can because it sounds good in here on Belton Platt and you're going to make your testimony good and say anything you can to load up on this man, aren't you?" Hewitt asked.

"I'm just going to tell the truth of what happened," Watson replied.

Hewitt raised a few inconsistencies between Watson's testimony and his earlier statement to the FBI, but Watson left the stand without contradicting his basic story. He'd been an effective informant. Several FBI agents also testified, corroborating Watson's story and describing how they stopped Belton in his Mercedes. At least as powerful as their testimony were the state's exhibits—the jewelry the FBI seized from Money Rock.

With FBI agent Steven Holland on the stand, Conrad handed over photos of thirteen pieces, which the feds had valued at $102,650, asking him to confirm they were the same ones he'd discovered in Belton's car. In addition to the Rolex and the ID bracelet that spelled "ROCK," there was a medallion of a lion's head, a ring with a lion's head, a heavy gold rope necklace, all of it the kind of jewelry that people expected a coke dealer to wear. Several actual pieces were passed to jurors for inspection.

Among those jurors was Ilene Dellinger, a twenty-nine-year-old vocational rehabilitation counselor who lived in the small town of Cherryville, west of Charlotte. Dellinger hefted each as it was handed to her. *This stuff is heavy*, she thought. They reminded her of the gold chains the television character Mr. T wore on *The A-Team*. She wondered who'd wear such things in real life. *Probably someone who wanted to show off*, she thought.

Once the prosecution rested, Belton insisted on testifying, despite Hewitt's advice to stay silent. Hewitt doubted that Belton would impress the jury and knew Potter disliked liars as much as he despised drug dealers. He worried his client was going to bury himself.

On the stand, Belton gave jurors an alternative narrative: He'd discussed buying a camera from Watson, but never cocaine. In Belton's version, Watson was the one who said he had cocaine, plus a gun and money in his car. Also, in Belton's recollection, Watson cursed a lot.

"He talking about, 'I got some dope and money in my D. car and my G.D. car,' you know, he was cussing."

Belton testified that when the FBI had stopped him and made off with his Mercedes, jewelry, and cash, he figured he'd been robbed by armed men posing as FBI agents. Why would the FBI want to steal his property? He was a simple businessman, owner of L&K Cleaning Service.

Dellinger, listening in the jury box, wasn't buying it. How could a man who made a living cleaning Burger King restaurants afford to drive a Mercedes with tens of thousands of dollars in cash and jewelry in his trunk? The more he talked, the less she believed. Dellinger also noted his confidence. Overconfidence, as she saw it.

Once testimony ended, jurors elected Dellinger forewoman. They began deliberating after lunch and reached a verdict before dinner. At 5:52 p.m., Dellinger told Judge Potter they'd found Belton and Gordon guilty as charged—guilty of conspiracy to sell cocaine and theft of government property.

Their sentencing hearing wouldn't come for a month. In the meantime, waiting in jail, the brothers got word that their dad had died. Alphonso Platt had been only fifty-eight, but his death came as no great surprise. After decades of alcohol abuse, his liver had given out. In his last years, Alphonso had been proud of his son's drug-dealing success, once bragging to Donna, Belton's oldest sister, that he deserved the credit for giving Belton his start. As Donna saw it, Alphonso Platt was the reason her brothers were headed to prison. "I have never known anybody so evil in my life," she recalled. "All I ever remember is seeing him drunk, mistreating his children, or trying to kill my mother."

Belton's feelings about his dad were more complicated. He hated the man for abusing his mother, yet loved him as a father. He and Gordon petitioned Judge Potter to attend his father's funeral. Such compassionate leave requests are often granted, but Potter said no. "The court cannot in good conscience subject the Marshal Service to the dangers of ambush or escape," he wrote.

Their sentencing hearing began on May 23, 1990, with the attorneys arguing over how much of Belton's past the judge should consider. Conrad wanted everything on the table, including Belton's role in the Piedmont Courts shootout. Hewitt reminded Potter that Belton's conviction had been overturned. He'd never been retried, and thus had no felony conviction. To base a punishment on testimony from an overturned conviction, Hewitt argued, was inappropriate.

But Potter concluded the state court testimony was reliable. He even let Conrad introduce statements police had taken from two men who didn't testify in the shootout trial—Louis "Big Lou" Samuels and one of Samuels's crew. These statements from Belton's enemies made him look even worse than he was.

When it was Hewitt's turn to present mitigating evidence, he called Carrie Graves to the stand. Belton's mother told Judge Potter that he'd been "one of the greatest sons that a mother can want to have."

Then came Rhonda Platt, Belton's twenty-eight-year-old wife. As she took the stand, the couple's three children—Lamont, Stephen, and Genesis—watched from their seats on a wooden bench near the back of the courtroom. Lamont was eight. Stephen was almost four. Genesis had recently turned two. None had legs long enough to reach the floor.

"Tell the judge," Hewitt urged, "what kind of husband and what kind of father he has been for the children."

"The best loving kind, you know, he always provided for us," Rhonda replied. "And he just been a father and a husband."

Hewitt pressed on, attempting to elicit something—perhaps a tender family story to soften Maximum Bob. "How has he dealt with his children, as far as doing things for them, and being a father to them?"

"How has he done?"

"Yes."

"Just been there, you know. Been there like a father."

If she had wanted to, Rhonda could have torpedoed her husband that day. She could have mentioned one of several out-of-wedlock children of which she was aware. She could have explained that her husband was often gone days at a time, that she'd never encouraged Belton's drug business, that she didn't need the jewelry or cars, that all she'd really wanted was him.

Instead, Rhonda had played along, but without enthusiasm. "I was just kind of done," she said later.

After she stepped down, Belton took the stand once more. Hewitt had warned him to be careful what he said, but this didn't seem to have registered.

Belton told the judge that much of the prosecution's testimony had been lies. "I did not conspire with no LaMorris Watson for no drugs or nothing like that." He'd been running a janitorial business since leaving state prison, making $160 a night. "I had five restaurants that I cleaned up every night." And he denied the prosecutor's assertion that he'd been a drug kingpin and menace to Charlotte since the Piedmont Courts shootout in 1985. He didn't even have a gun in Piedmont Courts, he told Potter, and "I have not been prone to use violence in any other kind of way."

Having spent many jailed hours contemplating his life, Belton had begun to recognize the damage he'd caused and the ways he'd failed his family. But he wasn't yet able to admit those failures—to agree that he was the gun-wielding, drug-dealing menace Conrad had described. Instead, he gave what Hewitt later described as "a rambling recitation," portraying himself as the person he aspired to be—a hardworking, law-abiding family man. He never apologized or admitted guilt, but he came close: "I've not been perfect all my life, but things change." He talked until Potter called a halt. "Excuse me, Mr. Hewitt," he interrupted. "I think we have a pretty good idea."

It's possible Belton would have fared better if he had confessed, pleaded guilty, and explained to Potter that he wanted out of the game. If he'd come clean, some assertions about his desire to change his life would have been more believable. He had signed up to take a real estate course at the local community college. And Carrie's Kitchen, though launched with drug money, had been a legitimate restaurant, not some cover for a drug ring, as the feds believed.

But maybe it would have made no difference. Not only was he going before Maximum Bob, but his conviction came when anxiety about illegal drugs hovered at an all-time high. Local news reports gave the impression that cocaine was everywhere—in an elementary school, where an eleven-year-old boy brought a crack rock to class, and in the county courthouse, where three teenagers were caught with coke in a restroom stall.[6] A month before Belton's trial, police caught a Mecklenburg Superior Court judge with cocaine in his car.[7] Charlotte would have ninety-three murders by year's end, more than double the number just two years earlier. Police attributed much of the surge in violent crime to cocaine, especially crack.

At the *Observer*, writing about cocaine had practically become Nancy Webb's full-time job. In January 1989, she kicked off a year-long series with a vivid story, "Cocaine: The Habit, the Hurt," that highlighted coke busts, violence, and addiction in Charlotte over the previous year. Her subjects, of various ages, races, and incomes, included a middle-class father whose addiction had drained his family's savings, jittery cocaine-exposed infants born at Charlotte Memorial Hospital, a courier nabbed at the airport with a one-pound package taped under his shirt, a high school dropout who died on a patch of dirt outside a housing project, shot through the heart because he owed money for cocaine.[8] In a column accompanying Webb's work, *Charlotte Observer* editor Rich Oppel underscored the severity of the area's illegal drug problem. Though not as bad as in larger cities, the problem is growing, he wrote. "And we in the Piedmont treasure our civilized, safe and moderate way of life—the very thing threatened by encroaching drug abuse, and the guns, crime, violence and other risks to our families that the scourge brings."[9]

The *Observer's* decision to zero in on illegal drugs in 1989 followed a tsunami of similar national coverage, much of it full of hyperbolic declarations, particularly about cocaine and crack. In 1986, *Newsweek* called illicit drug use an epidemic, "as pervasive and dangerous in its way as the plagues of medieval times,"[10] while the *New York Times* warned that crack use among teenagers was spreading from the inner city to "the wealthiest suburbs of Westchester County."[11] The War on Drugs, according to the prevailing narrative, was the government's fight against violent dealers who, in their quest for riches, poisoned people and ravaged neighborhoods. These were dealers lacking any moral compass, criminals "beyond the point of teaching and rehabilitating," as former first lady Nancy Reagan described suspects in a 1989 drug raid on a Los Angeles crack house. She had witnessed the raid, clad in her own LAPD windbreaker, as a guest of Police Chief Daryl Gates. The press had been invited too.[12] In this narrative, the people who use and sell drugs were viewed as making bad moral choices. That they might be jobless, depressed, or desperate wasn't part of the equation.

President Richard Nixon had coined the term "War on Drugs" in 1971, but President Ronald Reagan ramped up the war in the 1980s. In September 1989, his successor, President George Bush, devoted his first prime-time address to illegal drugs, holding aloft a clear plastic bag of crack that he said had been seized in Lafayette Park, across the street from the White House. Crack was "turning our cities into battle zones and it's murdering our children," he told the nation. He unveiled plans to spend billions to achieve "a victory over drugs," partly by nearly doubling prison and jail capacity, so casual users as well as dealers could be incarcerated.[13] Soon afterward, a record 64 percent of respondents in a *New York Times*–CBS News poll named drug abuse the nation's most pressing problem. Five percent cited the economy, while three percent cited the poor.[14]

Today, experts describe that stretch of time from 1986 to 1992 as a drug scare, similar to a Red Scare or a witch scare—a period in U.S. history when crusaders rise up to beat down an evil that doesn't exist, at least not at the maximum-danger level they describe. "Drug scares typically link a scapegoated drug to a troubling subordinate group—working-class immigrants, racial or ethnic minorities, rebellious youth," write Craig Reinarman and Harry G. Levine, sociologists who've published extensively on the subject.[15] After rising in the 1970s, overall drug use actually fell in the 1980s. Crack use did go up, but the only places it ever approached epidemic levels were poor, urban neighborhoods.[16]

About two weeks after President Bush displayed that bag of crack at his press conference, reporters uncovered the truth. It hadn't been seized across from the White House. Agents assigned to find crack for the Commander in Chief's photo op hadn't been able to locate anyone selling near the White House. They ended up luring an eighteen-year-old African American high school senior to Lafayette Park to make the undercover buy. And they didn't actually seize the crack. They bought it from the kid for $2,400 and let him go. National Public Radio's *All Things Considered* aired a story quoting men in Washington who'd been jailed for drug dealing. They told NPR that nobody sold crack in Lafayette Park because they'd never get a customer. Crack users lived in poor African American neighborhoods.[17]

So why was the president trying to convince Americans that crack was practically being sold on the White House's front porch? According to Reinarman and Levine, the War on Drugs as prosecuted in the 1980s by the Reagan and Bush administrations accomplished political goals unrelated to drugs. "The drug war was not effective or wise policy," they write, "but politicians promoted it nonetheless because, among other reasons, it provided a convenient explanation—a scapegoat—for enduring and ever growing urban poverty."[18]

Belton faced twelve to sixteen years under federal sentencing rules, but Potter had the leeway to impose a tougher punishment, known as an "upward departure," by documenting aggravating factors. Sitting behind the bench consulting his guidelines, the judge announced that he would bump up Belton's offense level because a gun was involved, then raise it again because he believed Belton had an extensive drug trafficking history, and then once more because Belton wasn't truthful on the stand. "So we have a category of three, offense level thirty-six, which would be 235 to 293 months," he concluded. "The court will impose a sentence of 290 months."[19]

And then it was over. Belton stood. Before a U.S. marshal led him from the courtroom, he turned to look at his family. Rhonda and Carrie sat crying. What shook him most, though, were the tears in his oldest son's eyes.

The sentence length didn't register immediately. He'd heard Potter say "months," and that's the word he'd focused on. He did the math once he got to the holding cell. Twelve months in a year. So 120 months was ten years, and 240 months was twenty years. And he still hadn't reached 290. He turned to Gordon, who'd just received a sixteen-year sentence of his own. "What he say they give me?" Belton asked.

Back in the newsroom, Nancy Webb also did the math, then typed her lead: "A Charlotte drug dealer's days of flash and cash ended Wednesday when U.S. District Judge Robert Potter sentenced him to 24 years in prison." She concluded with a quote from Conrad's boss, U.S. Attorney Tom Ashcraft, who noted there was no chance of parole. "This is really a significant sentence," he told her. "What's significant is the length. The guidelines call for 151 to 188 months."[20] By the time she wrote that story, Webb had published nearly 150 articles that included the word *cocaine*.

12

COMING OF AGE IN A
WORLD-CLASS CITY

Once Belton was convicted, Donna Brown, his older sister, did what she could to keep her brother connected with his children. Every week or two, she'd pile kids into her car and drive them to his prison—Atlanta in the first three years, then to Butner, North Carolina, where he was transferred in 1993. Usually she took Rhonda's three—Lamont, Stephen, and Genesis. Often, Kim went along, and occasionally Janie's children, LaToya and Lamont. They could make the 150-mile trip to Butner, near Durham, in under three hours, not counting a breakfast stop at a Hardee's or McDonald's along I-85.

Donna had been like a second mother to her siblings, and she still had that same take-charge personality, stepping in because her mother, Carrie, didn't drive and Rhonda, who had divorced Belton, wasn't eager to see him. "It was something I knew I needed to do, so he could stay in their lives," Donna recalled. "That was their daddy, and they loved their daddy." More than once, she found herself trying to explain his absence to his children. She'd tell them their father made mistakes. He hadn't left because he wanted to leave them, but because he had no choice.

To pass the time on the highway, Donna would lead the children in song. A day-care teacher, she'd have them belt out "Jesus Loves Me,"

Belton with his children in an undated photo at the Federal Correctional Institute in Butner, North Carolina. From left to right, Genesis, Belton, Kim, Stephen (in front), and Big Lamont. Courtesy of Carrie Graves.

perform "Row, Row, Row Your Boat" in rounds, and sing the theme song from *Barney & Friends*: "I love you. You love me. We're a happy family."

After they pulled into the prison parking lot, she'd make a mental rundown of prison rules and remind the kids about appropriate behavior. Toys, purses, and paper money had to stay in the car. To buy the vending machine food, which she found surprisingly good, she'd bring quarters in clear plastic bags. After confirming that all pockets were empty, she'd shepherd the children through security, with its required IDs and hand stamps, and into the visiting room furnished with utilitarian tables and chairs. The younger ones would run to their father as he came through the door. They'd hug his legs and clamor to be picked up. They'd kiss his face when he lifted them. After Belton and Donna claimed a table, they'd vie for his lap. Then Belton would fetch a Bible from a nearby table or from the prison guard's office. That's how they always began. Before the children could start a card game or request quarters to buy sodas, Belton would lead them in scripture readings and Bible study. Before anything else, they got the word of God.

After about a half hour, he'd close the Bible and ask the children about their lives, listening as they described school classes, friends, sports activities. The prison kept a stash of cards and games, and so they'd play Uno or spades or speed. Then they'd go to the vending machine for lunch—plastic-wrapped hamburgers, pizza, and chicken wings that they heated in the microwave. In good weather, they'd move to the patio area and snack on microwave popcorn under a sur-veillance camera's gaze. Years later, Janie's Lamont remembered how his dad taught him to make a special mix by dumping chips into the popcorn bag and shaking. LaToya recalled being puzzled by her fa-ther's incarceration. "I would ask, 'Daddy, why you here?' He used to take me down this long road, and by the time he finished, I still didn't know."

In those years, the prison in Butner periodically hosted Family Days, which featured an inflatable bounce house for the kids and real food—hamburgers, barbecue, trimmings—that inmates prepared and served in their dining hall. Belton's younger brother, Gordon, who was also doing time for the cocaine sting conviction, worked in the But-ner kitchen, where inmates had nicknamed him Cake Daddy. Donna swore the cakes he baked for those Family Days were the best she'd ever tasted. On those days, the children departed with goodie bags packed with whistles, paddleballs, and stickers. Sometimes Belton and the children posed for a family photograph. They'd gather in front of a backdrop—a beach or woodlands scene—with pots of bright yel-low mums arranged near their feet. Belton pulled his children close, holding Genesis, the youngest, in his arms. An inmate photographer snapped the photo. Since Butner inmates were permitted to wear street clothes, these photos didn't reveal that he was incarcerated. The resulting images—smiling children gathered around their father—could have been any American family.

In addition to visiting her brothers, Donna looked forward to seeing young men she'd known from the neighborhood, most serving time on drug charges. "People were so happy to see each other," she recalled. "It was like a family reunion."

The hardest part of the day came with the goodbyes, when a voice over the intercom told visitors it was time to leave. The children would hug their father a final time, then grow quiet as he lined up with other inmates at the visiting-room door. Sometimes they'd ask Donna questions: Why are the guards there? Why can't he come home?

Back in the car, Donna would offer a prayer and reassure the children they'd return soon. She'd ask if they had a good time, they'd reply that they did, and any sadness about leaving their father would appear to pass. Soon, they'd be back on I-85. *Thank goodness*, she'd think, *that children were adaptable.*

As Belton's children grew up in the 1990s, so did Charlotte, in ways both thrilling and tragic. The city had acquired an NBA team, then an NFL team. Construction cranes built office towers. NationsBank made the town its headquarters. By 1993, Charlotte's population was on par with St. Louis's and Atlanta's, and the city would soon overtake San Francisco as the nation's second-largest financial center. But that same year, though it was thirty-fourth in size, it ranked eighteenth in violent crime. By one measure, the per capita murder rate, it had surpassed New York.[1]

World class. The phrase had become the city's unofficial motto. *If we want to be a world-class city*, sentences would begin, followed by a description of something Charlotte needed (professional sports, political courage, a performing arts center, international flights) to bolster its status or reach a new benchmark. The scale of ambition would have been laughable, except that the city kept scoring victories. This was largely due to a burgeoning financial sector. A 1985 Supreme Court decision had relaxed interstate banking laws, allowing the city's two biggest banks, North Carolina National (which became NationsBank, and later Bank of America) and First Union National (later Wachovia, then purchased by Wells Fargo) to buy up financial institutions outside North Carolina. Their CEOs, Hugh McColl and Ed Crutchfield, were fierce competitors who seemed intent on matching each other merger for merger, acquiring properties in Florida, Georgia, Texas. McColl traced this intense drive to the Civil War. "After the war, the South was really a hugely defeated nation that was depleted of capital," he explained. "And unlike Germany and Japan after the Second World War, there was no Marshall Plan for the South. So we had to pull ourselves up by our own bootstraps, as I see it. And that drove me my entire career."[2]

McColl's underdog mentality permeated Charlotte, a city often confused with other places—Charlottesville or Charleston. Tourists flocked to North Carolina's beaches and mountains, not to Charlotte, in the state's southwestern Piedmont region. It wasn't the state capital. It had no scenic riverfront, no significant landmark or major historical destination. After George Washington spent the night in 1791, he'd called it "a trifling place," a fair description of what was basically a village at the crossroads of two Native American trading paths.[3] In 1800, its population was 276.[4]

But the nineteenth century had brought spates of good fortune. A few years after Washington's visit, a twelve-year-old boy playing in a creek on his family's farm outside Charlotte found a seventeen-pound rock that turned out to be almost solid gold. Once the nation's first gold rush was in full swing in the early 1800s, Charlotte won a branch of the U.S. Mint to process all that precious metal into coins. Though the city was a secessionist stronghold when North Carolina joined the Confederacy, U.S. General William Tecumseh Sherman bypassed the town during his southern march of destruction at the Civil War's end, leaving Charlotte undamaged and in excellent position to expand into textiles, distribution, and finance.

By 1908, the city had become home to the state's tallest building, erected when businessmen decided that a skyscraper would set the town apart. The Independence Building stood fourteen stories at Trade and Tryon Streets, the preeminent downtown intersection. Charlotte's W.J. Cash, author of *The Mind of the South*, scoffed at such stunts, noting that middling southern cities had little more use for skyscrapers "than a hog has for a morning coat."[5] But Cash was in the minority. In 1917, when a U.S. general scouted locations for a new military base, Charlotte had hustled to organize a hero's welcome—eight thousand of the city's fifty thousand residents attended his speech. The town won its army camp, and in the process doubled its population.[6] The city hustled again in 1940, when preliminary census calculations put the population just short of six figures, at 94,501. As a point of community pride, newspapers helped hunt down uncounted citizens, and after two recounts Charlotte pushed its 1940 census tally to 100,899.[7]

Growth was proof of progress, celebrated with zeal. To mark the arrival of the county's three-hundred-thousandth citizen in 1963, the chamber of commerce piled 300,000 chocolate kisses on the square at Trade and Tryon Streets. The publicity stunt backfired spectacularly. "In seconds little kids were being trampled, frantic mamas were screaming and the air was full of candy kisses," the *Observer* reported. Police and firefighters averted disaster by pushing into the scrum and flinging armloads of candy outward, scattering the crowd.[8]

The city reached a more consequential milestone in 1987, when the National Basketball Association awarded it an expansion team, the Charlotte Hornets. The news was deeply satisfying, a repudiation of critics who'd claimed the city's market was too small for professional basketball and dismissed its bid as a long shot. The only franchise Charlotte was likely to get, an out-of-state columnist had scoffed, was one with golden arches.[9]

The Hornets arrived to much hoopla. "At last," a *Charlotte Observer* writer gushed, "Charlotte can think of itself as a big city. The NBA has elevated it to major league stature, and the rest of the country is taking notice."[10] Evangelist Billy Graham, Charlotte's most famous native son, dedicated the new basketball coliseum, and on November 4, 1988, when the team played its first game against the Cleveland Cavaliers and lost by forty points, fans gave the Hornets a standing ovation simply for existing.[11] That first season, the team won only twenty of eighty-two contests, and still nearly every game sold out. The coming of the Hornets also created a new local hero. George Shinn, the team's majority owner, had made his millions with a sketchy for-profit college chain that was drawing federal scrutiny for high default rates on its taxpayer-backed student loans. This mattered little when basketball and city pride were involved. After all, as Billy Graham declared at the coliseum dedication, Charlotte was "taking its place among the great cities of America."[12] Confetti rained down as Shinn perched in a convertible next to Mayor Gantt and waved his way down Tryon Street in a ticker-tape parade.[13] Standing ovations greeted Shinn's speeches, which tended to be little more than a string of positive-thinking clichés: *Be proud of who you are. Know you're special because God created you. Count on good things to happen to you, and good things will happen.*[14]

Civic good times kept rolling into the 1990s. The Hornets lost most games and still managed to lead the NBA in attendance. NationsBank built its new sixty-story headquarters, Charlotte's tallest building, at Trade and Tryon Streets. The city planned a quarter-million-square-foot convention center that would attract big-time conferences and conventioneers. Progress was the city's cheerful refrain, yet issues of race and crime were the background soundtrack, helping shape certain decisions, including where the Hornets played their games. A coliseum downtown seemed an obvious choice, given that empty storefronts dotted the center city, a casualty of shopping malls and suburban sprawl, and that reviving downtown was a major goal. City leaders had officially declared the downtown "uptown," a more upscale appellation.[15] But leaders passed over two uptown locations for a third suburban site that citizens had preferred two-to-one in a poll.[16] It was seven miles southwest of the center city, convenient to interstates and airport, but not much else. For many white suburbanites, this was preferable to uptown Charlotte. "Race is a hidden agenda," historian Dan Morrill said of Charlotte's struggling uptown in 1992. "People say they don't like uptown, but what they're really saying is that a lot of people in uptown are black people." [17]

In 1993, Charlotte won a National Football League team, the Carolina Panthers, and it was Hornets hoopla all over again. The *Observer* declared, "TOUCHDOWN!" on its front page in "Christ-returns-to-earth-size type," as one writer later described it. [18] "Forever more," a reporter wrote, "this single decision will likely change the way people across the country feel about what lies between Washington and Atlanta." [19]

But this newest success came amid tragedy. Just three weeks earlier, October 5, 1993, two police officers, Andy Nobles and John Burnette, had responded to what sounded like a routine call—possible theft of a van near Boulevard Homes, a public housing project off West Boulevard, southwest of downtown. They made a traffic stop and approached the vehicle. The man inside bolted from the car into nearby woods. Nobles and Burnette pursued.

Minutes passed. Dispatchers tried and failed to raise the officers. Police blanketed the area and soon found their comrades, both face down in the woods, shot in the head. In a record-breaking year for murders, this was another first for Charlotte—two slain officers. Heightening the tragedy were the stories of the officers themselves, respected young white cops, both in their mid-twenties, among Charlotte's first to practice community policing. As they'd patrolled Boulevard Homes, they'd forged relationships and built trust with black residents, playing basketball with kids and chatting up adults who called them Andy and John. The gray-haired police chief's voice broke as he relayed news of the deaths. "A night that sent the city into mourning," one reporter wrote. [20]

Within hours of the shootings, police caught the killer, a black man with nineteen arrests and multiple criminal convictions. Thousands attended memorial services. Schoolchildren made condolence cards.

The deaths of Nobles and Burnette culminated a violent season. Among its victims: a five-year-old girl whose crack-dealer neighbor shot her by mistake, a sixteen-year-old boy murdered while walking to church, a seventeen-year-old mother killed during a robbery as she held her infant daughter.[21] There had been 48 murders in 1988, 80 in 1989, 121 in 1991. In 1993 that record would be broken with 129 murders—an increase of 169 percent in five years.[22] As body-count growth outpaced population growth, the *Charlotte Observer* launched a project to address the crisis.

The *Observer* had a new editor, Jennie Buckner, who'd arrived in August from Miami, where she'd been vice president for news at Knight-Ridder, the paper's parent company. Charlotte's crime had surprised her. "I just had an impression of a medium-sized city that was growing and had a lot of opportunity," she said years later. "Sure, every city had problems. But I was not expecting cops to be shot down. That was my naivety."

Though the *Observer*'s hometown coverage sometimes veered into boosterism, the newspaper also produced excellent journalism. It won its first Pulitzer Prize for Meritorious Public Service in 1981 for chronicling brown lung disease among textile mill workers and its second in 1988 for exposing the financial malfeasance at PTL Ministries, stories that led to evangelist Jim Bakker's 1989 criminal conviction in Maximum Bob's court. The newspaper's new crime project would be equally ambitious.

The first step was to figure out where crimes were occurring—a question harder to answer than it sounds, because Charlotte police didn't publish crime statistics by neighborhood. Ted Mellnik, the newsroom's database specialist, had convinced his editors to buy mapping software, and after months of negotiations with the Charlotte-Mecklenburg Police Department, he'd gotten his hands on data files of offenses by location. Now, by plotting violent crimes—murder, rape, robbery, aggravated assaults—he could pinpoint the city's highest-crime areas.

The results were dramatic. As Mellnik highlighted census tracts with Charlotte's highest crime rates, they formed a crescent of mostly black neighborhoods around uptown Charlotte. Their residents accounted for just 16 percent of the population, but they endured 54 percent of the city's violent crime.[23]

This wasn't the part of town where the newsroom's staff or middle-class readers lived. When reporters showed up in one of these neighborhoods, it was usually only to interview police and witnesses at the latest yellow-taped crime scene. But that was about to change. Buckner wanted to go deep. Reporters and photographers would spend countless hours talking to residents and learning about their lives. "I was concerned that it not just be, 'Here are Charlotte's most crime-riddled neighborhoods'—'mean streets' kind of reporting," she said. Instead, stories would highlight problems such as housing code violations, a shortage of good job opportunities, inadequate public transportation, lack of parks and community centers, repeat offenders who remained on the streets. "I wanted us to do something that would deeply inform all of Charlotte, including people in those neighborhoods."

The newspaper teamed up with local television and radio stations, organized town meetings where residents could air concerns, and asked city leaders how they intended to address problems. Liz Chandler, one of the lead reporters, familiarized herself with neighborhoods by cruising streets in her blue Honda until she was such a familiar sight that people waved when she passed. One of her best sources became Patsy Martin, a determined mother who'd lived down the street from the five-year-old girl who'd been mistakenly shot by the crack dealer in May 1993. Martin, who worked as a cook in the Allstate Insurance employee cafeteria, led the neighborhood association in Seversville, northwest of uptown, where an astounding one in nine residents had been victims of violent crime. Her three-block street had seen six killings in a single year.[24]

Chandler, an army brat who'd grown up in a dozen different places, had a knack for making people feel at ease. Martin liked her immediately, and figured newspaper stories could help the neighborhood's anti-crime efforts. Soon, Chandler was spending days with Martin.

She slept over on the living-room sofa in Martin's rental house, though occasional shouting matches outside made for restless nights. Once, when the neighborhood's electricity went out, she and Martin awoke to the rumble of Duke Power trucks idling at the top of the street, waiting for a police escort before entering the heart of the neighborhood. Sitting with Martin on the front porch, Chandler learned to spot subtle drug transactions conducted on public streets. Martin knew the neighborhood dealers, and she negotiated with them like a diplomat, inviting them to a fish-fry cookout in her yard, then warning them not to sell to kids or use children as their drug runners. Chandler marveled at how well Martin navigated the difficulties of daily life. She was particularly struck by a scene unfolding outside the house one Sunday morning in July—children standing on the corner, waiting for the church bus, as prostitutes and dealers crossed their paths, heading home from the night's work.

The *Observer* series, "Taking Back Our Neighborhoods," began rolling off the presses in June 1994, introducing its readers to neighborhoods just a few miles from their own homes, yet in a different world—streets where teenagers sold crack, prostitutes conducted business in vacant houses, and nightfall brought pops of gunfire. They also discovered hardworking residents like Martin who were trying to fight back, coping with violence and poverty unthinkable on leafy suburban cul-de-sacs. More than a few affluent white readers told Buckner they'd had no idea.

Over eighteen months, the *Observer* spotlighted crime-stricken neighborhoods, including areas where Belton had grown up and later sold cocaine. Cummings Avenue, where his family lived after his birth, was once solidly working-class. Now, thirty years later, it was a notorious crack haven, the focus of stories on absentee landlords who rented falling-apart drug houses. "It's like a zoo. Everybody do what they want to do. Just picture Cummings like a house infested with roaches," one dealer told the newspaper.[25]

This impoverished, violent undercity, the shadow side of Charlotte's progress narrative, was where most of Belton's eleven children were growing up. Several, including LaToya and Little Lamont, the two children he had with Janie, lived in Dalton Village. When nighttime gunfire erupted, Janie hustled them out of their beds and onto the floor or into a closet. Little Lamont recalled witnessing a shooting, apparently provoked by the theft of a beer, and how the victim's shoes came off as the bullet struck him and he hit the ground. Rhonda's sons, meanwhile, learned about gang life in the Hidden Valley neighborhood, home of the notorious Hidden Valley Kings.

Kim, Belton's oldest daughter, was seven years old when she saw her friend take a stray bullet to the leg. Kim had been beside her, but moved at the last second. "I was blessed because I got up. I would have got shot in the head." A few years later, she watched from her backyard in Dalton Village as men tackled a neighbor accused of being a drug snitch, pulled down his pants, and cut off his penis. Emergency workers attending the man held up a sheet to block neighbors' view. By then, Kim had seen the whole thing.

In junior high, Kim carried a box cutter in her backpack, protection against a Dalton Village boy who had threatened to rape her. When a school administrator found it, she was expelled. "The principal said they understood, but they had zero tolerance." She spent her eighth-grade year in an alternative school.

It seems logical to conclude that living amid this kind of violence might damage a child, but it took a major brain science study in the late 1990s—several years after "Taking Back Our Neighborhoods" was published—to explain exactly why. The Adverse Childhood Experiences Study found childhood trauma—an absent or depressed parent, abuse, neglect, exposure to violence—heightens a child's stress levels, creating higher cortisol levels. Without treatment, developing brains can be permanently changed, making a person more likely to erupt in anger and exhibit disruptive behavior, creating lifelong health and social problems.[26] Studies have also shown that children perform substantially worse on tests following a recent homicide near their home. "When they experience the shock of local violence, children appear to be less intelligent than they are," sociologist Patrick Sharkey has written.[27]

Perhaps the biggest challenge the "Taking Back Our Neighborhoods" project faced was persuading prosperous Charlotte to care enough to do something. The *Observer* appealed to readers' self-interest and civic pride, pointing out that taxpayers ended up footing the bill for violence, in the form of higher police and hospital costs, and that sagging property values in high-crime areas exacerbated the property tax burden in more affluent areas. "If we don't address conditions in the inner city, we'll follow Detroit, where jobs are leaving by the carload, or Atlanta, where the city is becoming poorer and more balkanized," Mayor Richard Vinroot told the newspaper. The city's community development director, meanwhile, trotted out a favorite local argument: "If we're going to build a world class city, we can't abandon the underprivileged."[28]

Yet the deep, abiding role that racism had played in creating these high-crime, underemployed neighborhoods went largely unmentioned. One of the first stories in the *Observer*'s series included several paragraphs on urban renewal, explaining how the city demolished black communities in the 1960s and '70s, how displaced families re-settled, and how the chaos hurt property values and destabilized the central city, which had lost 21 percent of its population since 1970.[29] This was accurate, as far as it went, but the summary didn't convey the massive tragedy of urban renewal—how it had destroyed businesses, scattered churches, severed community connections, and concentrated poverty in Charlotte. The *Observer* also didn't delve into the decades of discriminatory housing and economic policies that helped explain why black citizens were so much more likely than whites to live in Charlotte's poor, crime-ridden neighborhoods. This was a conscious decision, Chandler recalled. "We had long discussions about whether to include quotes and explanations about the vestiges of slavery, but everybody worried that calling out racism would shut readers down."

It was the late writer Gore Vidal who called our nation "The United States of Amnesia." How often we discuss the consequences of racism in passive voice, never saying who did what to whom. This is a powerful dodge, allowing white people to avoid the contentious process of assigning responsibility, to gradually erase difficult truths—even from history books. Charlotte had been adept at the dodge, discussing slavery hardly at all, segregation in the context of how white leaders had helped end it. After urban renewal destroyed the last of Charlotte's largest black neighborhood, Brooklyn, the Redevelopment Commission's executive director told a reporter, "There isn't any more Brooklyn. We ought to stop calling it that." He said he hoped the name would die, and it nearly did.[30]

By the mid-1990s, when "Taking Back Our Neighborhoods" was published, visible race discrimination—separate water fountains, segregated movie theaters—was three decades gone. Busing was keeping Charlotte's schools integrated, even if neighborhoods weren't. Many whites figured the playing field, if not level, was getting there. Plenty of black people were achieving, and that led some citizens to conclude that those who remained in poverty simply had personal deficiencies. They weren't trying hard enough. At the time, I was covering higher education for the newspaper and never worked on this crime series, but in newsroom discussions of race, the focus was often on reflecting diversity in our stories, which meant reaching out to sources other than white men. The "Taking Back Our Neighborhoods" team made sure to profile a high-crime white neighborhood to show it wasn't only black neighborhoods with crime problems.

Looking back, I know many in our mostly white newsroom believed America's playing field remained skewed. I certainly did. But I doubt we grasped the history that had brought us to this point. It was easy to condemn Jim Crow segregation. It was harder to explain the roots of economic inequality—to understand, for instance, that federal home loans that went mostly to white people created wealth that benefited their descendants for generations. African Americans had been lynched, denied the vote, paid less than whites, and excluded from jobs, schools, and colleges, yet many white Americans cried foul if this history came up, arguing that these were sins of the past, therefore irrelevant.

The *Observer's* series would have benefited from more historical context, but it succeeded in many ways—by shining a light on Charlotte's poorest neighborhoods, by forcing the city to pay attention. Hundreds of volunteers—nonprofits, businesses, and individual citizens—responded to the list of needs the newspaper published, offered help, donating goods, providing summer camp slots, tutoring. In 1995, "Taking Back Our Neighborhoods" was one of three finalists for the Pulitzer Prize for public service. In the journalism world, the project was groundbreaking, an example of what had become known as civic or public journalism—reporting shaped by the experiences and opinions of citizens, not institutions or public officials.

Still, when the newspaper concluded the series and took stock of its impact in December 1995, reporters summing up accomplishments were reluctant to claim lasting change. In a couple of neighborhoods, crime had dropped, thanks to ramped-up arrest sweeps and united efforts from neighbors. The city's community policing was a positive step. But a crackdown on crack houses had fizzled, and charities that initially jumped on the bandwagon had moved on to other demands. Though drug treatment produced documented results, a continuing bed shortage meant that addicts might wait months for help. Some neighborhoods had kicked out dealers. But those young men probably weren't turning in guns and applying for minimum-wage fast-food jobs. More likely, they moved to street corners where residents were less organized and more tolerant.[31]

Chandler had never spent so long on one project. When it was over, she couldn't say whether it had made a lasting difference in Charlotte, but she knew that it had changed her. The friendship she'd struck up with Martin became permanent.

13

THE CHRISTIAN INMATE

In July 1990, two months after Judge Potter pronounced his sentence, Belton arrived at the Atlanta penitentiary in leg shackles and handcuffs. Guards trained rifles on him as he exited the prison bus. A strip search followed, requiring him to squat and cough to ensure he wasn't smuggling contraband. He was handed soap and bed linens and sent to a cell in the Big House, an imposing building that reminded him of a haunted mansion, "one of those old prisons with ghosts running around." Built in 1902, the Big House was a sixty-foot-high granite fortress with a portico and belfry. Its exterior had changed little since completion. But its inmates and their crimes—that was a different story, a glimpse of twentieth-century America through the lens of incarceration.

Early prisoners included counterfeiters who'd tried to exploit flaws in the nation's young banking system and men who'd violated the 1910 Mann Act, also known as the White Slave Traffic Act, which was supposed to combat forced prostitution.[1] Socialist Eugene Debs, a founder of the Industrial Workers of the World, did a stint in the prison for sedition after he urged resistance to the World War I military draft. Gangster Al Capone became a celebrity prisoner in 1932, managing to wrangle cigars, a typewriter, and a rug to decorate his cell.[2] In the 1980s, the penitentiary's population included hundreds of Cuban detainees. They'd sailed to the United States during the

1980 Mariel boatlift and were being held indefinitely because Fidel Castro had refused to take them back. In 1987, days after the U.S. Bureau of Prisons announced plans to deport them back to Cuba, they'd rioted, torching buildings and taking dozens of hostages during an eleven-day uprising, the longest prison riot in U.S. history.[3]

By the time Belton arrived, the prison had completed a multimillion-dollar facelift to repair damage from the riots. The Cubans were gone, many either released or deported, and the inmate population was evolving once again. By 1990, half of the penitentiary's inmates were serving time for drug offenses.

Belton was happy to be there. Though locked in his cell at night, he enjoyed sunlight and fresh air during daily walks from building to building. This was a welcome change from his year in county jail, where outdoors had been the piece of sky visible only from a walled pen during recreation hour. He also appreciated access to washers and dryers, an improvement over the five-gallon laundry buckets he'd used in state prison. And Atlanta offered more educational opportunities. He enrolled in business law and Spanish.

The prison also provided a surprising new world of illicit activities. Inmates made poker game bets with quarters from their commissary accounts, and when gambling grew so rampant that the commissary ceased handing out quarters, the currency switched to postage stamps. Once the chow hall closed after dinner, resourceful prisoners used food smuggled from the kitchen to run in-cell food stands, heating irons to make grilled cheese sandwiches and boiling hot dogs in water heated with the live-wire ends of cords cut from appliances.

There was little an inmate couldn't buy in the prison's black-market economy. Moonshine was brewed from fruit juice fermented with yeast rolls. Syringes to shoot heroin were smuggled from the medical unit. Drugs and cigarettes managed to find a way in, despite strip searches. Some inmates continued running their drug operations, conveying instructions in coded phone conversations to men on the streets.

Belton could have done this too. Early on, two former associates offered a chance for easy money. *I've been looking for some work,* one told him during a phone call. *Talk to your people in Miami. See if they can get me some work.* This was a request for an introduction to Belton's Miami supplier. His friends offered him $5,000 for every kilo, which would go to Rhonda and help support Belton's family. He considered the proposition only long enough to remember his twenty-four-year sentence. "You're crazy," he told them.

His vow to go straight seemed stronger this time. For one thing, he had stopped professing his innocence. He admitted he'd broken the law and was paying the price. When inmates from Charlotte referred to him as Money Rock, he said to call him Lamont, the name he'd used since childhood. He got along well—"institutional adjustment has been considered excellent," Atlanta's warden wrote in a progress report. Despite being surrounded by men constantly breaking rules, Belton stayed out of trouble, uninterested in activities—gambling, drinking hooch, doing drugs, stealing, or "messing with gay boys," in his parlance—that he'd concluded were most likely to lead to infractions. The quarters he withdrew from his commissary account went for vending machine snacks during family visits.

Belton developed a near-monastic routine, starting with prayer in his cell before sunup. He dressed in his khaki prison uniform, then went to the chow hall for breakfast, unless he was fasting, which he did once or twice a week, believing the practice helped him receive God's word. Except for time spent exercising—walking the track, lifting weights, playing basketball—he devoted nearly every waking minute to his faith. He even organized a tithing system. He and other like-minded inmates put 10 percent of their prison wages toward commissary necessities—toothbrushes, deodorant, shower slippers—and then presented them as care packages to new arrivals. He made an immediate impression on Jeffrey Scott, who ran into Belton upon arriving in Atlanta in 1992. Scott, barely twenty-one, also a coke dealer, was fresh off the prison bus, from county jail in Knoxville. He'd been strip searched, handed soap and bed linens, and sent to his cell. As he entered his unit, a portly young inmate approached, hand extended, and asked Scott how he was doing. "What actually stood out to me was what he was wearing—a polka-dot pajama set," Scott recalled. There may have also been a robe. His recollection was that the polka-dots were black and white. "I was curious—how did you get that in prison?" (From the commissary, according to Belton.)

Belton Platt had smiled, introduced himself, then invited Scott to pray with him. Scott wasn't much of a Christian at that point, but the prospect of fellowship was comforting. He followed Belton into his cell, and when Belton dropped to his knees, Scott followed his lead. "I wasn't accustomed to praying in front of people," he recalled, but he felt power in Belton's words. "He prayed for me and my transition and for the other guys who came on the bus that day."

Belton worked at the prison as chaplain's orderly at the All Faiths Chapel, a job he'd requested. It paid considerably less than work in the prison factory, where inmates made mattresses and mailbags, but it gave him time for Bible study. After he cleaned the chapel and filled inmates' orders for greeting cards that Hallmark donated to the prison, he often retreated to a storage room furnished with desk and chair—a prayer closet that was an actual closet. This became his favorite place, a sanctuary where he continued the spiritual journey he'd begun when he discovered the teachings of Kenneth Hagin and his Pentecostal-based Word of Faith movement. He studied the Bible and listened to recordings of Benny Hinn, Morris Cerullo, R.W. Schambach, and other evangelists he admired. In the closet, Belton also contemplated his private sorrows. In May 1991, his wife, Rhonda, filed for divorce. It wasn't a surprise. Rhonda had warned that she'd leave if he went to prison. The two had seldom been happy together, yet Belton mourned the death of his marriage. "I felt that my family was destroyed," he said.

Within months of arriving in Atlanta, Belton began preaching. He'd been sharing his faith with fellow inmates since he arrived, striking up conversations in the recreation yard, trying to "win the compound for

Christ," as he put it. Preaching was a natural next step. Yet he was nervous about speaking to a crowd. Inmates who'd been leading Sunday afternoon services had to talk him into it.

He started with a prayer, then a scripture reading, then a sermon he'd scribbled down earlier, about God sending Abraham to the land of Moriah to sacrifice his son. Gradually, he relaxed, and when more than a dozen men responded to his altar call, he sensed God guiding him. Soon, he preached every Friday night and Sunday afternoon.

Prisoners who shared Belton's beliefs found him wise and charismatic. Many welcomed his kind acts. Some, like Scott, were less certain about Christianity, but found they deepened their faith as they spent time with him. Not everyone appreciated Belton's determination to deliver the Good News about Jesus Christ, however. Staff and inmates who had witnessed ephemeral jailhouse conversions were skeptical of the overly zealous convert. Belton was no longer a cocky drug dealer, but he struck some as a know-it-all Christian. The one time he nearly came to blows with another inmate, the argument was over Jesus.

The dispute began when a Muslim inmate named Hakim knocked on the steel door of Belton's cell one evening. Hakim wanted to debate Belton's beliefs. He challenged Belton to find one place in the Bible where Jesus called himself God. Belton, in the middle of Bible study, said he didn't want to argue. But he promised to deliver *three* scriptural citations to Hakim's cell when he finished.

Belton knew his Bible and had pondered the question of Jesus's divinity at length. He realized that nonbelievers often viewed Jesus as a prophet or wise man, but not the son of God. To Belton, certain about the Bible's literal truth, this made no sense. Jesus referred to himself as divine and allowed others to worship him, so if Jesus wasn't telling the truth, Belton reasoned, then he was a fake, a phony—a false prophet. How could a person believe Jesus was a good man and disbelieve what he said about himself?

Belton didn't tell Hakim all of that. Instead, he opened his Bible and pointed out several passages, mostly in the Gospel of John, where Jesus states, *I and the Father are one,* and *if ye had known me, ye should have known my Father.* But his interpretation, rather than appeasing Hakim, seemed to infuriate him. As they argued, Belton tried posing a question. If Hakim accepted the Old Testament as God's word, as he said he did, then he recalled that God directed Moses to make blood offerings for the sins of his people. "Hakim," Belton asked, "if Christ was not the supreme sacrifice for the sins of the world and if his blood didn't cleanse us from all our sins, how are your sins forgiven?"

Hakim's response was to grab Belton and push him out of his cell.

"Hold up, man," Belton said, trying to calm Hakim. But Hakim raised his fists. Belton raised his, unwilling to turn his back on a fight. Belton threw a punch, intentionally pulling it at the last moment, barely making contact. Then he turned to make sure the dorm officer wasn't around. That's when Hakim socked him.

Blood inched down the side of Belton's face. He retreated to a buddy's room, where he seethed with the anger that engulfed him when he felt disrespected. One inmate offered a shank. He declined. Fists would do fine. But before he confronted Hakim, he needed to change out of his slippery shower shoes. He asked his cellmate, Quin, to fetch his tennis shoes. Belton waited, hyped up. Minutes passed. Finally, Quin reappeared, empty-handed.

Lamont, he said, that is not you anymore.

Belton knew Quin was right. He shouldn't have let Hakim anger him. Later, Hakim apologized to Belton for punching him. Belton told Hakim he'd continue to pray that he'd one day accept Jesus as his lord and savior.

Belton spent three years in Atlanta. In 1993, outstanding behavior and work evaluations earned him a transfer to the Federal Correctional Institution in Butner, about three hours northeast of Charlotte. This was a good news. Butner, which included a psychiatric hospital and medium- and low-security units, was nicknamed "Club Fed" because of its amenities. Many inmates wore street clothes; it was possible to encounter a drug kingpin on his way to the tennis courts. The cell units were named for universities (Georgetown, Virginia, Clemson), and, if not for the fence surrounding the compound, an unknowing visitor might mistake the place for a college campus.

The best part of the transfer was that it put Belton closer to family and reunited him with his younger brother, Gordon, who'd been convicted with him. The two had been separated for nearly three years; Gordon hadn't even known Belton was moving until he arrived. The prison gave him a bed in Gordon's unit, though he was initially stuck in the hall because of crowding. The brothers embraced, talking into the night, and Gordon marveled at the change he saw. "It was like a glow when I seen him," Gordon recalled. "He just had this glow about himself. You can see stress on people's faces. But not on him. He was happy, one of few people I seen being happy in prison."

Gordon himself was having a tougher time. Though he'd made a name as "Cake Daddy," Gordon remained angry, blaming others, especially LaMorris Watson, for his conviction. Gordon was certainly guilty; he had been carrying that half kilo of cocaine for his brother. But his anger was understandable. Though he had earlier convictions for theft and breaking and entering, he'd never been part of his brother's drug operation, never profited from it. But because Gordon had gone along with his brother on the wrong evening, he was serving sixteen years. With Belton as his example, however, Gordon found it easier to take responsibility for his actions. "It just helped me to watch him," Gordon said. "He was a whole different person. The Money Rock was gone."

Prison life, by its nature, is a string of unvarying routines—mealtimes, guard counts, lights out—yet within those parameters, the inmates Belton encountered found many ways to do their time. Some passed the days in the TV room, eyes glued to the screen, ready to erupt at an unwelcome channel change. Others pumped iron. Some joined gangs or rebelled against the system, picking fights and spending half their life in solitary confinement. Some took up crafts practiced exclusively behind bars, such as sewing tapestries with thread unraveled from socks.

While in federal prison in Butner, North Carolina, Belton earned a diploma in residential carpentry from the local community college. Courtesy of Belton Platt.

Belton had a different strategy, which he described in a talk he wrote for a prison public-speaking class. "I know a lot of you, just like me, have lost a lot of things since coming to prison," he began. "Some have lost their wives. Some have lost their homes. Some have lost the respect of their children.

"But what do we do from here? Do we wallow around in self-pity? Do we cry, complain, or just give up? Do we just stop living?"

No. The best course of action, he said, was to "Get up and make something happen with your life. Don't set around and allow your life to dry up. Don't continue to make excuses for why you are here. Don't be afraid to make a change for the better."

That was what Belton did. At Butner, he earned a community college diploma in residential carpentry, volunteered as a literacy tutor, and pored over law books in the prison library as he crafted appeals. He took classes in WordPerfect, Lotus, and data processing. He preached, led prayer groups, and regularly walked up the hill to the hospital to sit with psychiatric inmates who'd been institutionalized for years. He prayed for their needs and assured them of the love of Christ.

As in Atlanta, he worked in the chaplain's office, a job he requested even though he'd initially landed one of the best gigs at Butner: inspecting eyeglasses that inmates made in the prison factory. He'd been so competent in that job that his supervisor accelerated his promotion. But he felt that the chapel was where he belonged.

The weight he'd gained living his Money Rock life had begun to disappear. He exercised regularly, avoided red meat, and took notes in nutrition classes. "Don't eat these: Butter, Margarine, oil, Crisco," he wrote. "Oils are liquid grease."

He honed his public-speaking skills through a program modeled after Toastmasters International. For two hours each week, inmates, many of them white-collar criminals, began with Table Topics, an extemporaneous speaking exercise that required members to stand and deliver brief responses to questions: *Describe the most memorable event of your life. What do you plan on doing when you get out of prison? You just won a scholarship to college, but there is one problem. . . . You don't have a high school diploma or GED. What would you do?* From there, they took turns delivering and evaluating speeches. Belton's communication skills had always been good, key to his drug-dealing success. This class refined those natural abilities, boosting his confidence before crowds. He accumulated certificates for "best speech," "best evaluator," and "most improved speaker," awards voted on by his classmates. As he became more adept, he began mentoring others.

Being locked away had barely put a dent in Belton's popularity with women. During his first decade of incarceration, he accumulated a stack of upbeat greeting cards and letters, several of which contained suggestive sentiments. Example: "Lamont, I wish I could reveal to you everything in my heart." He'd met the women while they were visiting incarcerated relatives or when they attended prison chapel programs with their church groups. None of the liaisons lasted, but a few were memorable, such as the love interest who tearfully admitted on the phone that she'd been unfaithful—with another woman. Belton was unfamiliar and uncomfortable with homosexuality, and the confession threw him for a loop: "Do I get upset? Do I get mad? I was so confused. Because it wasn't a man."

He began one relationship in 1997 with a Christian woman Carrie had urged to write her son. They began trading letters, and from photos she sent, Belton noted that she was slim and attractive. Soon, he was broaching marriage. At first, the woman, a family therapist who lived near Charlotte, insisted they keep things platonic. She wanted only to "aid you in upliftment and offer some diversion to your day," she wrote in May 1997. She also balked when he urged her to visit; she worried that associating with a felon could hurt her career. But by August, the platonic tone was no more. "I am in love with Belton Lamont Platt, 33½ years old, ex King Pin, Business man, Entrepreneur," she wrote in one letter. "I will expect total commitment, Romance throughout and Honesty in our union," she explained in another. She also suggested he lose some weight. "Can't Stand a Big Tummy!" When she finally made it to Butner, she arrived wearing dark glasses, Belton recalled, "trying to disguise herself to see the ex–Money Rock." Now, it was Belton's turn to suggest they keep things platonic. By year's end, the relationship was done.

Belton the federal inmate lived a surprisingly full life. And yet there wasn't a day he didn't long for home, and for his children. They sometimes talked by phone, but occasional calls, letters, and visits only emphasized deeper relationships he was missing. In 1997, for instance, Belton heard from thirteen-year-old Demario, the third of his eleven children. "I didn't have anything else to do so my mama told me to right you," Demario began, in a letter sprinkled with misspellings. He said he played linebacker and running back on his middle-school football team, and that a lone C on his report card had kept him off the A-B honor roll. Though Demario signed the letter "Love, Mario," his salutation suggested estrangement. It began not with "Dear Dad," but simply "Lamont."

It was no wonder they weren't close. Belton's relationship with De-mario's mother, Gloria Pruitt, had been about as slight as a relation-ship could be and still produce two sons—Demario and Derrick—in fourteen months. Several of Belton's children were just as distant. He'd never met one son who'd been adopted by the boy's maternal grandparents.

As Demario closed his letter, he raised the one question everyone kept asking: When was Belton getting out? "The other day your mama told me you where getting out soon," he told his father, "so were still waiting."

Many family members remained optimistic that freedom was just around the corner. His youngest daughter, Genesis, had a vision about his homecoming, which he described in his journal: "She saw me come to my mothers [sic] house with my mother screaming 'my son has come home.' She also said that the police just let me go. This vision was at a time when I needed a word from the Lord. It en-couraged me in such a special way." Belton's family believed freedom to be imminent because that's what Belton kept assuring them. In 1997, the family therapist he'd romanced, claiming she had the gift of prophecy, had insisted that it would be the year of Belton's release. Belton continued believing that if he prayed enough, he could make the change he wanted—it had worked when his state sentence was overturned—so he kept praying for a sentence reduction. Though he'd accepted that his incarceration was justified, he felt his sentence was excessive.

He had a point. For one thing, his sentencing judge, Robert "Max-imum Bob" Potter, famed for tough punishments, had piled on the time. Federal sentencing guidelines mandated twelve to sixteen years for Belton's crimes. But Potter bumped his time to twenty-four years with an "upward departure"—a finding of aggravating factors that fed-eral judges used in only 2.3 percent of cases the year Belton was sen-tenced. Those factors included Belton's participation in the Piedmont Courts shootout, which Potter took into account even though Belton's 1986 conviction had been overturned on appeal. In effect, Potter relied on evidence that hadn't been proven by a conviction. At the time, the law supported his action, but it would later be ruled unconstitutional.[4]

Punishment-wise, Belton was also a victim of terrible timing: His arrest followed the most extreme series of drug sentencing reforms in the nation's history. The Anti-Drug Abuse Act of 1988, for instance, set mandatory minimums for dealing and created much tougher penalties for possessing or selling crack cocaine, chemically identical to the powder form of cocaine, but more often used by African Americans. The law that most affected Belton was the Sentencing Reform Act of 1984, which had eliminated parole for all federal crimes committed on or after November 1, 1987. If you were convicted of a federal crime as of that date, you served 85 percent of your sentence. The law, championed to add consistency to a system that had produced wildly different sentences for similar offenses, ignored even the most outstanding good behavior and became one reason that prison times more than doubled for federal prisoners from 1988 to 2012.[5] Had Belton been charged two years earlier, he would have been eligible for parole after serving a third of his sentence—eight years. With his stellar record, he probably would have had a shot at parole. But without a successful appeal or pardon, he would serve 85 percent of his sentence, more than twenty years. These new sentencing laws were the reason he ended up sleeping on a bunk in a hallway when he arrived at Butner. The prison population was exploding. In 1988, as the new laws were first taking effect, there were just over 50,000 federal prisoners. By 2000, there would be 145,000.[6]

Belton had lost his first appeal in 1991, when the U.S. Court of Appeals had upheld his conviction, but he didn't give up. In 1996, he asked Bill Clinton for a pardon: "Mr. President, I know you will look at my petition, and say I wonder about this man. I don't know how many petitions even reach your hands, but I pray that this one does. I am not just another prisoner with a selfish ambition to get out of prison," he wrote. "I have done everything I've possibly could to better myself while offering encouragement to others to better themselves."

He was thrilled the day the mail brought a letter from the White

House. Then he opened it. "Your words of encouragement and support mean a great deal to me," President Clinton said. It was a generic form letter sent to the president's supporters, with no mention of Belton's plea for clemency.

Still he didn't give up. In 1997, he pinned hopes on a motion to vacate—or throw out—his sentence. He worked for hours in the prison library, filling a legal pad with notes on relevant cases, crafting an argument that cited ineffective counsel and errors in the prosecution's presentencing report. "I thank the Lord for using me to write such a good motion," he wrote in his journal. "I know that God has given me favor, and that I'm going home very soon." A fellow inmate typed and copied the motion for Belton in exchange for four books of stamps. After he sent it off, he telephoned family and friends and asked them to pray for him.

Judge Potter denied it.

Belton tried again in 1998, arguing for a reduced sentence based on his extensive rehabilitation. He followed the five-page motion with more than thirty pages of positive prison progress reports, academic records, certificates, and commendation letters, including one from a prison literacy teacher who noted the patience Belton exhibited tutoring inmates with learning difficulties. "Inmate Platt enjoys helping others," the teacher wrote, "and the positive attitude he projects helps set a productive atmosphere for the class." Belton even included his letter from President Clinton.

Again, Judge Potter said no. Potter wrote in his decision that federal rules prohibited Belton's claim, and he dismissed Belton's progress in prison, writing that while noteworthy, "his rehabilitative accomplishments are not extraordinary or exceptional."

Nothing in these responses to Belton's legal salvos offered encouragement, yet he kept trying. His need to connect with his children felt more urgent. By the late 1990s, most were teenagers. Their interest in weekend trips to prison had waned, and behavioral problems such as school suspensions were multiplying. His oldest daughter, Kim, had gotten pregnant at age fourteen and given birth to a son.

"They need a male figure in their life," Gloria wrote to Belton in 1997 about sons Derrick and Demario, then twelve and thirteen. Derrick, she complained, had run up $309 in charges after repeatedly calling an adult porn phone number. "Some where [*sic*] recently our paths has gotten mixed up because they have forgotten who the parent is in this house," she wrote. By the end of the decade, adolescent misbehavior was giving way to lawbreaking. At age sixteen, Lamont Davis, Belton's oldest son, was arrested for possessing crack and stealing a car. He got probation that time. Belton worried about the next time.

As Belton accepted his failings as a father, he thought more about larger societal problems. Parental responsibility became a topic for his sermons and public-speaking presentations. He suggested that courts order fathers to spend time with their children as well as pay child support. He wanted the government to do more, too, such as give tax incentives to businesses that offer jobs to low-income teens. "So many of our children are left with nowhere to go," he wrote, "but to the drug dealers, gangs, pimps, hustlers, for help in order to survive."

In one letter to his mother, Belton pleaded for more contact with his children. "I want to say a lot of things to them but I haven't had the opportunity to tell them," he said. "I know how to talk to them, they trust me, and want to hear from me," he wrote. "If everybody stop worrying about themselves and really see what is going on with my children's lives they will see that they need their daddy in their lives."

He told his sons that he loved them, that he would eventually be free, that he didn't want them making the mistakes he made. But their anger was growing, and he didn't know how to stop it.

14

SENTENCING A GENERATION

In 2000, African Americans made up 28 percent of Mecklenburg County's population but accounted for 70 percent of its felony arrests.[1] Each weekday morning, and then again in the afternoon, a fresh docket of those defendants arrived in Shirley Fulton's courtroom. From behind the bench in her black judge's robe, she'd scan her crowd, recalling lines from a James Weldon Johnson poem: *And far as the eye of God could see / Darkness covered everything.* Some days, she wondered where all the black men kept coming from, if the supply might eventually dry up and they'd run out of black people to prosecute.

As defendants waited for their cases to be called, those free on bond sat next to lawyers or parents, wives or girlfriends, or by themselves, filling benches that looked like church pews. The rest, the ones who didn't have or couldn't pay bond, came from jail, escorted by a deputy through an underground tunnel. They waited in a holding cell, then stood at the defense table with a deputy positioned slightly behind. They wore orange—pants and shirts, or jumpsuits—and rubber shower shoes over white socks. Their hands were cuffed in front of them. Sometimes their legs were shackled.

Fulton hadn't planned to be a judge, or even imagined it when she was a single mom working her way through Duke law school. But after she became a prosecutor, Mecklenburg County's district

Shirley Fulton's judicial portrait in the Mecklenburg County courthouse. Photo by Pam Kelley.

attorney, impressed by her intellect and steady demeanor, had championed her appointment to an open judicial seat in 1987, a year after Money Rock's trial. She got that appointment, then became the first black woman in the state to run for—and win—a judgeship on North Carolina's Superior Court, which heard felonies, major civil cases, and misdemeanor appeals.

Her career success had obscured a difficult personal time. In 1993, she'd found a cancerous lump in her left breast, had a lumpectomy, and was back to work before she finished chemotherapy. The cancer returned two years later, forcing her to confront the possibility of death at an early age. She enrolled in a trial study at Duke University Hospital, had a double mastectomy, then a five-day chemo treatment that blasted her cancer cells and depressed her immune system. Finally, she had a stem cell transplant. The ordeal permanently damaged her hearing, eyesight, and gums. Her fingers and toes sometimes felt numb. But the treatment worked. She was cancer free.

Recuperation had taken a year. She'd returned to court in 1997 with an assisted listening device and a new hairstyle—short and natural, replacing the longer straightened hair she'd lost during chemo. She told a reporter that cancer had forced her to realize that "tomorrow is not promised."[2] She vowed to slow down but instead got busier, enrolling in a local MBA program, something she'd wanted to do since law school. She attended weekend classes and graduated in 1998. She also became the county's highest-ranking judge. Shortly after her return, Mecklenburg Superior Court's senior resident judge retired. Fulton, next in line by seniority, stepped into the job, assuming responsibility for overseeing the local court system.

Soon afterward, she implemented a new process for administrative court—Courtroom 2201—to handle nontrial matters such as first appearances, pretrial motions, bond hearings, and guilty pleas, and move cases through the system faster. Then she assigned herself to 2201 permanently, figuring her ongoing presence would create consistency—similar punishments for similar guilty pleas. Also, no other judge really wanted the job, which was tedious and grueling. In other criminal courtrooms, a trial might end on Wednesday or Thursday, and the judge was done in court for the week. The docket in administrative court was never-ending. "I don't know how she did it and kept her sanity," one former judge told me.

She functioned as a sort of judicial project manager, spotting and fixing details—a missing lab result, unfinished discovery—that could derail a trial. On plea conference days, she met with lawyers in her chambers, listening first to the prosecutor, who described a defendant's crime and usually offered to reduce or drop some charges. Once she heard the defendant's side of the story, Fulton shared the sentence she'd impose. If the defendant decided to take it, he entered his guilty plea later, in the courtroom. With every plea, Fulton asked the same questions. This was part of the job's drudgery, repeating more than twenty required questions a dozen times a day. She kept the plea transcript in front of her, but knew it by heart.

"Do you now personally plead guilty?" she would ask.

Yes, defendants told her.

"Are you in fact guilty?"

Yes, they would say.

She could sail through a plea in ten or fifteen minutes, though they took longer when victims or defendants' family members wanted to speak. From victims, Fulton learned that the men standing before her had caused damage and heartache. From defendants' family members, she learned they had held jobs, loved their children, attended church. Considering its purpose, the plea process was remarkably business-like. Occasionally, however, a defendant's voice quavered, or a mother wiped tears as a deputy handcuffed her boy's wrists before taking him to jail. For a moment, judicial proceeding dissolved into tragedy.

Over time, Fulton grew discouraged with the way the system incarcerated and reincarcerated offenders. She sentenced young defendants knowing they'd probably return to their neighborhoods after prison, where they'd likely fall into old habits, increasing the chances they'd be back in criminal court again. She longed for another sentencing option—some sort of structured residential rehabilitation program where she could assign young men to work while learning life skills. She even imagined the curriculum she'd write for this nonexistent program. It would teach participants how to open a checking account, how government works, why they had a duty to vote in elections. It would push them to consider and discuss their values and introduce them to possible vocations—in law, medicine, science, business. It would encourage them to aim high, not low.

Convincing the state legislature to fund rehabilitation efforts was nearly impossible, however, even when they were proven to work. She'd seen this firsthand with the county's drug treatment court. In 1995, Mecklenburg County's judicial district became the first in North Carolina to launch a treatment court for felony drug possession charges. By agreeing to treatment, counseling, and drug testing, defendants could plead guilty and receive probation. If they stayed clean a year, their convictions would be expunged. The program required progress reports in court every two weeks, and backsliding was common, especially when defendants were just starting. But many eventually turned their lives around. When they stood before the judge describing new jobs and repaired relationships, courtroom visitors would applaud, sometimes fighting back tears. "It was amazing," recalled Steve Ward, the prosecutor assigned to the program in its early years. At about $2,500 per person per year, the program was also a bargain for state taxpayers, considering a year in prison cost more than $25,000.

And yet when state legislators were looking for budget cuts, the drug treatment court regularly got targeted for elimination. When that happened, Fulton hit the phones, lobbying legislators to save it. During her years as a judge, it always survived, but the exercise drove her crazy. "It was hard to understand why you would cut something that was working," she said.[3]

The situation wasn't unique to Charlotte. In America, fighting crime meant arresting and punishing, especially with drug offenses. One compelling discussion of this topic, titled "Insanity: Four Decades of U.S. Counterdrug Strategy," pointed out that the nation had to spend about fifteen times as much on enforcement to achieve results it got when it reduced demand for drugs by putting addicts in treatment.[4] The nation had been following this strategy—spending more to achieve less—almost since President Nixon declared the War on Drugs in 1971. For the first couple of years, Nixon did pump the bulk of his drug war money into treatment. Was it effective? "If one measures results by falling crime rates in major cities, the large-scale successful treatment of addicts, and a reduction in the availability of illicit drugs, the answer is almost certainly 'yes,'" writes Michael F. Walther, the U.S. Army lieutenant colonel and retired U.S. Department of Justice executive who authored the "Insanity" report. But then came Nixon's 1972 reelection campaign and the Watergate scandal. That's when the War on Drugs shifted resources from treatment to enforcement. "Despite evidence that a balance between law enforcement and demand-reduction could be effective, the need to be seen as 'tough on crime' allowed politics to trump a well-reasoned public policy and a strategy based on science-driven methodologies. Future drug budgets would reflect this shift in strategy."[5]

Fulton didn't need to read that report. She'd lived the situation it described. She only had to show up to see that black men predominated in Mecklenburg County's criminal justice system. Among citizens, this disproportionality resembled one of those optical illusion drawings—the young woman/old lady, or the vase and two silhouettes, entirely different pictures, depending on how you looked at them. Some people attributed the imbalance to societal factors—poverty, a lack of jobs and role models. Others agreed with a white county commissioner who described urban blacks as living in "a moral sewer of promiscuity."[6]

Many criminal justice experts blamed the system itself, which guaranteed more African American arrests because police disproportionately patrolled higher-crime black neighborhoods, where residents clamored for police protection. Through the late 1980s, "much of black America had remained committed to the War on Drugs, even supporting mandatory minimum sentences," James Forman Jr. writes in *Locking Up Our Own: Crime and Punishment in Black America.*[7]

But by the early 1990s, across the country, law officers and judges like Fulton had begun sounding the alarm that the nation's drug war had become a war on black people. Whites used drugs at the same or higher rates than African Americans. But in white parts of town—south Charlotte, for instance—drug deals went down behind closed doors. As a police commander in Chicago told a reporter, the black guy on the street corner has "almost got a sign on his back. These guys are just arrestable."[8]

Fulton didn't shy from discussing these racial issues with colleagues, though her calm demeanor usually disguised her passion. There was one day, however, when she revealed the depth of her frustration to Bart Menser, a senior prosecutor. The two had known each other since she'd joined the district attorney's office. Back then, he'd been a mentor, serving as lead attorney when she helped prosecute her first homicide trial. She'd had dinners with his family. He'd attended her wedding when she'd married in 1988.

Menser had been working in Fulton's courtroom that day, and he'd noticed she looked weary. When court adjourned, he approached the bench. "You seem down," he told her.

"You know," she replied, "I feel like I've put an entire generation of black men in prison."

On another day, Fulton had been reading through her docket when a defendant's name jumped out at her: Belton Lamont Platt. For a moment, she expected Money Rock. But when she reached his case, the defendant standing before her was a teenager, Money Rock's son.

Lamont was the fifth of Belton Platt's eight sons, and one of two named for their father. His mom, Janie, recalled that Belton had been easy to talk to when they met as teenagers, and she'd fallen in love long before he was rolling in money. They'd continued an intermittent relationship while Belton was married to Rhonda. Their first child, LaToya, was born in 1984. Two years later, Janie named her new son Belton Lamont Platt III and called him Lamont, like his father.

This was confusing, to say the least. Nearly five years earlier, Belton and Rhonda had named their son Belton Lamont. Janie's name choice became a sore point with certain family members, especially Carrie, who felt sorry for Rhonda and resented that Janie seemed to be advertising her adultery. To keep the two half brothers straight, Belton called Rhonda's son Big Lamont, while Janie's was Little Lamont. Janie had added the suffix "III" to her son's name to denote that he was the third Belton Lamont.

So Little Lamont grew up with Money Rock's name and the baggage that came with it. He'd been three when Belton went to prison, with no preincarceration memories, only photos of his dad holding him as a baby. He often heard stories that painted his father as a local hero, wealthy and respected on the streets. He didn't hear these stories from Belton, however. During prison visits and phone conversations, Belton never bragged about his life as Money Rock. Mostly, he tried to counsel his son to avoid his mistakes.

Fulton told me about her encounter with Little Lamont one of the first times I interviewed her. She couldn't remember when or why he was there, but seeing the son in her courtroom after prosecuting the father had made an impression. "It was a little sad, to see a pattern," she said. I couldn't find Fulton's signature on any of Little's Lamont's public court records; we concluded she probably handled a first appearance that didn't require her signature, likely for his first felony offense, which occurred on February 15, 2002. On that day, he'd skipped a class at Myers Park High School and made his way to the auditorium. The school was overcrowded—new school construction couldn't keep up with all the families moving to town each year—so the auditorium stage had been pressed into service as a classroom. Students were focused on writing scenes for an International Baccalaureate drama class. No one was paying attention to Little Lamont, near the curtains.

There happened to be an aerosol can of graffiti remover. He happened to have a lighter. He flicked the lighter, pressed the nozzle on the can. The stream of spray ignited.

The velvety stage curtains were dark green, one of Myers Park's school colors. They'd been treated with flame retardant, according to a teacher, but Little Lamont's makeshift blowtorch set a curtain burning. Someone noticed the smoke—smelled it or saw it—and suddenly students were abandoning half-written scenes, grabbing backpacks, hurrying offstage. As the fire alarm bleated, more than two thousand students spilled from exits into the winter air. Firefighters arrived in time to douse the fire before it could spread. The curtain was ruined, but the damage was limited. Eleven years later, the school principal at the time couldn't remember the incident.

Little Lamont had been sixteen for about a month in 2002 when he set the stage curtain on fire. In much of the nation, his case might have gone to juvenile court because most states at that time didn't automatically define offenders as adults until they were seventeen or eighteen.[9] He faced two felonies, burning a schoolhouse and malicious damage by explosives, each punishable by more than a year in prison. The severity of the charges reflected the circumstances of the incident—inside a school, where a fire could have been an epic tragedy. It likely also reflected the times. In the 1990s, school systems across the country began adopting zero-tolerance policies on violence. Police officers patrolled school halls, drug-sniffing dogs conducted locker inspections. A cafeteria fight once punished by suspensions now brought criminal charges.

To make matters worse, this wasn't Little Lamont's first offense. He'd been charged with two misdemeanors, trespassing and having a weapon on school property, two weeks before the curtain fire. He told me in a 2013 interview that he'd been consistently "bad" in school. He was adamant, however, that he hadn't been trying to burn down the school. It had been a mistake, and he'd hated when friends teased him about it. He was also adamant that he didn't want to discuss past offenses with me.

He spent more than a month in county jail before Janie and his stepfather paid his bond. Months later, a prosecutor dropped the explosives charge and Little Lamont agreed to plead guilty to burning a schoolhouse. Fulton never saw him after that single brief encounter in her courtroom. Another judge suspended his sentence, on the condition that he continue his schooling and pay $2,720.59, including $893.64 in restitution to Myers Park High.

He could avoid prison by staying out of trouble. But at sixteen, he was now a convicted felon.

Fulton recognized the irony of holding a workshop titled "Judicial Leadership in a Diverse Community" at the Duke Mansion in Myers Park, one of the whitest neighborhoods in town. The twenty-bedroom mansion, once the home of industrialist James B. Duke, was now a nonprofit inn and conference center, and the event, not the location, was most important. The 2002 workshop had been Fulton's idea, an outgrowth of work she'd done on Charlotte's Community Building Task Force, created in 1997 after police shot and killed two unarmed black citizens within six months and the city nearly exploded into riots. Its organizers had tapped Fulton to help lead the task force because she was widely respected, known for her ability to speak truth to power. The group had sought to dig deeper than previous attempts to smooth race relations, to address history and policies that continued to promote inequality in ways community leaders were only beginning to recognize. "The key is being able to say, racism is here in our town," one of the task force's organizers, former Charlotte mayor *pro tem* Cyndee Patterson, had told a reporter. "It's not that some people are lazy or some people are poor. You have to say it—it's systemic racism." [10]

With Fulton's support, the court system began a similar exploration a few years later. A 2001 survey had found that a large percentage of African American court personnel didn't think people of color were being treated fairly. That survey appeared at odds with an analysis of sentences in drug and traffic courts that hadn't found disparities by race. But perhaps court personnel were reacting to subtle systemic bias—longer sentences for crack cocaine charges, for instance, and policies that kept people in jail because they didn't have the money to pay bonds or court fees. These policies weren't discriminatory on their face, but they had a disparate impact on black people.

Fulton wanted judges to discuss these issues. That in itself was groundbreaking. Though Mecklenburg County's Superior and District Court judges spent time in the same building, they seldom gathered as a group. She'd been on the bench fifteen years, yet had barely spoken to certain colleagues. At a minimum, she figured the workshop would help her get to know her fellow judges. On Friday, April 26, 2002, court was shut down so Mecklenburg County's judges could do something they'd never done—spend a day talking about race, ethnicity, equality, and themselves.

The Duke Mansion's grounds bloomed with azaleas that morning. Arriving judges headed down the grand hall, a checkerboard pattern of black and white marble, then gathered at tables in the mansion's vast living room. The workshop started with breakfast and ended with evening cocktails. In between, guided by a facilitator, nineteen judges began excavating their own histories, exploring how each had life experiences that had shaped their worldview, and how their views affected decisions on the bench. Among the hottest topics that day: sagging pants. The subject arose as judges heard from an African American man who'd been a criminal defendant. District Court Judge Regan Miller, also African American, asked the young man if he realized his dress and behavior in court could affect the outcome of his case. Then Miller asked his colleagues the same question. In some judges' eyes, saggy pants and sloppy dress showed disrespect. Others, including Fulton, believed judges needed to consider defendants' personal situations. They might not have access to a shower or a washing machine. They might not be sleeping inside a house. An intense conversation ensued. Biases were pointed out, denied, acknowledged. There were moments of discomfort.

Several judges later described that day as a turning point—a demonstration that hard conversations about race were both possible and imperative if the criminal justice system was to be just. They also lauded both Fulton and her counterpart in District Court, the late Bill Jones, for visionary leadership. "They pulled the wool off the eyes. They made us talk about it," one judge told me. Another former judge said he believed the workshop made him fairer. "There was a good deal of confronting our own prejudices," he said.

The judges gathered three more times that year, with the final meeting in November 2002. Just a week earlier, Fulton had taken almost everyone by surprise by announcing that she'd be leaving the bench at the end of January. She'd informed people by letter so they couldn't try to talk her out of it.

When a reporter interviewed her about her decision, she admitted she was tired. "It's a constant battle," she told him. "There's never enough resources. And there's no promises that things will get better any time soon." [11] But she portrayed the move as a positive personal step—a decision to follow her passion. She was joining a law firm, and also would be volunteering her time with community development efforts to bring affordable housing, new businesses, and jobs to Charlotte's poorest neighborhoods, to explore opportunities "that pull at my heartstrings." [12]

What Fulton didn't tell the reporter was that she'd lost the idealism

she'd had as a prosecutor, when she believed she could make a difference by putting lawbreakers in prison. Four years in administrative
court had given her a stark look at a phenomenon still unnamed and
unknown to most of America. In Courtroom 2201, the mass incarceration of black men had played out before her eyes.

15
LOST BOYS

"Have I shown you Stephen's scrapbook?" Carrie asked. She'd retrieved it from her bedroom and plopped it on the coffee table. The three-ring binder was at least four inches thick, filled not only with photos of her grandson, but actual objects from his life, stuffed so full that its plastic-on-cardboard cover was splitting from its spine.

I'd come to rely on Carrie Graves's candor and good memory since reconnecting with her son, and I visited her often. At age seventy-seven, her Afro was gray. She remained opinionated, and enjoyed sharing said opinions. She announced her views with the buttons she wore (*Stop the violence against women*) and the T-shirts (*Juneteenth celebration*) and also on the front door of her public housing apartment, where bumper stickers declared that *Peace Begins at Home* and *A poor school is child abuse* and *Each of us matters to God*. Her home, Savanna Woods, was a "scattered site" public housing development built in the 1980s to address criticism that the city had stuck all its public housing on the west side. Unlike older and larger housing projects, these apartments, forty-nine units nestled on a middle-class street south of downtown, had never been plagued with violent crime. According to Carrie, their worst problem was gossip.

The apartment's compact living room, like the scrapbook, was chock full—with a sofa, coffee table, four chairs, bookshelves, a fifty-three-inch TV, African figurines, candles, Bible verses, children's books, videotapes, framed photos of children, grandchildren, great-grandchildren, and President Obama. Also, Carrie kept numerous boxes of papers. Because of her pack-rat tendencies, she periodically unearthed for me a letter or document or photo that illuminated something interesting about her life. But this scrapbook was more. It began with a Polaroid of a diapered Stephen in his father's arms and ended with the boy's obituary. In a family that had endured ample heartache, this was the saddest chapter.

Stephen had been born in June 1986, while Belton was in prison for the Piedmont Courts shootout. Belton and Rhonda pronounced his name *STEF-en*. But Carrie said it differently, with the accent on the second syllable—*Stef-AWN*—a choice that reflected her proprietary interest in this particular grandson. She'd felt a special connection, almost like she'd given birth to him herself. "If nobody ever loved me," Carrie said, "I know he did."

The scrapbook's first pages included typical childhood photographs—Stephen vacationing at the beach, playing in a pit of colored plastic balls, wearing a child-sized bow tie and double-breasted brown suit. There was a fifth-grade report card from Dilworth Elementary. He'd earned A's in every academic subject, but an N (needs improvement) in "Observes school and class rules." Carrie had deemed fair game anything that held Stephen's memory, so her book contained two of his long black locks, one braided, one not, to remind her of the braids he'd grown past his shoulders. She'd also stuffed into the scrapbook a sleeveless white T-shirt, yellow with age. The shirt and low-hanging jeans had been his signature outfit. And she'd included one of his Redman CDs, because Stephen loved rap. She recalled how he'd challenged her when she disparaged his music without listening to it: Didn't that make her the kind of person she hated—a hypocrite? She'd admired the rebuke; it had shown he was thinking.

Sympathy cards—"God cares" and "To encourage you" and "Just wanted you to know"—provided the scrapbook's epilogue. "In the sad times of life," one said, "it's part of God's plan for friends to help friends any way that they can." Carrie, long past tears, sat beside me, explaining the significance of each scrapbook item with her typical forthrightness and humor.

Absent from the scrapbook, however, was a reason for Stephen's death. For that, I asked Carrie and other family members. All described the losses he'd endured, first and foremost the father lost to prison. More than Belton's other children, Stephen had been angry, Carrie said. "He thought his daddy would never come home from prison." He channeled some of that anger toward law enforcement officers, whom he blamed for his father's absence.

Carrie saw Stephen often as he grew up. She'd moved in with the family on Ravenglass Lane during his preschool years, staying until the feds arrested Belton and seized the house. By Stephen's adolescence, Carrie's apartment had become a second home. He'd telephone: *Hey, Grandma. What you cooking?* He'd sleep on the sofa or floor, pulling his special blue blanket around his head. Carrie found Stephen to be mature, "older mind-wise than he was age-wise."

He'd been not quite four years old when he attended his father's sentencing in federal court and had little memory of a dad who wasn't behind bars. After Belton went to prison, Rhonda divorced him and became a beautician, working long hours to provide for Stephen and his siblings—Big Lamont, five years older, and their younger sister, Genesis. Rhonda also remarried, in a 1999 church ceremony with the white dress and bridesmaids she'd missed when she and Belton married as teenagers. Carrie catered the reception, a gesture meant to cool the bad feelings that had simmered between her and her ex-daughter-in-law since the divorce. Rhonda's husband, Ron, was new to Charlotte. He'd grown up in Buffalo, the youngest of eight children of a single mother. Like his stepsons, he was raised without a father in the house. He worked for a trucking company, and with their two salaries, he and Rhonda bought a new house—white with black shutters—in the east Charlotte suburbs.

Rhonda credited Ron with teaching her how to manage money, and from the outside, it seemed this newly blended family had gained a toehold in the middle class, away from drug dealers and violence. But the marriage ignited other problems. Stephen, twelve years old when his mom remarried, refused to be in the wedding party. He'd disliked his stepfather from the start, and their relationship never improved. That's one reason he often stayed with Carrie. By his teenaged years, he'd also found companionship with a group of boys and young men in Charlotte's Hidden Valley neighborhood, members of a gang called the Hidden Valley Kings.

When its first brick ranches and split-levels went up in northeast Charlotte in 1959, the sprawling Hidden Valley subdivision became a neighborhood for working-class whites who lived on fancifully named streets—Cinderella Road, Snow White Lane, Friendly Place. Rhonda grew up there, after her parents bought a two-thousand-square-foot house in 1974, helping to make the area one of Charlotte's first integrated neighborhoods.

Gang activity in those days meant the Outlaws and Hell's Angels, rival white motorcycle gangs that sold drugs and ran prostitution operations out of seedy massage parlors. Federal indictments ended their reign in Charlotte in the 1980s, but by 2000, street gangs such as the Crips and MS-13 had local presences. The Hidden Valley Kings, a homegrown bunch, became the city's largest gang, known for stealing cars and controlling the area's crack trade, and for a 2005 rolling shootout in which men fired at each other while driving down North Tryon Street.[1] Their infamy eventually earned them an episode on the History Channel's *Gangland* program, where a hyperbolic narrator described the Kings as having "taken over Charlotte's streets by any means necessary."[2] Big Lamont and Stephen fell in with the Kings because of proximity. Their grandparents—Rhonda's parents—still lived in Hidden Valley. Big Lamont told me that he'd joined at age twelve or thirteen and that Stephen followed several years later, around the same age.

Behavior problems came to overshadow Stephen's early academic potential. Both he and Big Lamont ended up at the Morgan School,

the county's school for violent and troubled students who'd been designated as "behaviorally-emotionally handicapped," a label disproportionately affixed to disruptive African American males. When the
brothers attended Morgan in the late 1990s and early 2000s, it was
little more than a holding pen, a fact that school system officials con-
ceded after overhauling the school in the mid-2000s.[3] One activity
Big Lamont recalled during his years at Morgan was watching music
videos in class. "If you wanted to learn," he told me, "you did that on
your own." There was one skill that Morgan students often mastered,
however: fighting. "Where I grew up, you had to fight. If you didn't
fight at Morgan, something was wrong with you. You had to prove you
could handle yourself as a man."

That white T-shirt in Carrie's scrapbook had been part of Stephen's
gang uniform, as were his cornrow braids and black-and-white bandanas. The family was unaware of their gang affiliation, Big Lamont
said. "They knew about the bandanas, but didn't know why we were
wearing them. All of us had cornrows, but they didn't really know
why."

Big Lamont described the Kings to me as "a bunch of people hanging out together," and argued that police tended to exaggerate their
criminal reach. "Basically, it was a friendship, all of us hanging out
together as friends." Still, he and Stephen were selling drugs and carrying guns. As young teenagers, they did small-time dealing as corner boys. The income gave Stephen money for video games, while Big
Lamont developed a taste for pricey clothing, rejecting bargains Carrie bought from Family Dollar in favor of fashionable urban brands
like Pelle Pelle. "If you didn't wear the dress code, you wasn't popular,"
he said. He liked to keep a Glock pistol in his back pocket for protection. During an argument, he might pull it out and fire a few rounds at
the ground. "As I got older, everything is for protection. When you're
in the streets, people be wanting to rob you."

The rules Big Lamont followed in Charlotte were the same ones Yale
University sociologist Elijah Anderson described in his 1999 book,
Code of the Street, a study of the informal rules governing interactions

among young, low-income African American men. At its heart, the code of the street revolved around respect. To earn it, a young man had to look right, wearing only certain clothing brands. He had to fight back if he felt disrespected, and he could raise his own status by disrespecting someone else, showing his nerve by taking another person's possession, messing with another man's woman, throwing the first punch, or pulling a trigger. Anderson describes this code as "a cultural adaptation to a profound lack of faith in the police and the judicial system."[4] Writer Ta-Nehisi Coates has called it "the code of men who have come to feel that they have nothing to lose." It appears ridiculous, even suicidal, outside its context, in a white middle-class world, Coates has written. But in neighborhoods where the code ruled, it was hard to opt out of the game.[5]

Carrie could see beneath her grandsons' tough street personas. She saw boys who played Nintendo on her TV, ate her cooking, then obeyed her orders to wash their dishes. But she wasn't naive. The code of the street demanded fearlessness, and neither had a fear bone in them, as she put it. She worried fearlessness would cost them their lives.

Before he had a driver's license, Big Lamont and a friend found an unlocked car in the parking lot of Charlotte Catholic High School, near Carrie's apartment, and decided to take a ride. Lamont claimed the wheel, cranked the ignition with a screwdriver, pulled into the street, and ended up crashing into a pole less than a mile away. "I ain't really know what I was doing," he recalled. By sixteen, he had convictions for car theft and cocaine possession. Stephen's story was the same. At sixteen, he was charged with possessing a stolen car and resisting a police officer. Their lives continued that way, undeterred by arrests, handcuffs, juvenile detention, jail, the threat of prison. And they weren't the only members of Belton's family who'd had brushes with the law. By their late teens, every one of his sons, all eight of them, had been charged with felonies.

It would be too easy to blame this criminal behavior on their father's absence, but Belton's incarceration surely didn't help. A growing body of research has found that a father in prison significantly increases chances that a child will have behavioral problems. In *Children of the Prison Boom: Mass Incarceration and the Future of Inequality*, authors Sara Wakefield and Christopher Wildeman say they've found that mass incarceration makes a "bad situation worse for disadvantaged children, resulting in increases in internalizing, externalizing, and total behavioral problems as well as substantial increases in physical aggression."[6] Mass incarceration, they argue, is one of the forces widening the nation's social inequality, "in the same league with decaying urban public school systems and highly concentrated disadvantage in urban centers as factors that distinctively touch—and disadvantage—poor black children."[7]

In the early 2000s, as Belton's sons accumulated rap sheets, crime in Charlotte was actually waning. Murders had peaked in 1993, the year Officers Burnette and Nobles had been killed in Boulevard Homes. Violent crime had begun dropping, not just in Charlotte, but across the nation, in what has been called "the great American crime decline." Experts have offered many theories to explain the decline: Mass incarceration took bad guys off the street, community policing proved effective, the youngest baby-boomer men reached their thirties, maturing out of prime crime-committing years. In neighborhoods, gentrification priced out bad elements. More prevalent air conditioning allowed people to stay indoors, reducing the chances of violent street confrontations. Cell phones played a similar role.[8] There may be some truth in all those theories, but in his book *Uneasy Peace: The Great Crime Decline, the Renewal of City Life, and the Next War on Violence*, Patrick Sharkey concludes that the primary drivers were mass incarceration, thousands more police officers on the streets, and an explosion of local community groups that provided social services and safe places for young people.[9]

And yet even as violent crime waned in Charlotte, one thing stayed the same. Young black men from low-income families continued to be disproportionately represented among victims and perpetrators. In Belton's family, the violence wasn't over. It was just beginning.

On a cold, clear Sunday evening, November 12, 2001, Maurice Leggett made a small decision that cost him his life. Like a stray dog seeking companionship, Maurice decided to follow Kameka Young home. Maurice, twenty-three, had been at the uptown bus station, where he'd struck up a conversation with fifteen-year-old Kameka and a seventeen-year-old named Sabrina Phillips. He said he was looking for some weed and just trying to be friendly. Later, Sabrina told police that Maurice's words didn't come out right. "He seemed like he was special," she said, and by that she meant he had some sort of cognitive disability. Maurice followed the two teenagers onto the no. 10 bus and got off with them near Boulevard Homes, the public housing project where Kameka lived.

Maurice, dressed in a blue track suit with a hooded jacket, sat on Kameka's stoop while she went inside and announced to several people, including Big Lamont, who was dating her sister, that some guy had followed her home. Big Lamont asked if the guy had money. Two people heard Big Lamont say he was going to rob him.

Minutes later, he tried. Sabrina told police afterward that she'd been outside, walking away from the apartment, when something told her to turn around. She saw Big Lamont, his right arm around Maurice's neck while another young man checked Maurice's pockets. Big Lamont pushed Maurice between apartment buildings, and "when they got like right between houses he like shot him and he dropped," she said.

The bullet pierced Maurice's jacket hood, entered the right side of his skull, exited the left. Sabrina ran to him as he lay face down on the sidewalk. She grabbed his hand tight, "like he was one of my own." For a moment, he grabbed back, then his grip loosened, and she knew he was gone. Police found three one-dollar bills, a dime, and three pennies in his pocket. He also had a library card, a match, and a state identification card, which he carried instead of a driver's license. Maurice didn't drive, because he was mentally challenged and suffered from seizures. "He was vulnerable in so many ways," his mother told a reporter. "He couldn't have fought them. So why did they have to kill him?" [10]

The shooting had taken place just off Burnette Avenue, one of two streets that had been renamed to honor police officers Burnette and Nobles after their murders. Sabrina picked Big Lamont out of a lineup of black men with braided hair. Police arrested him a few hours later in his girlfriend's apartment, practically at the scene of the crime. At the police station, he waived his rights and spoke to detectives without a lawyer.

"What happened tonight?" one detective asked.

"What happened—I shot somebody."

"Okay. How did it happen?"

"What do you mean how did it happen? I just shot him."

The interview went on like this, as detectives elicited details little by little. Big Lamont said he'd planned to rob Maurice, not kill him. He wasn't impaired by drugs or alcohol. He didn't use them. Despite detectives' continued questions, he refused to name his accomplice, his sixteen-year-old cousin, who helped rob Maurice. The code of the street forbade snitching.

"Okay. How do you feel about what happened tonight?" one detective asked.

"It shouldn't had happened."

"It wasn't intended to happen?"

"No. Cause it wasn't done on purpose."

"What was you thinking about when you just decide to shoot him?"

"I wasn't thinking about anything. I just pulled the trigger and it went off."

Prosecutors charged Big Lamont with first-degree murder. When they informed him they would seek the death penalty unless he pleaded guilty, it scared him. In September 2002, he pleaded to second-degree murder and got a fourteen-year sentence. Judge Shirley Fulton took the plea, not knowing Lamont Davis was another of Money Rock's sons.

Less than two weeks later, Demario, also one of Belton's sons, was driving to the beach with a cousin and two friends to celebrate his eighteenth birthday. On the way, according to police, he and his crew stopped in the small coastal town of Newport and robbed two shrimp sellers at gunpoint. After that, they drove to a convenience store in nearby Havelock. Demario's mom believes he was the victim of an attempted robbery. But police concluded that Demario's group was trying to rob two teenagers when one of them shot him. Demario's two friends drove off, deserting him. His cousin remained at his side as he bled to death in the convenience store parking lot.[11]

Belton learned of Demario's death when a prison guard summoned him to the chaplain's office and the chaplain told him to call home. Donna, his big sister, broke the news. Belton hung up the receiver and sat silently. Later, in his cell, he wept. Belton had loved the boy, even though their relationship had been limited to a few prison visits, phone calls, and letters, including the one in which thirteen-year-old Demario boasted about his football prowess and asked his dad when he was coming home.

He got a furlough to attend the funeral—his first in twelve years of prison. He made the 220-mile trip in the back of a corrections officer's car, stopping briefly at his mom's apartment to change into a suit from his green prison uniform before arriving at Alexander Funeral Home. Belton took the floor and gave the eulogy. God had told him, he said, that six young people in that room needed to find Christ, because Satan was trying to destroy their lives. "It could be one of my sons," he said.

At the time, both Big and Little Lamont were locked up and didn't attend. But sixteen-year-old Stephen, who was as close to Demario as anyone, served as a pallbearer. Demario was only two years older, but people said Stephen, craving a father figure, had looked up to his half brother. "It was almost like Mario was his daddy," Carrie said.

Belton had asked for an extended furlough to spend time with his grieving children, but he'd been given only one day. After the service, he returned to Carrie's apartment to change back into his prison uniform. It was time to leave; the corrections officer was waiting. As he was returning to the car, Stephen appeared. Belton pulled his son into his arms. He hugged him and told him he loved him. Stephen laid his head on his father's shoulder and cried.

Stephen was never the same after Demario's murder. In hindsight, the signs were clear. Rhonda recalled that he contemplated getting a job so he could help support the baby daughter Big Lamont had left behind. "I said, 'You can't save everybody.' I said, 'The only thing I need for you to do is go to school and be a child.'"

But he'd dropped out of school. Carrie noticed that he slept a lot. Rhonda could see he was drinking a lot. He'd even told her: I don't want to be here anymore.

"It was like he was telling the world, 'I don't give a damn about nothing,'" Carrie said. From prison, Belton urged family members to get him professional help. Carrie said she tried but he didn't want to see a therapist. Rhonda offered to get him counseling or to sign him up in the Big Brothers program. "He said he didn't want to talk to nobody, if it couldn't be his daddy. I think he wanted his daddy to be there, and he didn't have that. That played a big part."

On June 26, 2003, about eight months after Demario's death, Rhonda picked up Stephen from her parents' house in Hidden Valley. She didn't know it then, but realized later that he must have retrieved a gun he'd hidden in the backyard.

Once home, she went to the laundry room to fold clothes. She could hear the phone beeping as Stephen tried to dial his girlfriend. They'd fought earlier, and his girlfriend wasn't answering. He paced the hallway, a photo of Demario in his hand.

"Why you walking around with that picture like that?" she asked.

He shrugged.

He went into his room and turned on his rap music.

She heard a noise, a pop.

"Stephen, what was that?"

She opened the door. He was on the floor near his bed, gun on his lap.

Most people who commit suicide with a gun, about 75 percent, shoot themselves in the head.[12] Stephen, with his choice, seemed to be making a statement about the losses he'd endured. The photo of Demario lay beside him. He'd shot himself in the heart.

For the second time in eight months, Belton was called to an office and instructed to telephone home. Again, he spoke to Donna, his older sister. Again, he got a furlough to attend his son's funeral. The family held the service at the church Carrie had attended for years, St. Luke's Lutheran, located down the street from her apartment. This liberal, predominantly white church was outside the part of town most of Stephen's people frequented, so Carrie included directions in the obituary: "Use city bus #19." Many of Stephen's friends found their way, and the sanctuary filled with young black men in white T-shirts and low baggy pants.

Again, Belton preached, not so much about his son's death, but about getting right with God. He warned the young gang members in the pews that Satan was out to destroy them: "God told me to ask you: Who will it be next time?"

Later, at Oaklawn Cemetery, Carrie spotted several young men gathered around the coffin. She went to investigate and found they'd slipped a fifth of vodka in the casket and placed a joint under Stephen's collar. She retrieved the joint, broke it up, and threw it away. She couldn't reach the vodka.

Belton returned to prison. By this time, after burying two sons, he might have concluded that God was out to destroy his family, out to punish him for sins his prison sentence hadn't covered. Instead, he focused on his faith in Christ, determined to look beyond despair and find God's redemption. Redemption became a major theme in the autobiography he'd begun writing. By January 2004, after filling yellow legal pads with tales of his childhood, his cocaine dealing, his trial and conviction, after recounting his religious growth and his success ministering to other prisoners, he came to the part of his story where Stephen died. Belton described his pain, his powerlessness to help Stephen. He wondered if God had deserted him. But he didn't hold that doubt, not for long, because he knew Satan, not God, had taken his son's life. When he recounted Stephen's funeral, he finished by describing gang members who came forward during altar call, their lives changed as God moved in such a mighty way. "As a result of that service," he wrote, "several people gave their lives to Christ and many were delivered from several years of bondage. To God be the glory for all He has done."

16

THE LOVE OF HIS LIFE

At Butner, Belton had the crème de la crème of federal corrections—a landscaped campus with tennis courts, street clothes instead of uniforms, prison chow that included Gordon's dense pound cakes drizzled with powdered-sugar icing. He'd taken public-speaking classes and honed his preaching skills. He'd reconnected with Gordon and developed close friendships with inmates who shared his faith. Then, in 2001, as all was going well, he requested a transfer. He moved to Seymour Johnson, a minimum-security prison camp on a U.S. Air Force base in eastern North Carolina, about an hour farther from Charlotte. The decision perplexed nearly everyone who knew him and upset friends and family, especially his mother and a woman he'd grown close to who lived near Butner and visited regularly. "They thought I was crazy," he told me. But Belton said he was only following God's orders. *Seymour Johnson*, God had said.

As I had come to know Belton, I learned that God talked to him all the time. I believed he was sincere when he reported acting on God's direction. Still, it was hard to equate his reality with my own. God never spoke to me, except metaphorically, when I witnessed beauty or experienced love or grace. I asked a prison chaplain who was a friend of Belton's to explain how it felt to have God speak to you. He told me to think of it as a strong intuition that you're meant to do something.

Belton said it was sometimes like that for him, and sometimes clearer: He heard an audible male voice, not from somewhere in the room, but from his inner ear.

Both their descriptions echoed those of Stanford University anthropologist T.M. Luhrmann, author of *When God Talks Back: Understanding the American Evangelical Relationship with God.* For her book, Luhrmann spent hundreds of hours listening to Christians, like Belton, who experience God "immediately, directly and personally." [1] It's a huge demographic. In a 2006 Pew Research Center survey, 26 percent of U.S. respondents said they'd received direct revelations from God. Luhrmann found that believers who experienced these revelations usually developed their ability over time, learning to attend to their minds and emotions in specific ways to find evidence of God. By persisting, "they begin to experience a real, external, interacting living presence," she writes. "In effect, people train the mind in such a way that they experience part of their mind as the presence of God." [2]

Belton had to shut out thoughts and distractions to hear God's voice. "Sometimes I'd say Holy Spirit, could you turn up your volume, so I can hear you?" He didn't always know God's purpose—why he was supposed to go to Seymour Johnson, for instance. But the order had come loud and clear, and he obeyed.

He liked the prison when he arrived in July 2001. Though he had to wear a uniform again, this one dark green, he had more freedom to move about the grounds. The camp housed only low-risk inmates who supplied the Air Force base with cheap maintenance and landscaping labor. The property didn't even have a fence around it.

Belton turned his spiritual focus toward seeking the Lord's presence, having been inspired by Tommy Tenney's bestselling *God Chasers*, which advocates having an intimate relationship with God. He tended that relationship in an unlikely place—the chapel bathroom, where he found solitude he couldn't get in the chapel. He spent hours there, sitting on a chair he'd pull into the space or kneeling on the hard tile while he prayed and listened for God. He also reconnected at Seymour Johnson with Barry Washington, an inmate who'd known

Belton in his first years at Butner. Washington saw a change in his friend: He was no longer picking arguments about scriptural interpretations, insisting on being right. He had matured.

Belton again worked with the prison's chaplain, and this one enlisted him to help teach Bible classes. The two had just completed a class on a Monday night in July 2002 when a new, white-haired inmate stepped forward to shake hands. Jim List, a sixty-two-year-old minister from West Virginia, was starting a thirty-eight-month sentence for mail fraud and filing a false tax return.[3] Among the camp's many white-collar felons, his background was particularly exotic. A New Zealand native, he'd grown up in Africa with missionary parents, emigrated to the United States for Bible college, and eventually went to work for Tampa-based Greater Ministries International. List impressed inmates with his tales of Africa, particularly stories of making and eventually losing a fortune in gold and diamond mines there.

List's role with Greater Ministries had landed him in prison. As an elder, he'd earned a good living—at least $160,000 in commissions, according to prosecutors—by signing up fundamentalist Christians to "gift" money to a program that was supposed to double their offerings in months.[4] He told Belton that the program had blessed its members by providing them with monthly payments, delivered in cash via U.S. Priority Mail. Government regulators took a different view. By 1998, three states had ordered a halt, charging that the program's promises amounted to selling unlicensed securities. At some point, investors' monthly cash payments stopped.

After his arrest, he and Susan, his wife, sold their West Virginia house to cover attorney costs. Strapped for money, they relocated to Myrtle Beach, South Carolina, where friends offered free use of a modular home. By the time a Tampa federal jury convicted Greater Ministries founder Gerald Payne and other top leaders in March 2001, national media had reported widely on how the ministry bilked thousands of Christian investors out of several hundred million dollars, pulling off one of the largest swindles in American history.[5] Stories described hucksters ripping off gullible and greedy Christians in a Ponzi

scheme that required constant cash from new investors to pay divi-
dends to earlier investors. "Faith and Mammon" was the *Forbes* magazine headline.[6] The scheme had appealed to people who mistrusted
the government and believed in the late 1990s that the Rapture would
arrive with the new millennium. Ministry leaders peddled diet supple-
ments that guarded against the effects of end-time plagues and talked
of founding a sovereign nation where no government would have ju-
risdiction. For $10,000, donors were promised a passport, a driver's
license, and one square foot of land in this new nation, which was to
be called Greater Lands.[7] Greater Ministries leaders also bragged that
they owned African gold mines, though when regulators moved in,
they found few actual investments.[8]

List wasn't at the top of the Greater Ministries hierarchy, but as a
church elder he knew enough to have value to prosecutors. Taking
his attorney's advice, he cooperated and pleaded guilty. Still, he told
Belton he didn't understand what he'd done wrong.

Without knowing Jim List, it's impossible to know his motivations:
Did he realize he was swindling people, or was he so blinded by dollar
signs he couldn't see the implausibility of his promises? In one affidavit
from the case, a duped Pennsylvania man who had invested through
List wrote that when he asked List to explain the puzzling financial
statements he got from Greater Ministries, the minister admitted he
didn't understand them either. List tried to help the man withdraw his
money—investors were supposed to be able to get gifts back at any
time—but the Tampa headquarters delivered only excuses.[9] Maybe
List was as duped as his investors. Susan, his wife of fourteen years,
said he believed the investment program was legitimate and that its
profits were funding good works around the world. He was a good
man, she said, whose lust for money clouded his judgment. "That was
a hindrance in his life for sure."

List and Belton bonded almost immediately, having discovered
they shared a dream—to build an international ministry. Belton was
certain God had brought them together when he learned that List's
ministry was named Rock Ministries International, the same name

he'd chosen in 1993 to give the ministry he planned to build. Before long, List had ordained Belton and was introducing him as the man who would be joining him in ministry once they were released.

Belton was particularly drawn to Jim List's fatherly demeanor. He wrote in his journal that he wanted to spend all his time with List. "I guess he's filling a space in my life I always wanted filled. That being a father who loved me and believed in me." They ate and prayed together, and nearly every day, the two logged several miles on the prison's outdoor track, discussing their beliefs and planning the organization they'd build once they were free. They were about the same height, medium build, and except for List being white, they might have been mistaken for father and son as they trudged around the track. During prison visits, Belton came to know Susan and the couple's friends. Before long, Belton was referring to Jim List as "Dad."

December 20, 2002, dawned gray and drizzly. It was a Friday, and because Belton fasted most Fridays, he hadn't met List for breakfast. Instead, after donning a raincoat and skull cap, he found List outside at Base Detail Check Out, where inmates waited to be transported to work assignments. The two men talked until List noticed his bus starting up. As he took off to catch it, Belton called after him to take his hat. List was one of the prison's oldest inmates, and Belton felt protective, worried he'd catch cold. By the time Belton reached the bus, it was pulling away. He stood worrying, skull cap in hand, as his spiritual father departed.

After List left for his prison job, Belton went to the chapel for Friday prayers. He was leaving around noon when an inmate approached and blurted out: Did you know Jim is dead?

"Don't play like that," Belton scolded.

No, the man said. He died. He died on his job.

Belton stormed down the hall, searching for anyone who'd been with List that morning. Quizzing inmates, he learned a heart attack had killed List before he even reached the hospital. His death came only two months after Belton's eighteen-year-old son Demario had died of a gunshot while attempting a robbery. At the time, List had consoled Belton, saying he felt sure the Holy Spirit had intervened when the bullet pierced Demario's chest, giving him time to get right with God before he died.

As Belton tried to reconcile his faith in God's goodness with another personal tragedy, he told himself that List was in a better place. That certainty settled on him one afternoon shortly after List's passing, as he waited in his room for a guard to check him off during the four o'clock count. Prison counts, conducted five times every twenty-four hours, required inmates to be at specific locations so their presence could be verified. The counts also provided an unremitting reminder that an inmate's life was not his own. That afternoon, it occurred to Belton that Jim List would never have to stand for a count again. Belton looked heavenward, out the window of his cinderblock cubicle. "Dad, you're free now," he said.

With List gone, Belton became concerned about Susan, the woman he called Mom, or Mrs. List. "He kept calling me all the time checking on me," Susan recalled. "He said God just kept placing on him so strong that he was to take care of me. He didn't know what all that meant, but knew it was something."

At fifty-three, Susan was trim and attractive, with shoulder-length brown hair and thick eyebrows that framed her face. Her style—sensible heels, delicate gold hoop earrings, below-the-knee hemlines—reflected her personality, neither flighty nor flashy.

As a conservative Christian, she believed God made women the weaker vessel, yet had proven herself unbreakable during her husband's ordeal. When his arrest forced them to move from West Virginia to Myrtle Beach, she found secretarial work in the local prosecutor's office. Once List began his sentence, she drove more than three hours to visit him most Saturdays and Sundays, arriving by eight in the morning, making the return trip home in late afternoon. She'd met Belton as he volunteered in the visiting room, distributing Bibles and games, entertaining the children of visiting families.

Jim List's funeral was two days after Christmas, and by the new year,

Susan had returned to work. On a Friday night after her first week back, she gulped down two Tylenol PMs, climbed into bed, and pulled up the covers, hoping for unburdened rest. Instead, Belton dominated her dreams. He was clad in prison-issue gray shorts and shirt, jogging toward her. Then he stopped, leaned forward, and kissed her. Like Belton, Susan based decisions on communications from God. She awoke certain that this had been a God-given dream. She had never intended to return to Seymour Johnson. But on that Saturday, she hit the highway. She was behind the wheel before the sun rose.

Belton was both pleased and unsettled to see her. Under the visiting room's fluorescent lights, Susan sat at a table with her arms crossed, explaining she'd dreamt about him, omitting the part where they kissed. Belton told her about the final conversation he'd had with her husband, before List climbed aboard the prison work bus.

In the days that followed, both experienced God nudging them toward each other. Susan initially tried to ignore it. During a phone call, Belton asked what the Lord was saying to her.

"I can't talk about this right now," she told him. "I just can't handle this right now."

A prison romance was the last thing she wanted. She had a grown son from her first marriage, which had ended in divorce. She'd met Jim List in 1988 after he visited her Tallahassee church to solicit for a mission project. Two husbands were enough. Still, Belton kept calling.

For Belton, God's intention had become clear: Susan was the woman he was meant to marry. On January 6, 2003, three days after meeting with Susan in the visiting room, he wrote his mother: "I truly know that this is my wife, sent from God. She's everything and more I asked God for in a wife." Giddy with love, he drew smiley faces between several sentences. "Boy, I thank God I didn't make any of those other women my wife," he wrote. "I'm in love for the first time in my life, and I'm completely satisfied! Now don't you faint hearing me say this. (Smiley face) I am, mama, I am finally happy."

Susan was an unlikely partner, not only because she was the widow of the man he'd called Dad. At fifty-three, she was also fourteen years

his senior. And she was white. Not a small point. Despite copious philandering, he'd never been involved with a white woman. Until Jim
List came along, his only close white friend had been Adam Gilbert,
his elementary school pal. As he'd grown to love Jim List, he couldn't
help noting the irony that God had given him a white spiritual father.
It wasn't that he disliked white people, but he'd often formed opinions based on race—disapproving of mixed marriages, rooting for the
black man in any fight or athletic competition. "My coming up in an
environment where color and race has always been an issue, uncon-
sciously, I had some uncircumcised areas in my heart when it came
to racial matters," he wrote at Seymour Johnson in his autobiography,
referencing Biblical descriptions of a circumcised heart, which was
one that had been purged of sin.

Not surprisingly, many of Susan's family and friends were appalled
at their relationship, as were Belton's fellow inmates. Some disapproved of interracial couples. Some wondered if Belton was taking advantage of a grieving widow. Some were disturbed he wanted to marry
the woman whom he had only recently referred to as "Mom."

There was also the issue of timing. Belton and Susan got together
so quickly that people wondered if their attraction predated Jim List's
demise. They said no, and it would have been impossible for them to
see each other behind List's back, but some inmates smelled betrayal.
By the time Belton proposed to Susan in February—two months after
List's death—their relationship was the talk of the compound. Inmates
who'd been friends passed Belton in the hall without speaking. As
he and his friend Barry Washington were walking the track one day,
Washington broached the subject on everybody's mind: "The only
thing, Lamont, why so early? Why you in such a rush to do it?"

A valid question. He wasn't getting married to have sex, because
federal prison didn't allow conjugal visits, and he had years left to
serve. He wasn't marrying for money. Susan had little. For nearly an
hour, the two men paced around the track and debated. Washington
urged Belton to wait a while, maybe six months. Belton assured Washington he hadn't planned any of this. But God had convinced him that

he and Susan should marry and build a ministry together. God's curious instruction to transfer to Seymour Johnson now made sense, one more step in his plan.

Eventually, Washington, who had himself become a minister in prison, accepted that Belton was following direction from God. "I can't fight against the Lord," he recalled. He told Belton that he and Susan had his blessing.

April 3, 2003, was perfect for a wedding—sunny, eighty degrees, pink azaleas blooming in the prison courtyard. A magistrate presided in the visiting room as the bride and groom exchanged vows. Susan wore a tan shift and matching jacket with appliquéd hem. Belton wore his short-sleeved hunter-green prison uniform, its shirt tucked into a belted waist. He was slim now, thanks to exercise and fasting. Carrie, the only family member in attendance, wore a flowing brown-and-yellow African-print dress, big earrings, big necklace, colorful bangles that climbed her wrists, and an African cloth headband that reined in her Afro. She was pleased her son was happy. Susan, often first in line on prison visiting days, had impressed Carrie with her loyalty. After the vows, the two newlyweds posed for photos. Belton pulled Susan close, his arm around her waist. They smiled.

Once they married, inmate gossip faded. But with all their differences—race, class, age—people wondered if the marriage would endure. Susan's biggest concern early on wasn't that Belton had once sold cocaine or instigated a shootout. She knew those days were over. What nagged was his romantic history: He'd cheated on every woman he'd ever been with.

But Belton had changed, through prayer and study and ministering to others, and also with the help of a tool familiar to countless memoirists—writing. While filling notebooks and legal pads with sermons, speeches, and a forty-thousand-word autobiography, he saw his past actions with fresh eyes. "Instead of staying home with my little boy and being a father to him," he wrote, "I ran the streets and instead of a father I became only a baby maker. That Rolex looked good on my arm, but the price I paid was a little boy's love. The Mercedes Benz I drove was nice, but what it cost me was two of my sons' lives. All the women and money were nice, but what they cost me was my home, the love and respect of my wife and 24 years of my life."

Belton was no longer that man he described, but marriage had highlighted new shortcomings. His personality remained strong—bossy, some would say. When he and Susan had a disagreement, he often responded with anger. Setting about to fix those faults, he again put pen to paper to share his revelations with men aiming to be the husbands God wanted them to be. The result: a how-to guide he titled *Ministry of the Husband*.

When Belton and I first reconnected, he gave me that book, a paperback with a cover displaying a couple's hands softly clasped. He'd self-published it with the financial help of a friend, a retired professor in Charlotte who'd become a faithful pen pal. At the time, I skimmed a few pages and put it aside, appreciating the effort but dismissing the book as the product of sexist beliefs I didn't hold. When I finally read it, I saw that I'd been too hasty. Yes, some assumptions—the husband's job is to teach his wife God's word, for instance—would make feminists shudder. But Belton had come a long way, considering what he once believed:

> I remember being taught that the woman is to serve the man. I was laid back, and women took care of me. Whatever I asked them to do, they did. That was the way it was supposed to be (so I thought). Listen to me men! We carry this same attitude into our marriages! . . . God did not bring you your wife so she could be a slave and serve you; He brought you your wife so you could serve as an example of His love.[10]

He tells men to respect their wives, admit mistakes, and love unconditionally, as Jesus did. He counsels that lavish material gifts—fancy cars, jewelry, big trips—aren't important. "The most important thing for my wife is my love for her," he writes. "She would rather live in a box on a hill with all my love than a mansion without my love."[11]

In their first years, of course, Belton and Susan didn't even have a box on a hill. They had prison—the visiting room, and a visiting-room table, where they sat holding hands, talking, and studying the Bible. They showed affection with hugs, kisses, and other small gestures. Susan loved the way Belton placed his hand at the small of her back when they walked together. It made her feel secure.[12]

Even behind bars, Belton scored a few romantic coups. With the help of Barry Washington, who got out in 2004, he sent Susan red birthday roses. He also bought her two inmate-crafted needlepoint pillows. They were red and heart-shaped, with "Susan," needlepointed in white on one, and "Belton" on the other. Susan propped them next to each other on her bed and took a picture. She tucked the photo into an envelope and mailed it to her husband as a reminder. Until he could join her, she and the pillows would be waiting.

Belton and Susan Platt at Seymour Johnson Federal Prison Camp after their marriage in 2003. Courtesy of Belton Platt.

17

FREEDOM

On April 27, 2010, a sunny morning at the Federal Correctional Institution in Bennettsville, South Carolina, Belton changed from gray prison sweats to navy trousers and a shirt with a button-down collar. He embraced Susan, supplier of these new clothes. He hugged goodbye to Chaplain Ron Apollo, who turned to Susan with tears in his eyes. "I'm going to miss this guy," he said. Belton slipped into the passenger's seat of Susan's red Chevrolet Aveo, and, once on the highway, asked for her phone to call his kids. He flipped it open, stared, handed it back. He didn't know how to make it work.

The last time Belton had seen freedom was 1989, before cell phones, before the internet, back when drug violence, not foreign terrorism, was what most unnerved Americans. While Belton was doing time, the nation had elected its first black president, but also surpassed Russia to claim the world's highest incarceration rate. By 2010, the number of African American adults under some type of correctional control had surpassed the number enslaved in 1850.[1] The ramifications had just begun piercing America's consciousness.

While the world changed, so had Belton Platt. He'd studied carpentry, public speaking, financial planning, the Bible, and earned an inch-thick stack of certificates attesting to his accomplishments. He'd accepted blame for his failures as a father, his adultery, his crimes, and he'd cultivated a faith that sustained him through hard times and setbacks, one of which came when the prison system transferred him hundreds of miles from Susan, to Manchester, a correctional institution in the Appalachian Mountains of eastern Kentucky. "When things like that happened, I didn't like it, but I trusted God," he told me. "I figured God had something for me to do." In Manchester, Belton was startled to find that only a small minority of inmates were black. He'd had no idea America locked up so many white men. He organized a prison ministry, as he had elsewhere. He also found a public way to announce his changed heart: by renouncing his old name. Belton had rejected his drug-dealer nickname years earlier, back in Atlanta, insisting that no one call him Money Rock. Everyone—inmates, his family, Susan—knew him as Lamont, the middle name he'd been called since birth. Lamont had been cocky, unable to shrug off an insult, unwilling to walk away from a fight. In prison, that tough persona provided a means of self-preservation, even after he accepted Christ. But he'd gradually shed it, and in Manchester, he made the change official, burying his old self, literally. During an outdoor exercise period, he wrote "Lamont Platt" on a piece of paper, along with attributes— pride, a quick temper—that he associated with his old personality. He tore the paper up, dug a hole with a stick, poked the paper into it, covered it up. From then on, he went by Belton Platt.

Bennettsville, South Carolina, two hours from Charlotte, became his final federal prison stop. He'd been diagnosed with a heart irregularity, and Bennettsville had better resources to treat the problem. Back to the South—and to Susan—he went. When a subsequent cardiology exam found him perfectly healthy, he was permitted to remain there, a development he attributed to God's miraculous ways.

Ron Apollo arrived at the Bennettsville prison soon after Belton, in 2008. It says something about the reputation Belton had built as a preacher—and also about the intimate world of federal incarceration— that Apollo had heard about Belton Platt at his previous chaplaincy in Jesup, Georgia. Inmates who'd gotten to know Belton in Butner or Atlanta or Seymour Johnson talked about the inmate pastor who'd turned their lives around. Apollo, a Pentecostal minister, had become a prison chaplain after sixteen years in the military. He joked with inmates that he always knew he'd end up in prison, but he'd never expected to be paid for it. As a teenager growing up in a trailer park next to a housing project in Raleigh, North Carolina, he'd earned cash as a low-level drug runner. One night, an officer caught him red handed, but then, for reasons Apollo never understood, she let him go, telling Apollo not to make her regret her decision. Apollo became a believer in second chances. In Bennettsville, Belton became his *de facto* assistant pastor—preaching, leading Bible studies, helping some eighteen faith groups organize their worship services. He also headed up the Christian Community Locker, which equipped new prisoners with personal hygiene items. He even became a head cook in the kitchen, catering the warden's staff meetings with made-from-scratch apple turnovers and cinnamon rolls.

When Belton was released in April 2010, it was to a halfway house to begin the final six months remaining on his sentence. Susan dropped him off at the squat yellow-brick building in Florence, South Carolina, about an hour from the house she was renting in Conway, near the coast. Before they kissed goodbye, he gave her about three hundred dollars to pay bills. This, along with fifty dollars he kept for himself, was his total prison savings, the money with which he was supposed to make a new life.

For many former inmates, adjusting to freedom—finding a job and place to stay, resuming control of their daily lives—can be more challenging than incarceration. Belton recalled a few days of panic before he landed his first job, but otherwise, he adjusted easily. In many ways, he was fortunate. Susan worked as an administrative assistant at a law office in Conway, so her income covered their basic needs. He also had an uncrushable optimism and an entrepreneurial knack for making his own luck—the same skill that had made him such a good drug dealer. If you dropped him in the middle of a desert, he once told me, "you come back a year later, I'm going to have a house, a wife, a dog in the yard. A store on the corner. God has just blessed me."

Belton had taken a job as a cafeteria cook, but he was soon job hunting again when he realized his boss was shorting his pay. He showed up at Ryan's steakhouse on Highway 501 in Conway one morning before it opened, ducking in through a back door while a supplier made a delivery. Brad Doughty, the manager, told him that they were closed and had no openings; Belton left his résumé on his way out, then telephoned a couple of times. Doughty rarely hired ex-felons, but Belton's persistence won him over. Soon, he was wearing a black chef's hat and jacket, grilling steaks to order and carving roast beef as a display cook on the buffet line. He became one of Doughty's best employees— punctual, good with customers, eager to work as many $7.50-an-hour shifts as he could get. He drove to work in a high-mileage Jeep Cherokee, payment from his former cafeteria boss in lieu of back wages he'd owed Belton.

After four months in the halfway house, Belton served the final sixty days of his sentence through home confinement, meeting curfews and making daily check-in calls. Home at this point was a raggedy two-bedroom that Susan had rented on Powell Street just outside Conway's business district. It had cracks in the floors, broken glass in the yard, and a thriving water bug population. Word on the street was that next-door neighbors were running a crack house.

Settling in Conway hadn't been the original plan. For years, Belton had seen himself returning to his hometown, to his mother, his now-grown children, his friends. But as his release date approached, he'd asked his case manager to change his post-release destination— Conway instead of Charlotte.

Who do you know in Conway? the case manager asked.

No one, as it turned out. Conway seemed a peculiar choice—a town of seventeen thousand, known to vacationers as the place they bypassed right before arriving in Myrtle Beach. It wasn't on the coast, but was near enough that surrounding highways were dotted with gift shops and fluorescent-colored billboards advertising swimsuits and towels, cherry bombs and boogie boards.

Belton said God had directed him to choose Conway over Charlotte, and Susan agreed this was wise. She'd observed that her husband was nearly incapable of saying no when anyone sought his help. He'd been like that as a drug dealer too. "You give him a sad story," one former dealer had told me, "he give you the shirt off his back." Susan suspected that if Belton lived in Charlotte, demands from family and friends would hinder the ministry mission she believed that God had for him.

The case manager accepted this venue change better than other family members, including Belton's mother, who exploded when he called with the news. "God ain't told you nothing like that," Carrie scolded. "Your kids have been waiting for twenty years. They're hurting for their daddy. You've got grandchildren who don't even know you."

The decision, Carrie said later, "busted my bubbles for a while." She'd wanted her son close because she loved him. Also, he was dependable and could drive her places. Also, for years, she'd dreamed of reopening Carrie's Kitchen, their short-lived family restaurant, seized by U.S. marshals after the FBI charged Belton. In time, however, she made peace with his decision. Susan was her son's first priority, and Carrie knew Susan wasn't keen on Charlotte. "I guess it was selfish on my part. I just wanted him to be here, close."

Belton was still on home confinement when he and Susan opened their living room for Sunday worship services. The first week, the congregation numbered two, three if you counted Susan. But it didn't take long for word to spread that a house on Powell Street next to the crack house was holding Sunday church and giving away meals. Belton and Susan prepared full dinners—fried chicken, beef and gravy, starches, sides—served on paper plates after worship. Often, worshippers came hungry, broke, depressed. "He gave me something to eat, and prayed for me," one woman recalled. "It just seemed like that was where I was supposed to be."

As months passed, the service attracted a dozen, or fifteen, or twenty people, even the young men from next door, who listened to Belton's witnessing in exchange for the good food. Belton and Susan funded this endeavor from their own pockets. After one service, checks forged with Belton's name began showing up at local grocery stores. Someone had snuck into a back room and stolen his checkbook. Attendance kept growing, crowding the living room until they moved the operation to a small chapel a friend had built in his backyard, then to a rented office building on Highway 378. They put a homemade sign in the front window: Rock Ministries Church International. He'd been waiting to use the name since 1993, when he wrote "Rock Ministries" in his Bible in the Atlanta Penitentiary. By late 2011, worshippers were squeezing into the office space. There were offerings now, though often meager. Once, examining the collection basket after a service, Susan joked: Praise God, we got a whole dollar. But Belton was already planning his next step. He telephoned Ron Apollo with the news: He was quitting Ryan's steakhouse to launch a full-time ministry and find a permanent church location.

Financially, the move seemed risky, even to a believer like Apollo. "You sure God told you to do that?" he asked.

Belton was sure, and he had Susan's full support. By this time, the union they'd forged following their hasty prison courtship had become unbreakable. They'd built it over seven years of phone calls and prison visits, navigating through Susan's worries about her husband's history of philandering, arguments that Belton tried to win by announcing he was head of the house, and, in May 2009, yet another violent death.

Susan had entered the visiting room in Bennettsville prison and announced that they needed to talk. Belton knew from the look on her face that something terrible had happened. His first thought: his mother. But it was yet another son—Derrick, younger brother of the late Demario. Derrick had been driving in Charlotte when an unknown assailant shot him from a passing car.

He was only recently out of jail. At twenty-four, Belton's son had spent more than six years behind bars. He'd pleaded guilty to shooting two men with an assault rifle. He'd had cocaine-related convictions too. But family members said he'd just enrolled in community college; they were optimistic that he'd turned a corner. And then came several men in a Toyota Camry, one shooting Derrick in the head as he drove down a busy street. Derrick's Chevy Malibu veered toward a day-care center, coming to rest only feet from a building where children napped.[2] When Belton heard these details, he imagined his son expiring in the Chevy's driver's seat. He imagined God helping Derrick stop that car. He sobbed, and Susan held him.

With Susan, Belton could drop his defenses, exposing old grief that coexisted with his confidence. He often described her as the hero of his story—the woman who rescued him, just as she'd rescued stray animals as a little girl. "I was a lost dog and a stray cat," he liked to say. Susan described Belton with similar appreciation: "I've just never had anyone love me and care for me like he does." They insisted their courtship arose from God's instructions, not mutual attraction. Whatever the case, they seemed well matched.

In April 2012, in a simple white church just outside Conway's city limits, Belton Platt celebrated Easter Sunday. The location, in a mostly white area, seemed an odd fit for the mostly black congregation, but the century-old church had been empty and on the market since its Methodist owners had consolidated three small congregations into one several years earlier. By the time Belton found the building, they were ready to deal, accepting his offer to rent for six hundred dollars a month with an option to buy. The church was in good shape, with a graceful white steeple, colorful stained-glass windows, red carpet, and matching red cushions on its wooden pews. Rock Ministries had moved in a few weeks before Easter, dedicated the building the previous Sunday, and had already set up a clothing ministry in the small fellowship hall. The marquee on the lawn advertised the new occupant: Rock Ministries Church International, Apostle Belton L. Platt. There was not a thing international about the church, but Belton liked to aim high.

Belton preaching in 2012 at Rock Ministries Church in Conway, South Carolina. Photo by Diedra Laird, courtesy of the *Charlotte Observer*.

He now had assistant ministers, including Tracy McGuire and his wife, Stephanie. Like Belton, McGuire had served time for selling cocaine. They'd met in Butner, working for the prison's eyeglass manufacturing operation, becoming close friends who nurtured each other's faith. They reconnected when Belton got out of prison, and the McGuires relocated to the Conway area with a goal of starting their own ministry. For several months, until they got settled, the couple and their children stayed with Belton and Susan. This was not at the raggedy Powell Street rental, but in a six-thousand-square-foot brick house, practically a mansion. Friends of Susan's—a police lieutenant and his wife—had offered the house when he took a job as a police chief in Alabama. The upside: Susan's friends charged reasonable rent, and there was plenty of room for anyone needing a place to stay. The downside: It sat on twelve acres in Green Sea, an unincorporated community north of Conway, thirty miles from the church. Belton and Susan did a lot of driving.

The Easter service began at 10:30 a.m. with Tracy McGuire reading from Colossians 3 and Stephanie McGuire announcing, "Happy resurrection day!" then belting out Israel Houghton's bouncy gospel hit "All Around": *Let the nations sing, let the people shout. Let your kingdom come, pour your spirit out! Manifest, manifest your love. Manifest, manifest your love.*

People arrived over time, as if it were a drop-in event, with the crowd eventually growing to about fifty worshippers. Some wore jackets and ties, Easter dresses, fancy hats, but some also wore jeans. A leather-skinned white man, self-described as "kind of homeless," prayed in sweatpants and T-shirt. During an altar call, assistant ministers laid hands on one fellow while he wept audibly. "Oh, God. Oh, God," he called. "I'm sorry, God." An usher passed a box of tissues.

Noon was approaching when Belton finally took the microphone. Belton typically didn't write his sermons. Instead, he prepared by finding a quiet place, where he'd kneel and meditate on his message. On this day, he gestured toward the distraught man, still at the altar. "This is why he died," Belton declared. "This is why he was resurrected, to set the captives free. To heal the brokenhearted." He continued: "He's the Lord of glory. Holy! Righteous! Perfect! And he became what you are. That's why I can walk free from guilt and condemnation—because he became what I was. So I can become what he is."

Belton often cited his own transformation as proof that God could help anyone change. That he was two years out of prison, living with a wife he adored, fulfilling his dream of preaching before his own congregation made a compelling argument for the power of faith. But he emphasized that prayer alone wasn't enough. So while beseeching the room to accept Jesus, he dispensed advice. "If you want your life better, it's going to take making better choices," he said. "It's important to set goals, to write down your vision. Look at your neighbor. Say: If you want to be blessed, work." Repeat after me, he instructed children in the audience: "I am in school . . . preparing . . . for my future."

By 12:45, Belton's forehead shone with perspiration. Still to come was Holy Communion, a monthly event at Rock Ministries, celebrated with individually packaged wafers and sealed plastic cups of grape juice. Before Belton could finish the reading—"And when he had given thanks, he brake it, and said, Take, eat: this is my body, which is broken for you: this do in remembrance of me . . ."—a few children had peeled open their juices and gulped down a midworship snack. The service ended at 1:20 p.m. Attendees stood and stretched. Belton reminded them about an upcoming clothing distribution. "If you know anyone who needs some clothes," he told the group, "we have them back there to be a blessing."

18

TRYING TO MAKE A CHANGE

The day after the Easter service, with schools closed for spring break, Belton and a dozen church members gathered to serve a meal to children who lived in a Conway public housing project called Huckabee Heights. It was a perfect day for a picnic—the weather warm, the spring grass freshly mown. People set up plastic tables, unloaded containers of potato salad, fired up charcoal grills for hot dogs and burgers. A retiree named Cleveland manned the deep fryer, dropping chicken pieces into bubbling oil. Many kids who spilled out of apartments already knew Belton from the after-school program the church had launched. As two little girls greeted him near the concrete basketball court, he pulled them close, one on each side. "These my babies here," he said.

Belton had always had an affinity for children, and they were often drawn to him. He'd begun speaking to groups, where he counseled young people to avoid the path he'd taken, as a drug dealer and as a teenager unprepared for fatherhood. He also taught in a teen pregnancy prevention program, where he urged boys to avoid sex if they weren't ready and use condoms when they were. Several thank-you notes proved they'd paid attention. One adolescent told Belton he'd learned "you can really get things if you don't use a condom" and that you shouldn't have sex just "to show off in front of your home boys."

When Belton lectured on topics like these—sexually transmitted diseases or the foolishness of selling drugs—it was with a sober demeanor. In lighter moments, his affectionate, fun-loving streak emerged. He gave hugs with intention, knowing that some children had never experienced a fatherly embrace, and when he joined kids on a basketball court, it was like he was a boy again, back on Dalton Village's blacktop court.

Belton had dressed planning to play basketball, in a gray sweatshirt, but before he could start a game, he was intercepted by a five-year-old who needed help with hair braids that felt too tight. He obliged, focusing on her small head as he loosened offending elastic bands. More children arrived, and there were more hugs. A grinning boy smacked his hand with a high five, then nodded toward the court, where children were scrimmaging with a young man, skinny in a sleeveless white T-shirt and low-hanging jeans.

"Is that your son there?" the boy asked.

Lamont Platt, also known in the family as Little Lamont, had come to Conway from Charlotte at his father's urging. He'd been staying with Belton and Susan for a week. He'd learned to operate a pressure washer and riding lawn mower at Belton's direction, and he'd pronounced himself committed to following his father's guidance. "Whatever he needs me to do, I'm trying to do it. I'm trying to get where he is now."

Little Lamont had landed in state prison at age seventeen, less than a year after getting probation for setting fire to the curtain in his high school auditorium. He'd been convicted for assaulting a man to steal forty dollars and for violating curfew. His probation was revoked, and he started a cycle that became his life—incarceration, probation, back to prison after messing up probation or committing another crime. Now, at twenty-six, he didn't have a car, driver's license, or permanent address. He'd done various day labor jobs—construction, moving company, warehouse work—and hadn't kept one more than a month. When he wasn't locked up, he usually stayed with his mom or sister. They were the most important people in his life, and after his most recent prison stint, he'd tattooed his mom's name on the right side of his neck—*Janie*, in looping cursive. On the left near the front, *Toya* was inked in the same script.

When I interviewed Little Lamont, he always gave thoughtful answers but also balked at certain questions, such as why he lit that spray can in the high school auditorium. "What you asking for is the details, what was going on at the time," he told me. "I don't want to talk about it." When I pressed, he finally talked about how friends teased him for trying to burn up the school. "It's funny to them. It's not funny to me. It wasn't my intention. I wasn't thinking about the criminal part of it. I was a child, a kid." Little Lamont had a curious mind, and a knack for flipping our interviews so I ended up answering his questions. He wanted me to define words I used—*crescendo*, for instance. And because he asked, I found myself describing my religious beliefs, which were tenuous, and admitting that I'd smoked weed in college.

He didn't only question others. He'd thought a lot about his own motivations, trying to understand why he couldn't stay out of trouble, why it was that when authority figures told him to do something, he felt compelled to do exactly the opposite. He'd had behavior problems at a young age, talking back and acting out, especially in school. He assumed his upbringing played a part. He'd lived with his mom and sister in Dalton Village, the same public housing where his father was raised. Drugs were everywhere. Neighbors smoked weed and crack, and stray bullets were so common that Janie sometimes slept during the day, while her kids were in school, so she could be awake to move them to a safe place in the apartment when there was gunfire in the middle of the night. But Little Lamont's family didn't think these difficulties—or his father's absence—explained everything. Janie had married a sheriff's deputy when her son was thirteen, so he'd had a father figure, at least for a while. "I did everything I could," she told me, "but Lamont always been a troubled child. I can't say why."

His brothers' deaths had devastated him. Outsiders wouldn't necessarily expect Little Lamont's family of half siblings to be close, given the betrayals that had gone into creating it. But after Belton went to federal prison, there'd been a kind of détente. Several mothers had made peace, and most of the children came to know each other. No one ever referred to half brothers or half sisters. They were brothers and sisters, connected by the father who was not there.

Little Lamont had been in the county jail when Demario was killed in 2002. He didn't find out until after the funeral, when an inmate gave him a newspaper clipping about the murder. "My mom didn't want to tell me because she didn't want me to flip out," he said. "That was a tough pill to swallow."

Stephen's suicide came eight months later. He and Stephen, six months apart in age, had grown up playing basketball, discussing rap music, and trying to convince their mothers to drive one of them to the other's house so they could hang out. He had again been in jail when Stephen shot himself. "I wish I was out because he might could have talked to me." He wondered if he could have dissuaded him. "There was much love between us." A jail chaplain had given him the news. This time, the jail released him for the funeral.

Since he was a boy, Little Lamont had read his Bible. In prison, he'd spent hours studying it, and his deep interest gave him a natural connection with his dad. After Belton launched his Conway church in 2012 he'd also begun holding Friday night worship services in Charlotte. These services, at a church in a working-class neighborhood near downtown, were a big commitment—a 150-mile drive from Conway, plus a $50 weekly rental for the church. With attendance at two or three dozen, the collection plate offerings covered little more than gas. But Belton insisted he was following God's direction. He said he felt an obligation to preach in Charlotte, "to build up what I had helped tear down." The weekly engagement gave him a continuing tie to the city, drawing new people and old friends, some of whom remembered when Belton was Money Rock, or even before that, when he was Lamont from Dalton Village.

And they'd drawn Little Lamont. He'd shown up just a couple of weeks before his Easter visit to Conway, arriving with his mom's Bible in a worn leather case. Belton greeted him with a hug, rubbing the top of his head. "Boy, you looking good," he said. "I'm proud of you."

"I'm trying to make a change," his son replied.

Belton viewed his preacher role as a kind of spiritual mail carrier, delivering the message God had given him. On this evening, that message seemed meant for Little Lamont. "How many of you wish you would have walked away from some things?" Belton began. In the sanctuary, hands went up, including his son's. "I wish I would have walked away from some things," he continued. "It cost me twenty-one years of my life." The good news, he said, was that change was always possible, though it didn't always happen on schedule, as quickly as one might hope. He recalled a story from the Gospel of John about the invalid in Jerusalem who suffered for thirty-eight years before Jesus healed him. The lesson was that God hasn't abandoned you, no matter what you've been through. "You don't have to believe this," he told worshippers, "but God has told me to tell you your season is about to change."

As the service neared conclusion, Belton called on worshippers to dedicate their lives to Christ. Recorded gospel music swelled. Little Lamont rose from his pew and approached the front of the sanctuary, where he stood, hands in pockets, with more than twenty others.

Belton made his way down the line of worshippers. He poured oil from a small bottle to anoint each person. He lay hands on them and prayed for each in turn. When he reached Little Lamont, he placed both hands on his head. His gold wedding band flashed as it caught the light shining from the ceiling. They stood like that for a long moment, father and son.

Soon after, Little Lamont accepted Belton's invitation to visit him in Conway. At the picnic, he interacted easily with Huckabee Heights children. At one point, he sat on the basketball court tying a boy's shoe. Later, he asked to borrow Belton's car keys to drive a child to a nearby bathroom. Belton reminded his son that he didn't have a license and couldn't risk even a short drive. Little Lamont nodded in agreement.

The previous day, sitting in a pew after Belton's church service, Little Lamont had talked with me about his past. "My attitude was real bad," he said. "I wouldn't listen to anybody." He, too, had followed the code of the street, the rules demanding that a man fight any perceived disrespect. Now he was trying to be more mature, slower to take offense, more like his father.

"It's a learning process. I'm growing every day," he said. "It's helpful because he's my father. When he's ministering to other people, I sit back and listen. I can actually say that being in his presence, I've built a better relationship with God." They had prayed together, and now, he said, "it feels like me and God are on the same page."

Belton had encouraged Little Lamont to stay in Conway longer, but shortly after the picnic, he returned to Charlotte. Three weeks later, a police officer arrested him near his mom's house in the Cherry neighborhood. The charge: possessing a crack rock and resisting arrest. He didn't have much crack, but the officer caught him within three hundred feet of a school, which made the offense more serious. Again, he went to county jail. By year's end, he was back in prison.

19

SUSAN AND MASHANDIA

Six thousand square feet would have been an excess of rental house for two people, except that Belton and Susan were almost never alone. With four bedrooms, they welcomed houseguests who needed a place to stay, for a few days, weeks, months, even years. Some, such as his friend Tracy McGuire and his family, they knew well. Others, including a family living out of a minivan, had been strangers.

The third chapter of 1 John undergirded their generosity: *My little children, let us not love in word, neither in tongue; but in deed and in truth.* For Belton and Susan, providing shelter was a way to love in deed. A few houseguests tested the limits of Christian hospitality, however, particularly one woman who critiqued the family's dinner menu, telling Belton that she and her daughters preferred pork, fried foods, and beans flavored with ham hocks over chicken and fish the Platts served. The mother and two daughters, who'd been evicted from their motel with no place to stay, had been living with the Platts for months. By the time the woman found a job, Belton was so ready for their departure that he paid for a week in an extended-stay motel until their apartment was ready. That was in early 2013, and he and

I happened to be talking on the phone when the woman texted him. "Let me read something to you," he said, pausing our conversation. She was complaining about her motel room: *I thank you for the room. You put us way on the beach. Do you not know how far this is from my school and work?*

After the woman and her daughters moved out, with one house-guest remaining—Sidney, a young church member who served as Belton's driver on his trips to Charlotte—Susan declared a house-guest moratorium. Then, less than a week later, she changed her mind. She'd been standing in her kitchen when she had a vision: Mashandia Williamson gathered there with her children. God was telling Susan to take them in.

Mashandia was a member of their church, thirty-three years old, a bookkeeper for the local Kmart. She had four children, ages eight to seventeen, and was trying to build a new life after leaving the father of her two youngest. She'd been attending a Seventh-Day Adventist church, but switched to Rock Ministries after hearing Belton preach at a funeral. "I felt so much love, the presence of the Lord there," she recalled. She joined the choir and took a part-time job doing church finances, which led to a deep friendship with Susan. "I thought of her as a sister, the way we would joke and carry on," Mashandia said. "I knew God was doing something with us."

She'd grown up near Conway, became pregnant at fifteen, and had four children by age twenty-five. She'd been living with her mother after fleeing a rocky thirteen-year relationship. Her seventeen-year-old son had one bedroom. She and the three younger children shared another, just big enough to fit a king-size mattress and bunk beds. She was desperate for her own apartment, but found herself sabotaged by her credit history. Three rental agencies had rejected her.

It was Saturday when Susan called with her invitation. Stay as long as you want, she said. Mashandia had been doing her mom's hair. She finished attaching extensions and informed her kids they were moving to Pastor Platt's and Ms. Susan's house. Her oldest son stayed with his grandmother; she and the three others packed clothing into black garbage bags, filled the trunk of her Mercury Sable, and arrived by dinner. Susan led them upstairs to their new bedrooms—one for Mashandia and her oldest daughter, Endegé; one for Karheem and Queen.

Except for her beautiful smile, Mashandia's appearance seemed designed to avoid attention. She dressed modestly and had cut her hair short; for some reason, it had begun falling out. She also followed Seventh-Day Adventist teachings that forbade jewelry or makeup. When she arrived at the Platts' house, she often would break into tears, especially when dealing with her children's fathers. Belton recalled that when he tried to step in and help, "she'd argue and fuss with me. I ended up getting the brunt of what everybody else had done to her." At first, he told Susan he thought Mashandia might be crazy. She'd grown up with an abusive, alcoholic father and endured toxic relationships. She was unsure whether this new living arrangement would work out, but she didn't have another plan.

As months passed, her worries eased. Mashandia pitched in with cooking, cleaning, and laundry, while Susan sometimes drove the children to school. Sidney, the Platts' other houseguest, was like a big brother to her children. Belton was a father figure. Mashandia became so comfortable in her new family of choice that she'd team up with Susan when she argued with Belton. "We kind of laughed and joked and picked on Belton a lot," she said. "Once I knew I was accepted in the home and didn't have to go anywhere, I was okay." Belton ceased questioning her sanity. "She became someone I could trust," he said. "And she really cared about me and Susan."

Belton, meanwhile, packed his days with activities. He preached and led Bible study at Rock Ministries, drove to Charlotte to deliver a weekly sermon, counseled youth in a pregnancy prevention program. When a childhood friend's ailing stepfather needed help with his insurance company, he studied, passed the licensing exam, and became certified to sell insurance in South Carolina. He told his personal redemption story on Christian radio and television. During an anti-violence rally in Charlotte's Grier Heights neighborhood, where he'd once sold cocaine, he apologized for his dealing and delivered a say-no-to-drugs speech that brought handshakes from police officers in the crowd.

His tendency was to take on too much. At day's end, he'd fall asleep during conversations with Susan, sometimes midsentence. He did the same thing during our phone interviews—literally nodding off as I was asking a question. Susan scolded him, complaining she only saw him when he was exhausted. He vowed he'd do better, and they carved out Friday date nights, often staying home while Belton cooked dinner.

The new year began with good news. In January 2014, a judge granted Belton's motion to end his five-year probation early. He'd argued for the early termination by explaining that probation kept him from volunteering in certain places, like schools and the local jail. He supported his argument with letters from heads of nonprofits describing his good works. When he called to tell me he was off probation, he sounded as happy as I'd ever heard him. Finally, he said, he felt truly free.

Later that year, in August, Belton attended the International Congress of Churches and Ministers conference in Chattanooga, Tennessee. Browsing a book display, he struck up a conversation with a man named David Sellers, a self-described Christian entrepreneur who'd spent his career launching restaurants.

"Know a good place for lunch?" Belton asked.

Sellers had a ready answer. He owned a restaurant, Luii's, not far away. That afternoon, when they again crossed paths at the conference, Belton told Sellers he'd enjoyed his lunch. They sat down to talk, and Belton told his story.

Sellers liked to help ministers start businesses. When he met a pastor who impressed him, he often lent his expertise gratis, believing that a steady income from a business allowed pastors to focus on ministering instead of offerings. He was familiar with Conway. He told

Belton it was good location for a restaurant. He said Belton should consider launching one.

"I wish I had my journal," Belton replied. He recalled that while in prison, he'd written in his journal about a prophecy he'd received from God: One day, he'd open a restaurant in Conway.

Sellers told Belton to pray about the project and let him know if he wanted to proceed. "I can make that possible," he said, "as soon as you want to do it."

Belton didn't have to pray. "God already told me to do it, and you're here."

They agreed he'd duplicate Sellers's Luii's restaurant, a casual eatery that offered something for everyone—pizza, wings, hoagies, hamburgers, even fried baloney sandwiches. Back in Conway, Belton zeroed in on a former Pizza Hut on Highway 501. It was a prime downtown location, though the empty building, infested with roaches and plagued with mold from a leaking roof, needed major renovations. Sellers helped negotiate rent with the owner and gave Belton both the restaurant concept and his advice, free of charge. Belton began scouting for used equipment. It all seemed like major good fortune.

Susan, however, was contending with health issues. She was still working in the law office in Conway and also led the church's women's fellowship on Saturday mornings. For more than a year, she'd had back pain, which she initially attributed to a fall she'd taken. She was also having urinary tract infections. A diagnosis eluded doctors. For months, she got by with ibuprofen and back massages from Belton and Mashandia. Then her stomach and chest began bothering her. The conclusion was gall bladder inflammation. She scheduled gall bladder surgery in September 2014, relieved to finally have a diagnosis.

The procedure itself went fine. The report afterward was devastating. There were spots on her liver, and tests found cancer. More tests brought worse news—Stage 4, already in her lungs and lymph nodes.

Susan and Belton told only a few people, including Mashandia and Pastor Apollo, the prison chaplain in Bennettsville who'd become a close friend. Doctors doubted chemotherapy would help, so she declined it. Instead, she and Belton asked God for a miracle.

Belton told me about Susan's illness in a Christmas Eve phone call. The prognosis was grim, he said, but the family was praying and remained hopeful. At one point, he fell silent, then sobbed.

With Susan growing sicker, Mashandia quit her bookkeeping job to be her caregiver. She kept up the house, and while Belton was working, she ferried Susan to appointments, administering oxygen and medications. On nights when he was preaching in Charlotte, she and Susan would lie in bed, watching movies or episodes of Kenneth Hagin's ministry programs. Gloria Tadlock, one of Susan's best friends, marveled at how well Mashandia attended to Susan's needs. "Susan loved her so much," she said. "It was obvious to me that God had planted her there to take care of Susan."

The illness was soon impossible to hide. Thin and weak, Susan attended church with an oxygen tank, its clear, narrow tube attached to her nose. "We would call for prayer, she would stand, and we would pray for her," Mashandia recalled. "She just wanted to trust and believe God, so that's what we did."

At home, Susan found solace in music, falling asleep while listening to her favorite CD of soaking music, a kind of Christian music popular in prophetic churches. Believers used soaking music to quiet their minds, to soak in God's presence like a sponge and become filled with the Holy Spirit. Its melodies were soothing and repetitive, not unlike New Age music, and as Susan spent more time in bed, she'd listen for hours. Mashandia downloaded the album to her phone so Susan could listen when they were away from the house.

By February 2015, Susan was under hospice care, using liquid morphine and fentanyl patches for pain. But she was insisting on attending an upcoming church women's retreat in the North Carolina mountains. She'd planned the event and was looking forward to seeing a friend from Florida she'd invited to speak. As the date approached, Belton urged her to cancel, fearing the trip would be too difficult. "Ms. Susan wasn't trying to hear that," Mashandia recalled. "She was like, *I'm going*." Mashandia drove. When it was time for opening remarks, Susan was there, wearing a black sweater, tweed pants, and an oxygen tube. Mashandia stood beside her holding the oxygen tank while Susan leaned on the lectern and welcomed attendees.

She lived another month. By late March, she'd been admitted to Grand Strand Hospital in Myrtle Beach. Belton and Mashandia stayed with her, both sleeping in her hospital room. One morning, Mashandia was moving an air mattress when she knocked over a flower vase. She caught it, attempting to hold both the mattress and vase as its water dripped from Susan's nightstand. Susan laughed. Are we having fun yet? she said. "She was still high-spirited, still Ms. Susan to the end," Mashandia recalled.

Belton wasn't faring as well. He thought he was hiding his distress from his wife, but Mashandia knew Susan could see through it. Once, as Susan struggled to breathe, he lost his temper, ordering a nurse to get a mask that would deliver more oxygen. Afterward, Susan, embarrassed, apologized for his outburst.

Shortly before she lost consciousness, while Belton talked with a visitor, Susan asked Mashandia for a final favor. Take care of Belton, she said.

Belton was still hoping for a miracle. But others, including Mashandia, believed Susan had accepted death. After Susan's grown son arrived from Florida, he pulled Belton into the hospital hallway, where he suggested that perhaps they were prolonging Susan's suffering on earth. He reminded Belton that Jesus built many mansions. Surely God had a mansion for his mother.

Belton took the words to heart. He returned to Susan's side, leaning in close as he took her hand. "Baby, you know I love you," he said. "I

kept you on earth longer than I should have. Apologize for me when
you see Jesus."

She was sixty-six when she died on March 27, 2015. The funeral
was April 3, Belton and Susan's twelfth wedding anniversary. It was
also Good Friday. At Rock Ministries Church, arriving mourners
approached the white casket, adorned with a spray of pink roses,
to view Susan's body. By the time the service started, pews were
full. Some guests stood in the aisles. There were church members, friends, co-workers from Susan's law office. Many of Belton's
family members had come from Charlotte to pay their respects—
Carrie, his siblings, two daughters, and three sons who served as
pallbearers.

Belton entered from the back, tearful and unsteady, the funeral director holding his arm. The service proceeded with songs, liturgical
dance, a eulogy from Pastor Apollo. Gradually, the mood lightened.
When Stephanie McGuire and Mashandia sang an anthem of spiritual deliverance, people rose to their feet, bouncing, clapping, singing
along: *No more shackles, no more chains, no more bondage. I am free,
yeah!*

Two months later, in the same sanctuary, Belton convened church
members to announce that he and Mashandia were planning to
marry.

The scene played out like a repeat of Belton's decision in 2003 to
marry Susan just months after her husband, Jim List, died of a heart
attack. Inmates had felt betrayed on List's behalf. Now people felt betrayal on Susan's behalf. Church membership dropped. Rumors flew
about Belton cheating on his dying wife. Even Carrie, who almost
always took her son's side, thought the hasty marriage disrespected
Susan.

Still, the marriage proceeded. They exchanged vows on June 3,
2015, in a pretty garden courtyard in Bennettsville. Apollo officiated.
They honeymooned in Niagara Falls.

If anyone had asked, they would have said they weren't in love. This was an arranged marriage, with the arranging done by God. Pastor Apollo had encouraged their union. Months earlier, not long after Susan's cancer diagnosis, Apollo had awakened from a dream that he believed contained a prophecy. In the dream, he learned that Susan would die, and that Belton would marry Mashandia. He didn't share the prophecy with Belton; he didn't think Belton could take it. He did tell Mashandia. Stunned, she pushed the information to the back of her mind to focus on Susan. She believed that was the best course with a life-changing prophecy, to shelve it and wait to see if God brought it to pass. "You have to do that to keep your sanity," she said.

Later, in a telephone conversation, Apollo told Susan God wanted her to know that her prayers had been heard. She and Belton had been looking for a new house in Conway. She'd been praying to find one. The Lord was building a house for her, but not one made with the hands of men. "The Lord's getting ready to take you home," the pastor said. "You're going to be at peace."

Susan wept, telling Apollo she'd been praying for someone to take care of Belton. Apollo assured her those prayers would be fulfilled. Susan didn't mention Mashandia by name, but her response made it clear to Apollo that she wanted Belton and Mashandia to be together. She has already been taking care of me, Susan had said.

Apollo shared this story with Belton after Susan died. They'd met for lunch at a Bojangle's in Bennettsville. "The Lord told me to tell you it's okay," he said, urging Belton to marry. "That's who Susan wanted you to be with, and that's what you've been praying about."

After their marriage, Belton and Mashandia continued to grieve. "I was still in love with Susan," he recalled. "It was like part of my soul was snatched away." They struggled for months. A few times, he threatened to leave, and Mashandia was ready to let him go.

Once again, there was that question, the one Belton's friend Barry

Washington had raised when Belton married Susan in 2003. Why so quickly?

Belton's answer was the same: This was what God wanted. Belton knew people would disapprove, but Apollo had counseled that the devil would try to use women to destroy him. "Just being alone, it makes you vulnerable," Belton said. "Because Mashandia was around me, they could not get to me."

In time, mutual respect grew into love. Belton marveled at Mashandia's humble spirit and desire to serve God. He praised her and her daughter Queen for their faithful ministering as he mourned Susan. God had blessed him with Susan, and now with Mashandia. If he got nothing else in this life, he said, that was enough.

It's easy to believe Susan would have approved the marriage. She'd seen how much Belton had depended on her, that for twelve years she'd been his emotional anchor. She knew he'd need someone to fill that role when she was gone.

But Mashandia had another theory about why God had put her with Belton. "I don't think it's so much for me and Belton," she said. She suspected God was working for her children. He wanted them to have a loving father "so the cycle wouldn't repeat what I went through with my dad." At the same time, God was giving Belton a second chance as a parent.

Mashandia explained this in late 2016 as we sat at a table in Luii's, where she was working the lunch shift. "The first year was tough," she said. They'd been mourning Susan, dealing with church turmoil, navigating a new life with their blended family. "I still had to wrap my mind around everything that had taken place, because to me, you're Ms. Susan's husband."

Mashandia was no longer the tearful woman who'd moved into the Platts' house. She wore makeup and jewelry. Her hair had ceased falling out and she styled it in long twists. But those were only superficial changes. She credited Susan with helping her find inner-strength amid a custody battle with her oldest daughter's father. "With Ms. Susan backing me, telling me I could do it, I fought, and won." She was determined to make marriage to Belton work, she said, because she didn't want to mess up God's plan.

Belton and Mashandia Platt in 2017. Courtesy of Belton Platt.

20

HOMECOMING

By the time Big Lamont strolled into his party on December 13, 2015, family and friends were already gathered at tables, eating and talking. Music pulsed as children played on the dance floor beneath a twinkling disco ball. Off to the side, a professional photographer had set up his portrait backdrop. What a difference twelve hours made. That morning, Lamont had been North Carolina Offender No. 0634806. Now he was guest of honor.

His mom, Rhonda, had been promising this welcome-home party for months, and it was bigger than he'd imagined. He made his way around the room, shaking hands and accepting hugs. Several people handed him money. An aunt gave him a handsome Movado watch. Carrie beamed, clasping her grandson's left hand in both of hers. His sister, Genesis, greeted him, as did Kim, Antonio, and Elijah, his half siblings. Also in attendance was his daughter, who'd been a toddler when he went to prison in 2002. Now she was a sixteen-year-old with a star-quality smile. She was also the mother of a seven-month-old son who was meeting his grandfather for the first time.

Big Lamont had been upset when he learned his daughter was pregnant. Telephoning her from prison, he'd warned that "all that responsibility going to fall on you." But he'd gotten over it, concluding that he couldn't be mad at her when he'd done the same thing as a teenager.

At the party, Lamont took his grandson in his arms. The boy's hair was styled in little knots for the occasion, and he wore a tiny pair of True Religion jeans. As Lamont held him, the child sucked his pacifier, studying his young grandfather's face.

The party, the food—most all was Rhonda's doing. She'd begun before dawn that morning, driving a hundred miles east to Hoke Correctional Institution. Lamont had changed into the clothes she'd bought him—jeans, a checked collared shirt, new Timberland boots. Once back in Charlotte, she'd dropped him at a barbershop for a fresh cut. By late afternoon, she and other family members were hauling aluminum pans filled with fried chicken, barbecued chicken, green beans, potato salad, macaroni and cheese, cabbage, yams, and banana pudding to a nightclub called the Charlotte Area Club House, which advertised a clean and sober environment, though its parking lot smelled of weed. Rhonda continued working as guests arrived, setting up a buffet line, then dishing out servings as people came through with disposable plates. She finally took a break to pose with her son for the photographer she'd hired. Big Lamont, a head taller than his slim mother, stood behind her and draped one arm over her shoulder. They smiled as the camera flashed.

Big Lamont was thirty-four years old. For the last fourteen of those years, he'd lived in various correctional institutions tucked off highways in small North Carolina towns—Tabor City, Raeford, Laurinburg, Polkton, Elizabeth City—out of sight and mind of most citizens. His prison time, unlike his father's, had been hard and angry. While Belton had learned to preach, found a wife, and baked cinnamon rolls for prison administrators, Lamont had accumulated dozens of infractions. Guards wrote him up for threatening staff, disobeying orders, using profane language, flooding his cell, tampering with locks. In 2009, at Tabor Correctional Institution, he was charged with two counts of assaulting a prison officer. Lamont said he'd had permission to be in the library, where he was studying. He said he'd been minding his business when a guard entered and told him and a couple other inmates to leave. According to a police report, Lamont cursed and pushed one corrections officer, then pushed and grabbed a second officer who'd stepped in to help the first. Both responded with pepper spray.[1] He was convicted, sentenced to seven additional months, and sent to the hole, which meant solitary confinement—a cell with a steel toilet, sink, and a thin mattress on a hard bed.

Smaller than parking spaces, these cells kept inmates isolated for all but an hour or two each day. Many states had stopped or curtailed the use of solitary confinement, heeding studies that showed prolonged time in isolation can create or worsen mental disorders. But during Lamont's incarceration, North Carolina relied so heavily on what it called "restrictive housing" that human rights groups condemned the state's practices as cruel and unusual, the equivalent of torture.[2] He'd been sent to the hole often, including a two-year stretch in Tabor City. His time in solitary totaled nearly three and a half years.

I'd visited Lamont in early 2015 at Scotland Correctional Institution in Laurinburg, halfway between the coast and mountains, near the South Carolina line. The high-security prison, off a main road lined with tall pines, had more than three hundred of its cells designated for solitary confinement. He'd recently gotten out of one, returning to the general population earlier than scheduled, he told me, because solitary stayed full, and his space was needed more urgently for another inmate.

Lamont was six foot one, 230 pounds, with a round face and shaved head. His right forearm bore Charlotte's telephone area code, "704," a popular tattoo among Charlotte-area inmates in North Carolina's prisons. "They call it 'The 4,'" he said. "The 4 stick together." As we talked, I never saw the temper documented in his prison records. Despite his size, he sometimes seemed childlike. He told me that he shared his father's keen business talents, and he wasn't bothered that he hadn't heard from his dad in a while. "I'm not used to being paid attention to." He often widened his brown eyes as he talked, which made him appear earnest, sometimes incredulous.

When I asked Lamont what happened the night Maurice Leggett was killed in 2001, he shifted the conversation to the actions of others—the younger cousin who was involved, and the teenager who erroneously told Lamont that Leggett had money in his pocket. He should have listened to his girlfriend, who warned him not to do it. "Women make better decisions. Men make bad decisions. Period. They move too fast." Lamont noted that a boy who'd witnessed the murder when he was twelve years old was now a fellow inmate in Scotland Correctional Institution. He mused that his own bad behavior had probably affected the young inmate. "I set a lot of bad examples for a lot of little kids," he said.

Though he'd spent more than three years in the hole, Lamont talked casually about the experience, the way a person might describe a long, tedious commute. He told me he spent days reading books, including his Bible, Sun Tzu's *Art of War*, and Milton William Cooper's *Behold a Pale Horse: Exposing the New World Order*, a conspiracy-theory treatise that covered UFOs, the War on Drugs, and the assassination of President John F. Kennedy. He was also able to converse with inmates through the walls of adjacent cells. "Something you do in the hole, you argue all day, to kill time," he said. He left his solitary cell primarily for showers and recreation, which meant being transferred to an outdoor enclosure for an hour. He didn't believe his time in the hole had damaged him. He thought he had endured it pretty well.

At that time, freedom was less than a year away, and Lamont had begun contemplating his return to life on the outside. "When I step back in the environment, you never know what's going to happen. You get around your friends again," he said. Some in Lamont's family described him as a follower. He agreed. "I want to stay away from people. That's when I get into trouble."

Yet Lamont responded well to his father. My daddy, he called him. When Lamont was confined in Tabor City's prison, before his transfer to Scotland County, Belton's house had been just a fifteen-minute drive across the state line in South Carolina, and for months he'd visited regularly. Tabor City proclaimed itself "Yam Capital of the World" and touted its Yam Festival on its welcome sign. It didn't advertise that its largest employer was actually a fifteen-hundred-bed prison. Tabor

Lamont Davis, who Belton called Big Lamont, at his 2015 welcome-home party. Photo by Pam Kelley.

Correctional Institution was one of six state prisons built in the late 2000s to relieve inmate overcrowding, and local leaders had welcomed it as an economic boon to the depressed area.[3] Lamont had arrived shortly after it opened.

When Belton visited, he parked in a lot in front of the gray, low-slung main building, inside a high fence topped with razor-wire spirals that sparkled in sunlight. Lamont was usually in solitary confinement, so they talked through glass, Lamont in handcuffs secured with a chain around his belly. Often, they discussed Lamont's plans for postincarceration life. One option was to stay with Belton and Susan in South Carolina. But Lamont, who wanted to be near his daughter, planned to return to Charlotte. Before Belton left, they'd bow heads, and Belton would ask God to prepare his son mentally, emotionally, and spiritually to leave prison. They couldn't hug goodbye, but each told the other he loved him. Belton visited for months, until the prison system moved Lamont in late 2012 to Scotland Correctional Institution.

On the night of Lamont's party, Belton and Mashandia, driving to

Charlotte from Conway, were among the last to arrive, and their entrance launched a new round of hugs and photos. The last time Belton and Lamont had both been out of prison was 1989. As oldest son, Lamont had the most memories of his father—treats his dad bought neighborhood kids from the ice cream truck, a surprise birthday bike, the spanking he got after playing with his mom's gun. He also remembered watching Judge Potter sentence his father in a courtroom. He'd been eight, didn't understand everything that was happening, but knew it was bad. "My father was my idol, really," Lamont told me. "He was just snatched from me. It been tough on any kid that lose their favorite role model."

In 2001, when Lamont was in jail facing the murder charge, Belton had prayed from federal prison and called family members for updates, but was otherwise powerless to help. At the party, as he watched Lamont posing for photos and accepting hugs, he described the day he learned prosecutors were threatening the death penalty. He'd dropped to his knees, crying out from his cell: "My son. My son." Then he heard God answer his cry. "He said, *He's my son too*," Belton recalled. "I was so focused on the fact that he was my son, I never even gave a thought to the fact he was God's son as well."

21

LIFE ON THE OUTSIDE

On January 4, 2016, three weeks after getting out of prison, Big Lamont woke, dressed, and prepared for class. He was living with his mom, sleeping on the living-room sofa in the two-bedroom apartment she shared with Genesis and her daughter, Honesty. Before Rhonda went to work, she drove him to the Center for Community Transitions, a nonprofit that helped people rebuild their lives after prison. He joined seventeen ex-offenders—a bigger group than usual—for the first job-readiness class of the new year. As 9 a.m. approached, smokers took final drags on cigarettes before heading inside. Coffee drinkers filled cups from a big urn in the classroom. Lamont and his classmates claimed seats around tables.

"Good morning!" At the front of the room, Erik Ortega, one of the teachers, introduced himself. Ortega had a booming voice, a Bronx accent, and a talent for delivering straight talk with humor. He always told his classes that they obviously sucked as criminals, given that they'd all gotten caught. This line usually got a laugh, partly because Ortega was a failed criminal too. At nineteen, he'd been arrested at JFK airport with a suitcase full of cocaine. He served six and a half years. When he got out, he slept on a cot in his mom's apartment and learned the challenges of life as a felon. When he applied to McDonald's, his application was rejected.

Over the next two weeks, Lamont sat through lessons on résumé writing, proper dress, job-search strategies. He and classmates also practiced mock interviews, explaining their criminal records to prospective employers. Doing this effectively was an art—focusing on strengths such as work ethic and punctuality, but telling the truth about offenses. The trick was to acknowledge guilt without excess details. The process sometimes reduced ex-offenders to tears.

The Center for Community Transitions, which had been helping ex-offenders reenter society since the 1970s, had seen its clientele grow as the nation's prison population ballooned. Every week, more than a hundred people found their way to Mecklenburg County after completing jail or prison sentences. Often, they'd left prison lacking basics like proper clothing and transportation. Many ended up in homeless shelters.

President George W. Bush first thrust the reentry issue into the spotlight in 2004 during his State of the Union address. "America is the land of second chance," he said, "and when the gates of the prison open, the path ahead should lead to a better life."[1] But more than a decade later, odds for success remained long. About two-thirds of people leaving incarceration were rearrested within three years of release.

The city of Charlotte had joined the national Ban the Box movement, eliminating the *Have you been convicted of a crime?* question on job applications, an effort to assure applicants that a criminal record wasn't an automatic disqualifier. But many private employers still refused to hire felons, especially those convicted of violent crimes. The classes at the Center for Community Transitions didn't guarantee a job, but statistics showed they improved the chances.

Lamont left the program's graduation ceremony feeling optimistic. He had an edge over many classmates, he figured. He'd had felony convictions—car theft, cocaine possession—from a young age, which gave him experience job-hunting with a criminal record. Even before his murder conviction at age twenty, he'd worked for a grocery, fast-food stores, and a company that made wooden pallets. He was sure he could do it again. "A job's a job," he said. "I take any job."

Two weeks later, he had one—with a day-labor company that sent him to work sites around town. He drew several demolition assignments. Construction was booming in uptown Charlotte, and there was plenty of work to be had tearing down buildings to make way for new development. "Everything you could tear something up with, we used it," he said. "Hammers worked best. You can bust a wall with a regular hammer."

Rhonda, ready to be done with chauffeur duties, bought him a used car once he passed his driver's test. "I studied the book for like a month," he told me. He also discovered social media on the Android phone she gave him. He created accounts on Snapchat, Instagram, and Facebook, where he posted unsmiling selfies and a photo of his grandson dressed in Michael Jordan gear. To mark the birthday of his late brother, Stephen, he shared a slideshow on Facebook of blurry childhood photos set to music. "HAPPY BIRTHDAY BABY BROTHER RIP," he wrote. At one point, he changed his status to "in a relationship."

Once he had a car, he paid his grandma regular visits. He'd lounge on the loveseat in Carrie's living room, and they'd talk about old times and favorite foods. When they had cookouts, he'd help with the grill. Sometimes he telephoned to see if she needed to be driven somewhere. He was vigilant about keeping appointments with his parole officer, avoiding his old neighborhood, Hidden Valley, and staying away from certain friends, declining offers to hang out. "No point," he told me. He'd seen men released from prison only to get locked up again. "I guess I just embraced my freedom more," he said. "I ain't thinking about going back."

After several months at day labor, Lamont returned to the Center for Community Transitions, hoping to find work that paid more than $10.50 an hour. He tested to qualify for a Goodwill course that taught construction skills such as reading blueprints and using power tools. But the program required seventh-grade math and reading skills, and he scored too low. Instead, he took a counselor's suggestion to check out a Charlotte company called High-Temperature Technologies.

Lamont wasn't sure what High-Temperature Technologies actually did when he showed up for his interview, and that wasn't surprising. HTT filled an obscure niche in the nation's power industry, making and installing a sealing system that improved the efficiency of power-plant boilers. Workers often installed the material while harnessed to scaffolding several stories high.

The good part of the job was the pay—$12 an hour with substantial overtime. It wasn't full-time work, however. A couple of sixty-hour weeks at a power plant in New Mexico or Texas might be followed by a string of unpaid days. Jobs were mostly in fall and spring, when energy consumption was lower and power plants were able to shut down boilers for maintenance. This seasonality was a big reason the company relied on what its owner, Jenifer Gelorme, called "second-chance hiring." HTT didn't ask about criminal records, and when new hires needed bank accounts or driver's licenses, staff members helped them navigate the bureaucracy. "A lot of our guys haven't been given a lot of guidance," Gelorme said. "We try really hard to help people become grownups."

Deploying these employees to far-flung locations created challenges. Lamont, like many of HTT's new workers, had never flown on a plane or navigated airport security. To minimize glitches, HTT supervisors kept crews together as much as possible, handled boarding passes, did head counts, and generally operated like high school teachers leading field trips.

Lamont started work in October 2016 after completing safety training and passing a drug test. Over the autumn, he worked at power plants in South Carolina, Virginia, and New York. When he was between jobs, he visited his dad in Conway. He'd accompany Belton on errands, just like he did when he was a little boy.

With the coming of winter, the HTT work wound down, and after the holidays, Lamont decided he needed a change of scenery. When Belton agreed to give him a job at the restaurant, he headed to South Carolina.

Luii's had opened in September 2015, just in time for a record-breaking October rainfall that flooded much of Conway but spared the restaurant. For several days, it stayed packed. Belton and Mashandia worked morning to night, barely pausing for bathroom breaks. "If business was that good every day, I'd retire early," Belton said later.

By the time Lamont moved to Conway in January 2017, Luii's had established itself as a family restaurant with free drinks for kids, senior discounts, and contemporary Christian background music. Once a week, Belton led Bible study in the dining room.

Belton and Mashandia lived a minute's drive from Luii's, in a downtown neighborhood shaded by live oaks hanging with Spanish moss. They'd moved shortly after the marriage to a roomy ranch house. Belton, determined to be a good father to Mashandia's children, assured them that they had great potential, that they could make straight A's and become everything God told them to be. He also expected them to follow his rules. Along with standard parenting prohibitions—no cursing, smoking, alcohol, or drugs—he required them to address elders as *ma'am* and *sir*, and he forbade secular music. He believed lyrics celebrating sex, violence, and bad behavior affected listeners, sowing such conduct into their hearts and minds.

Mashandia viewed Belton's parenting as a blessing. Endegé was preparing to graduate from high school. Her oldest son would soon enter the Navy. The two youngest had made the honor roll. "I needed help with my kids and didn't even realize I needed it," she said.

When Big Lamont arrived, Belton trained him as cook and dishwasher, though not as a server, given his dicey people skills. He proved reliable, sometimes showing up early for shifts. But he had a tendency to argue and balk at taking orders, at work and home. Sometimes he just lost his temper, "acting crazy," as family members described it. Once, he had a loud, obscenity-laced argument on the phone with his girlfriend while standing in the street outside the house. He announced in front of Mashandia's children that he didn't follow other people's rules. Belton had seen similar tendencies in all his sons. He knew where they got it. "They got my blood in them," he said, "That part of me I don't like seeing in them."

Belton believed that prison and solitary confinement had damaged Lamont. "That boy who went in that hole, all he had was himself, his books, and his philosophy of life. He wasn't out interacting. He feels like he has all the answers, and thinks he's normal. He's still a boy trapped in a man's body, because he was in the hole all them years."

After six months, Belton told Lamont to move out. "I'm training my kids to be one way, and he had a whole other concept of life," he said. Lamont had a good work ethic and giving heart. But Belton couldn't abide his behavior.

It was June 2017, not long after Lamont had returned to Charlotte, when I met him at American Deli, a fast-food place that shared a parking lot with a payday lender. At the counter, he ordered wings and asked the server to make his drink a combination of peach, fruit punch, and lemonade. As we settled at a table, we were joined by the cousin of Lamont's who'd been his co-defendant in Maurice Leggett's 2001 murder. His cousin had recently moved to a halfway house in Charlotte, the last stop before completing his federal sentence on a gun violation. "I actually just got me a job today," he said. He smiled, exposing the silver grill he wore on his teeth. The job was with Lamont's new employer, a company that manufactured masonry reinforcement products. Lamont, who'd moved back with his mother, had been hired after learning about the place from another cousin. Now he was packaging wire pieces, 360 to a box. "Easiest job I ever had," Lamont said. "Might be there twenty, thirty years."

Lamont reiterated what his dad had told me—that they'd parted amicably. "We still cool," he said. He understood that Belton wanted his new children "to succeed better." But while Belton couldn't abide Lamont's disrespect, Lamont couldn't stand his dad's rules. "I ain't got time to follow the rules he put on his kids."

We'd talked for about forty minutes when Lamont announced he had to leave. He needed to return his cousin to his halfway house before curfew. Before he left, I broached a subject we'd never discussed. I'd been thinking about the government entities that had affected his life—the school system that dumped him in an inferior program for troubled kids, the state prison that failed to provide mental health counseling and kept him in solitary confinement for lengths of time that experts described as torture. Theoretically, voters had the power to change these situations.[2] Lamont had completed his probation, and in North Carolina, that meant he'd regained his right to vote. All he had to do was register. I wondered if he planned to vote in the next election.

"Nope," he replied.

Had he ever voted?

"Nope."

Did he pay attention to politics?

"Nope."

Why not?

"I don't like none of them."

22

UPRISING

The police just shot my daddy four times for being black . . . ! My daddy ain't do nothing. . . . They just pulled up undercover. . . . My daddy don't got no motherfucking gun . . . !

This was how news of Keith Lamont Scott's death broke in Charlotte, via a distraught young woman streaming on Facebook. Scott's daughter, Lyric, recorded herself cursing and screaming at clusters of cops, their hands on hips, faces like stone, only flimsy crime scene tape separating them from her rage.

Fifteen minutes in, she began shouting: *My daddy is DEAD! They shot my daddy. They killed my daddy.* The phone camera in her hand recorded jerky images—the grass, the sidewalk, the blacktop beneath her feet as she paced the scene, the sounds of her gulping sobs as she wept. The live stream continued for more than an hour.

It was a warm, sunny Tuesday afternoon, September 20, 2016, and it would become the day Charlotte was unmasked, its racial failings eclipsing its gleaming New South image. Keith Scott had been sitting in his Ford Explorer, waiting for his child to get off the school bus, parked in his townhome complex in the University City area, northeast of uptown. He was forty-three, a married father of seven. A motorcycle accident had left him with a traumatic brain injury.

Police were looking for another man, not Scott. But they

approached after seeing a gun and marijuana cigarette in his car. When he got out, they said he was holding the gun and ignored commands to drop it. In a police video, you can hear an officer shouting: "Drop the gun!" In Scott's wife's video, you can hear her shouting to police: "Don't shoot him!" Brentley Vinson, the officer who shot him, was also black. Scott did have a gun. Police recovered it near his body. But there were no photos or video that showed him holding it. Experts said his brain injury may have interfered with his ability to follow directions, especially shouted orders. His wife had yelled to police: "He has a T.B.I. He's not going to do anything to you guys. He just took his medicine." [1]

By 9 p.m., Lyric Scott's video had been viewed nearly a half million times.[2] By early Wednesday morning, a gathering that began near the shooting scene spilled onto Harris Boulevard and nearby Interstate 85. Angry protesters shut down the highway with traffic cones, trapping motorists, looting the contents of a tractor-trailer, smashing car windshields, lighting fires.

"There is about a hundred people in the middle of the street and they won't let nobody by," one woman told a 911 operator. "They have these construction cones. They won't let nobody through. . . . They're harassing people. Banging on people's cars."

"And what are they doing with these cones?"

"It looks like they protesting something. . . . They just all in the street, just *We want justice*. . . . Oh my God, they're coming through these cars," the woman said. "I can't back up. I can't go straight."

"Do you see any weapons, ma'am?"

"No, I don't see any weapons. People are standing on these people's cars now. They just won't let us go through."[3]

Police used tear gas to break up the highway blockade around 3 a.m.[4] The next night, demonstrations moved uptown, where law enforcement again attempted crowd control with tear gas and flash-bang grenades. Outside the Omni Hotel, a bullet was fired into a group of demonstrators, killing a twenty-six-year-old named Justin Carr. Police charged a civilian with the murder. Activists claimed that an officer had shot Carr. The governor declared a state of emergency and called in the National Guard.

The city had never seen this level of violence, not during the civil rights movement, not during school desegregation. At a press conference Thursday morning, Mayor Jennifer Roberts looked stricken. "We have a long tradition of working together to solve our problems," she told reporters. "The events that we saw last night are not the Charlotte that I know and love."

The Charlotte that Roberts referenced was finally a major city—second tier, certainly, but seventeenth largest in the country, with an uptown that could plausibly be described as bustling. Four years earlier, it had hosted the 2012 Democratic National Convention, and if the city had been a debutante, the DNC would have been its coming-out party, a spotlight dance on the world stage. Some 35,000 convention visitors had packed into uptown, which sizzled briefly with the star power of Los Angeles and the eccentricity of Portland. With Comedy Central broadcasting *The Daily Show* live from Charlotte, host Jon Stewart praised locals. "You're the nicest people," he said. "It's really kind of annoying." President Obama's plane had barely left the ground before speculation began about what Charlotte might host next.

"I don't think the city will ever be the same," then-mayor Anthony Foxx had told a reporter. "This event took us a long way in the minds of the world community."[5] There was talk of landing the Super Bowl, or even something bigger. "Longer term," Foxx said, "we should begin thinking about the Olympics."[6]

The next time Charlotte made national headlines, in 2014, it was because of what the city lacked. A new study had found that social mobility in America varied widely by location. By analyzing U.S. income tax records, researchers at Harvard and the University of California discovered that the chances of improving one's station in life were highest in the Great Plains. They were lowest in the Southeast—former slave states—and in areas with large African American populations. In San Jose, California, whose social mobility rivaled Denmark's, a child born in the poorest fifth of the population had a 12.9 percent chance of making it to the top fifth. But a similar child born in Charlotte had only a 4.4 percent chance, "far lower than anywhere else in the rich world," as *The Economist* put it.[7] When the study ranked fifty of the nation's largest cities by social mobility, Charlotte came in last.[8]

The United States bills itself as the land of opportunity, a place where people easily pull themselves up by their bootstraps, but research shows that's long been more myth than fact. The chances of escaping poverty in America aren't nearly as good as they are in Canada, or Australia, or most other wealthy countries.[9] The new study found Charlotte's social mobility to be some of the worst in the developed world. Census data also portrayed a city of haves and have-nots. More than 25 percent of Charlotte households made more than $100,000 a year, a percentage much higher than North Carolina as a whole. And yet its poverty rate had almost doubled since 2000, from 10 to 18 percent, one of the biggest jumps in the country. One of every three census tracts was deemed high-poverty, meaning at least 20 percent of the tract's residents were poor. African Americans, who made up about a third of the population, were roughly three times as likely as whites to live in poverty.[10] "We've been so focused on building the prosperity, we just haven't paid attention to what's happening in our county," the county commission chairman said.[11]

In fact, one sign of inequality—school resegregation—had been staring Charlotte in the face for years. In 1999, a federal ruling had ended thirty years of court-ordered busing. Judge Robert Potter, the judge who'd sentenced Belton, had concluded that busing was no longer necessary because it was unlikely "that the school board will return to an intentionally-segregated system."[12]

Potter's reasoning ignored the fact that busing had only treated the symptoms of segregation. It never cured the root problem—housing segregation, created largely by the government's own policies. When busing died, school resegregation surged. Belton's high school, West Charlotte, once a national symbol of integration success, lost virtually all its white students. By 2017, about half of Charlotte-Mecklenburg's black and Latino students attended schools that were less than

10 percent white. Poverty levels at seventy-six schools were so high that everyone got free lunch and breakfast because it was easier than sorting out the few kids who didn't qualify.[13] At the end of the day, they went home to largely segregated neighborhoods, much like children who'd lived in Piedmont Courts in the 1960s.

And now the protests, the looting, the violence. Carrie had been glued to the television in her living room on that first evening, alarmed as she watched protesters lobbing water bottles at police, who responded with tear gas. A black man shot dead by police hadn't surprised her—she'd seen that before—but she was shocked by the ensuing violence. Usually, Charlotte tamped down unrest before it got out of hand. In 2013, for instance, an officer had killed a black man named Jonathan Ferrell, a former college football player who'd been seeking help in the middle of the night after wrecking his car. The officer was white, and Ferrell, unlike Scott, had no weapon. The state's decision to charge the officer with voluntary manslaughter helped ease community tensions, as did a group of black barbers who organized "Cops and Barbers" sessions, where their clients and neighbors could meet police leaders in town hall–style meetings. The officer went free following a hung jury and mistrial. Even then, Charlotte remained peaceful.

The precipitating cause of the 2016 uprising was Keith Scott's death. But the anger went deeper. "They got us in failing schools without adequate resources and then you don't have the education to get jobs," a man with a bullhorn told protesters in Marshall Park. "Then they want to talk about black-on-black crime. Why does black-on-black crime exist? It's because we are living in a community of deep poverty perpetuating black-on-black crime. And that's why we got police terrorism running rampant in the city."[14]

Many issues came up in the days following the protests—police shootings, resegregated schools, and urban renewal and highway construction, which destroyed and cut off black neighborhoods. People talked about Jim Crow laws and even slavery. "Four hundred years of racial inequality is part of why we find ourselves here today," Dr. Ophelia Garmon-Brown told the *Charlotte Observer*.

Garmon-Brown was co-chairing a task force trying to address the city's lagging social mobility. "If we are not focusing on institutional racism and the inequality," she said, "things will only get worse."[15]

Minimizing or at least reducing racial inequality in Charlotte had once seemed a goal within reach. In 1984, when President Ronald Reagan came to town and criticized busing as a failed social experiment, the *Observer* rebuked him: "Charlotte-Mecklenburg's proudest achievement of the past 20 years is not the city's impressive new skyline or its strong growing economy. Its proudest achievement is its fully integrated public school system."[16] The tone of superiority reflected the civic mood. Having elected Harvey Gantt their first black mayor, and with court-ordered busing keeping schools integrated, "people thought they had conquered something," Gantt told me in 2017.

Gantt, seventy-four, a retired architect and respected elder statesman in Charlotte, remembered how the city used to be. "We thought very highly of ourselves," he recalled. "But I'm not so sure we didn't cover over some things."

In the months following Scott's death, various nonprofits and educational groups organized discussions around the city. One evening, a group called Race Matters for Juvenile Justice presented a program on brain science to explain implicit biases we all carry. Another night, a district court judge took the stage to describe how he grew up in Myers Park unaware of his white privilege. A museum screened a documentary that explored what it means to be white in America. "It's just the norm," one young woman told the camera. "White is the good thing."

Charlotte had so many race-related panel discussions and lectures that one sometimes conflicted with another. An advocacy group led ongoing discussions of Michelle Alexander's *New Jim Crow: Mass Incarceration in the Age of Colorblindness*. A nonprofit gave bus tours, pointing out the impact of urban renewal and highway construction on black neighborhoods. The Levine Museum of the New South opened an exhibit called "K(NO)W Justice, K(NO)W Peace," one of the nation's first to explore the impact of police-involved killings.

It was late November when Mecklenburg District Attorney Andrew Murray completed his investigation of Scott's shooting death. In a press conference resembling a courtroom argument, he presented video and images, showing the process he used to decide whether to bring charges against the officer. What Officer Vinson saw, he said, "was a man who had drawn a gun when confronted by police, exited a vehicle with gun in hand, and failed to comply with officers who commanded him at least ten times to put the gun down." [17]

Murray told the room he was fully convinced that the shooting had been lawful. Officer Vinson wouldn't face charges. That night, dozens of protesters gathered outside Charlotte-Mecklenburg Police head-quarters and marched uptown, chanting for justice. One banner read: "How to get away with murder: Become a cop." [18]

23

SOUTHSIDE HOMES

When the banged-up white pickup rattled into Southside Homes with its grocery haul, Carrie Graves's neighbors were waiting to help unload. The driver parked in Carrie's front yard, and out of the truck bed came boxes of fragrant peaches and fat onions, bricks of sharp cheddar, almond-topped breakfast pastries. More neighbors arrived, heading to a folding table in the yard, now loaded with food. Items disappeared nearly as fast as they were set out, with people filling their bags and wire carts, eager to get groceries out of the thick July heat and into air-conditioned apartments.

By 2017, food giveaways were a Saturday ritual in Carrie's corner of the sprawling public housing project called Southside. Each week's donations were different, depending on surpluses and sell-by dates at Trader Joe's, three miles away but in a world where shoppers sought free-range chickens and milk from grass-fed cows. There might be ground chuck, ash-rind brie, or rosemary focaccia. Sometimes the truck brought cellophane-wrapped flower bouquets that spent their final days withering in a container on Carrie's porch. Produce dominated on this Saturday—blueberries, grapes, potatoes, tomatoes. When a neighbor boy appeared, Carrie's son Gordon called him over and pressed two quarts of strawberries and a bag of apples into his arms. "Take this stuff here to your mom," he said.

While residents filled bags outside, Carrie, wearing a Luii's ball cap from Belton, worked in her cramped living room, using every empty surface to sort food she'd set aside for family members. A gallon of milk waited on the linoleum. Peppers, tomatoes, onions, and avocados filled her easy chair. A tub of tzatziki and a pepperoni package nestled in the corner of the loveseat, which also held an ottoman, stacked on top to free up floor space.

Carrie had started these giveaways five years earlier, on the back patio of her former apartment in Savanna Woods. A connected friend had helped her arrange the donations. When she was relocated to Southside in 2014 as Savanna Woods underwent renovations, the food pantry simply changed address, serving a new group of public housing residents. One neighbor, Deatrice, was so grateful that she'd begun looking for an organization to honor Carrie, preferably with a cash prize. After filling her cart, she confided to Gordon, out of Carrie's earshot, that she planned to contact Cam Newton, the Carolinas Panthers' quarterback. Newton had dressed as Santa for Southside kids at Christmas. Maybe he'd make another visit. "He loves publicity," she said.

Deatrice had heard that Carrie's family was related to Martin Luther King Jr. This wasn't the case, as far as anyone knew, but the rumor had a ring of truth, given Carrie's activist history and passion for politics. Before the 2016 election, she'd convinced a nephew to drop her off uptown so she could watch President Barack Obama campaign with Hillary Clinton. While waiting to get inside the Charlotte Convention Center, she gave an interview to a reporter from Europe—Switzerland, as she recalled. Two days before the election, she offered her views on her front porch as a visiting activist recorded her on Facebook. Wearing a baseball cap covered with political pins and a shirt commemorating Obama's first inauguration, Carrie told viewers to make sure they voted in down-ballot state and local races. She also had a message for young people who weren't planning to vote: "You ain't got no business griping and grumbling about anything. Because you're the reason—and people like you—are the reason we get all these nut heads in our federal government and our state government."

"What I heard," the young activist said, "is a lot of young people who were part of the protests now don't want to vote."

"Oh really, why?" Carrie asked.

"Because they just feel nothing ever changes."

"And that's why," Carrie said. "Because they have that kind of attitude. Why stop? Be a part of something. Even if your kind of thing that you wanted to get passed, if it don't, you can feel good that *Doggone it, I tried, and I'm not going to stop.*"

"You're never going to stop?"

"No. That would be so bad for all my grandkids, and my great-grandkids."

When Donald Trump beat Hillary Clinton two days later, disappointment wasn't strong enough to describe Carrie's emotional state. As President Trump's first year in office unfolded, she ranted regularly, referring to him as Satan's brother. But she viewed Trump's election as the fault of citizens who failed to vote, not as a system failure. By the summer of 2017, she was on to the next election, debating who would get her vote in Charlotte's Democratic mayoral primary.

At eighty-one, Carrie lived on food stamps and a monthly Social Security check of $807. She paid $437 a month for the two-bedroom public housing apartment she shared with Gordon, who was on disability. He had a broken car and no money to fix it, so when Carrie needed to go to the doctor or Walmart, she relied on friends or on the city's elderly transportation service. A chunk of her Social Security money went for necessities—soap, deodorant, laundry detergent, paper towels—that weren't covered by food stamps. Protection pads weren't covered either, and she had to buy them regularly for an overactive bladder that was growing worse with age.

Arthritis in her knees and spine was getting worse too. She struggled to climb the stairs to her apartment's only bathroom, and slept in the living-room easy chair, which she found more comfortable than her mattress. She refused to consider senior housing. "I don't want to live with no old people," she said. She'd also refused offers from Donna and Belton, who'd both urged her to move in with them. She didn't want to live in someone else's house.

She hadn't wanted to relocate from Savanna Woods to Southside, either, but had assumed it would be temporary. Her understanding had been that she'd return to Savanna Woods after renovations and move back into her same apartment. Then she learned she wouldn't get her old unit. At first, she accused housing authority officials of misleading her and wished aloud for a house of her own. By the time the Savanna Woods apartments were ready, she'd decided that if she couldn't have her old place back, and since nobody seemed to be giving her a house, she'd just stay in Southside.

In truth, she'd grown to like Southside's neighborly ambience. At food giveaways, people picked up extra for neighbors who couldn't attend. Wheelchair-bound residents were pushed to the food table, then back to their apartments. "Country," is how Carrie described Southside's atmosphere. "You know, you holler out the back, *Hey, you got any butter?*" In the summer, Carrie's screen door creaked with comings and goings—neighbors saying hello, Big Lamont stopping by after work, Gordon stepping out for a smoke. Some evenings, family and friends convened for backyard cookouts. When she babysat Honesty, her eight-year-old great-granddaughter, children congregated on her front porch. "A porch full of chaps," she said. "Something magnetic about that porch." From her chair on the porch, she could converse with neighbors while cars and city buses rumbled down Fairwood Avenue. Occasionally, someone would honk or wave: "Hey, Grandma!" Crime didn't worry Carrie, despite occasional gunfire and a violent crime rate twice the city average. She figured she was safe as long as she minded her own business. Also, police were always cruising by. She speculated they got contact highs from neighbors who smoked weed.

Southside had 381 apartments. They occupied forty-one acres off South Tryon Street, a couple miles southwest of uptown. It was the city's largest and oldest remaining public housing, having outlasted others, including Piedmont Courts, which had been demolished and replaced with new mixed-income developments. When it opened in 1952, Southside had been "a low-rent housing project for Negroes," an attractive alternative to substandard slums. One of its first tenants, according to a newspaper report at the time, was Harriett Robinson, a young widow with three little girls. She'd been renting a single dark room in a house where the water spigot and community bathroom were on the unheated back porch. In her new two-bedroom in Southside, her living room was empty "because she has nothing to put in it," the reporter wrote, but "she isn't complaining about anything at all. It's so fine to have plenty of space and a good bathroom and plenty of light that she doesn't mind the empty living room." [1]

Seven decades later, Southside's winding streets were lined with mature leafy oaks, and though it lacked the style and amenities of newer mixed-income developments, it had sidewalks, open green lawns, and sturdy red-brick buildings that had been renovated in the 2000s. Affordable housing was hard to come by in Charlotte, especially near uptown, and with rents capped at 30 percent of income, demand for Southside apartments was so high that the waiting list was closed.

Few areas illustrated the story of Charlotte's stalled social mobility as well as Southside. Residents were mostly African American. Often, they came from families who'd lived in Charlotte's poor, black neighborhoods for generations. This set Southside apart from the city as a whole, so full of newcomers that people joked it was hard to find natives. Many Southside residents struggled with illness, depression, addiction. Seventy percent were unemployed, and they lacked access to the kinds of relationships and networks that middle-class people used to find jobs or help their kids get into the right high school or college. In a lot of ways, Southside had barely changed since 1952. Racism had created the development. Jim Crow had never really disappeared.

It's unlikely that South Tryon Street motorists passing Southside's apartments contemplated their history. But some may have wondered how much longer the public housing would last. Charlotte's crime had

plummeted from its early-'90s peak, and people clamored to live near
the center city. For the first time in history, whites were moving into
mostly black neighborhoods. Southside's newest neighbors included
breweries, a craft coffeehouse, a grocery with a wine bar. A half mile
away, high-end apartments were rising. The housing authority said it
had no plans to demolish or redevelop Southside, but among residents,
the rumor mill buzzed with talk of the project's eventual demise. Carrie and her neighbors knew they were living on valuable land.

In June 2017, nine months after Keith Lamont Scott's death, *Charlotte
Magazine* hosted a public discussion titled "How a Broken System Led
to Two Charlottes." The venue was Lenny Boy Brewing on South Tryon
Street. If you accepted that there were two Charlottes, then Lenny Boy,
with its organic beer, kombucha, and Saturday morning yoga classes,
exemplified the prosperous, gentrifying one. After outgrowing one
building, it had renovated this cavernous warehouse and become a
magnet for millennials and their dogs, a friendly neighborhood craft
brewery that also happened to be next door to Southside Homes.

Connected to its taproom, Lenny Boy had a high-ceilinged space,
perfect for large events. That's where two hundred people gathered
for the discussion, some ordering an IPA or lager before settling into
folding chairs. There were four panelists—the superintendent of
Charlotte-Mecklenburg schools, a city council member, an assistant
public defender, and the coordinator of the Charlotte-Mecklenburg
Opportunity Task Force, created to address the city's subpar social mobility. Together, they were familiar with most of Charlotte's
shortcomings.

The public defender, Toussaint Romain, had taken to the streets
during protests, wearing a white shirt and tie, urging calm as he stood
between angry demonstrators and riot-geared police. He kicked off
the evening's discussion by challenging its entire premise—that Charlotte suffered from a broken system. "My friends, the system is not
broken," he told the crowd. "The system is working as it was designed
to work from the founding of the country."[2]

Carrie Graves in 2017 on her porch in Southside Homes. Photo by Pam Kelley.

No one tried to argue otherwise. In fact, the mobility task force had said as much in its report, urging the community to "Acknowledge the significant role segregation and racialization have played in our current opportunity narrative." To drive the point home, the report included a 1935 map of redlined Charlotte, tangible proof of a major federal policy that thwarted African Americans' efforts to buy homes.

In a city where good manners often eclipsed honesty, the discussion at the brewing company had uncomfortable moments. "White folks, why are you not asking questions?" demanded Patrice Funderburg, a self-described social justice provocateur. "It's not our job to teach you what to do with us."[3] Later, she made a point that drew applause. "Anybody in here live in Southside Homes?" Hearing no response, she continued: "How do we have a forum that talks about two Charlottes when only one Charlotte is in the room?"

One Saturday morning not long after the Lenny Boy event, Carrie sat in a patio chair on her porch, waiting for the truck with the Trader Joe's groceries. On her lap, she held her great-grandson Michael,

Genesis's sturdy eleven-month-old, who alternated standing, squat-
ting, and grabbing at anything in reach. Carrie babysat him often, despite her arthritis. I'd asked how she managed the lifting and carrying.
"Jesus," she'd responded. "That's the best I can tell you."

She'd been to the doctor that week, and her knees were feeling better, thanks to steroid shots. A nurse practitioner had given her two
prescriptions. One ordered an orthopedic mattress for back support.
The other said she needed a ground-level apartment for her safety. A
ground-level apartment meant moving again, perhaps to another unit
in Southside. Carrie said that was okay, depending on where, because
some locations in Southside were preferable to others.

When she wasn't ranting about Trump, Carrie usually described
herself as content. She was in public housing, where she didn't have
to worry about keeping a roof over her head. Her sons were all out
of prison, as was Big Lamont, Belton's oldest son. She was especially proud of Belton, and enjoyed telling people about his church
and restaurant in Conway. She took delight in grandchildren and
great-grandchildren and found purpose babysitting Honesty and
Michael. On summer days, when tinny music signaled the ice cream
truck, she'd fetch her change purse to get a dollar for Honesty. She
chuckled at Michael's antics, even when he fussed or flung a toy. "It's
amazing these babies have their own mind when they come out of
their mamas' butt," she said.

She didn't covet wealth, and she explained why by recalling stories
about unhappy rich white people she'd known when she worked as
their babysitter or cleaning lady. "I thought all these people had all
this peace, and, you know, prosperity, and all this kind of stuff. And
then I learned they whored around too." Money didn't buy happiness,
in other words.

Still, she wished for a house. She'd clearly thought a lot about her
dream house, because when I asked about features she'd want, she
rattled off specifications: a dining room that would sit ten or twelve.
More than one bathroom. A kitchen with lots of cabinets and storage
space. At least four bedrooms, so she'd have two extras for guests—not

just family, but people down on their luck who needed a place to stay. "People do have some bad troubles and things," she said. "I'm just blessed, that me and my kids have never had to stay in the shelter or out on the street."

Such a house was unlikely, she realized. Then again, she enjoyed thinking about it, and who knew what the future held. "I'm always expecting miracles," she said. If she had a breakfast nook with a kitchen table, she could drink her morning coffee and read the newspaper while sun streamed in. With a big dining room, guests wouldn't have to walk outside with their plates when she served Christmas and Thanksgiving dinners. On an expansive front porch, Honesty could play with friends or read books. And for Michael, there would be soft green grass. The boy needed a yard. He was already taking his first steps. Soon, he'd be running.

EPILOGUE

I arrived nearly an hour before the 2017 Charlotte City Council swearing-in was scheduled to start, but still too late to get a seat in council chambers. Hundreds of well-wishers had already staked out the government center lobby on that historic December evening, chatting and hailing friends as they stood in a line that snaked around the room. It was the first time in memory, or maybe ever, that citizens had elected such a youthful council, with six of eleven members under forty years old. It was also the first time they'd chosen an African American woman, Vi Lyles, as mayor. And then there was Braxton Winston, the most surprising first of all—the only council member to launch a political career after facing down a line of riot police.

Winston was a father of three, Davidson College graduate, a videographer working several part-time jobs to pay the bills. He'd been driving home the day Keith Lamont Scott died when he saw flashing lights and protesters. He joined the crowd. As tensions rose and police launched tear gas, he stripped off his shirt to use as a mask. That's when a newspaper photographer captured his image—an African American man, bare-chested, with dreadlocks, sagging pants, and exposed boxer shorts, standing with fist in the air. With that single photo, he was famous.[1]

When protests finally quieted, Winston didn't. He became part of Charlotte Uprising, a new coalition seeking police accountability and social and economic equity. One evening, he stood before City

Council demanding the mayor's resignation, charging "crimes against the humanity of the City of Charlotte." Before long, he was running for council. Davidson College's president donated to his campaign. Retired Bank of America chairman Hugh McColl—the man instrumental in building present-day Charlotte—mentored him.[2] Winston won an at-large seat, a stunning accomplishment for a political novice. His win drew congratulations from both Chelsea Clinton and hip-hop artist Common, who'd tweeted after the victory: "We can be the change we want to see in our society!"[3]

To take the oath of office, Winston, thirty-four, had donned a tweed jacket and Oxford blue shirt, though he still maintained his long hair. When it was his turn to give remarks, he waited, grinning, until twenty seconds of applause subsided. "We have work to do," he said. "It is our time to be warrior advocates for our people."

Unlike Winston, Vi Lyles was an insider, but the former city administrator had defeated the incumbent mayor with a similar message, describing herself as an instrument of change, eager to "build opportunity for all in our city." With business titan Hugh McColl backing Winston, with leaders pledging to build more affordable housing, create livable-wage jobs, and address inequality, it was no wonder that the evening's mood was hopeful. This incoming city council represented a new chapter. Still, the big question remained: Could Charlotte overcome its past?

As I watched the swearing-in from an overflow room, I thought about Carrie's unsuccessful council run in 1969. She'd been on a slate of progressive black candidates; none had prevailed. The winners that year had been all male and all white, except for a moderate black incumbent who whites viewed as a safe choice. By contrast, this new mayor and eleven city council members were mostly nonwhite—a first-generation immigrant from India and six African Americans. Back in 1969, Carrie had declared that blacks in Charlotte were ready to govern themselves. That declaration was coming true. Mecklenburg County, with its growing Latino and Asian populations, wasn't even a majority-white county anymore.

And yet Charlotte still had segregated neighborhoods, segregated schools, and a black poverty rate triple the white rate. The deep roots of systemic racism wound themselves around everything—health, wealth, educational attainment. Even elected officials who wanted to change the system had had little success. Richard Rothstein writes in *The Color of Law* that undoing nearly a century of residential segregation requires solutions "both complex and imprecise," applied with the understanding "that it will be impossible to fully untangle the web of inequality that we've woven."[4] The Opportunity Task Force said something similar: "Our community is not unique. We live in a country that faces the inheritance of inequity daily, but has very little sense of how to address it together."[5]

The anniversary of Scott's shooting death had brought a new wave of civic soul-searching—lectures, panels, and discussions, all aimed at finding a way to move past racism and inequality. One evening at the Levine Museum of the New South, I'd sat at a table with seven strangers, eating fried chicken and chewing over questions we'd been assigned to discuss: *What issues did Scott's death bring to the surface? How can we foster understanding, compassion, and justice across difference? How can we restore trust and improve community-police relations? How can we address our city's greatest challenges and opportunities?*

To my thinking, the city's greatest need was affordable housing. Average monthly apartment rent had topped $1,100, while the minimum wage was stuck at $7.25 an hour. The fight for $15 an hour hadn't made it to North Carolina. Nearly half of Charlotte renters were considered rent-burdened, meaning they spent more than the recommended 30 percent of their income on housing.[6] The largest deficit was housing for very low-income people—families who earned 50 percent or less of the median income.[7] These people worked $9- or $10- or $11-dollar-an-hour jobs in retail, fast-food, day care, landscaping, construction. Their labor kept the city running, but increasingly, they couldn't afford to live in it.

I couldn't imagine poverty waning until there were thousands more affordable housing units to address a crisis-level shortage, until neighborhoods became more integrated, by both race and income. If we didn't address housing, our schools would stay largely segregated, and low-income citizens would remain cut off from what sociologists called "social capital," connections to opportunities that help people get ahead.

At my Levine Museum table, I'd broached this topic, arguing for affordable housing in middle-class neighborhoods. One of my dinner companions, a young African American woman, jumped in with a question: How would my neighbors feel about welcoming those people? She meant people who needed rent subsidies, people likely to be black. She had a good point. Middle-class homeowners regularly fought attempts to build affordable apartments in their neighborhoods. At another housing event, a legal aid lawyer had made the same point, explaining why so many landlords refused to accept tenants who relied on housing vouchers: "The reason that a lot of landlords will not accept vouchers is because they associate them with low-income black people, and they don't want to say that."

This was how many conversations unfolded. Yes, there were solutions, at least theoretically, but all the game-changing ones came with multimillion-dollar price tags or social, political, and legal roadblocks. In North Carolina, cities didn't have the authority to raise the minimum wage or require developers to include affordable units in new housing projects. And the state didn't forbid landlords from rejecting potential tenants who needed government housing vouchers to pay their rent. A dozen states had laws prohibiting these automatic rejections, which had a disparate impact on minorities. But not North Carolina.

In one way, however, the city had made progress. Many of its leaders and a decent number of citizens had embraced a more complex, malevolent view of local history. In doing so, they'd come to understand present-day racial inequality. Chalk up a win for all those forums and roundtable discussions. If conversation alone could transform a place, Charlotte would be a burgeoning utopia.

But people were growing impatient with lack of action. Critics lamented that much of the business community wasn't invested, and that leaders lacked political will. Even former Mayor Harvey Gantt, usually an optimist, had sounded frustrated at a community breakfast as he described the city's low-dose commitment to affordable housing, drawing applause when he called for more: "People who are not affected by it, who are living in million dollar homes, should be saying *Do it.*" One young journalist writing in the *Charlotte Post*, the city's African American–owned newspaper, had been more blunt: "It's time to put up or shut up."[8]

As Charlotte tried to move forward, America as a whole seemed to be regressing. The Trump administration had signaled its intention to stay the incarceration course, with U.S. Attorney General Jeff Sessions ordering federal prosecutors to seek maximum penalties in all criminal cases.[9] On a visit to Charlotte to announce a new task force to address violent crime, Sessions said little about the task force and took no questions from reporters, but he made his tough-on-crime message clear. Without mentioning Keith Lamont Scott or other African Americans killed by police, he assured law enforcement officers that the Trump administration had their back. "Police are not the problem," he said.[10] He also didn't address the city's lack of economic mobility, or discuss childhood trauma, lack of living-wage jobs, or other factors that led people to commit crimes. "I wish we had a better solution than jail," he said, "but we don't."[11]

Charlotte's crime was rising. The eighty-five homicides in 2017 represented a twelve-year high. Murders, usually by gunshot wound, involved drugs, domestic violence, robberies, arguments. The increase was starting to look like a trend, not a temporary uptick. No one knew why, though one council member suggested a correlation between rising crime and loss of hope about the future.[12] Most victims were men, and most of the men were black.[13] This statistic might have prompted major headlines if they'd been another race or gender. But the violent demise of black men—that was the way it always was.

Many of the dead had been in their teens or twenties, their lives not so different from those of Demario, Derrick, and Stephen. Though gone for years, Belton's three sons weren't forgotten. Carrie never tired of recalling her favorite stories about Stephen, and Genesis carried his name on her right arm, tattooed inside a winged heart. Gloria Pruitt, who'd lost both Demario and Derrick, had kept their clothing, shoes, photos, drawings, letters—anything that triggered a memory. They still appeared in her dreams, sometimes as little boys, sometimes at eighteen and twenty-four, their ages when they died. In her dreams, they were always smiling.

Remembrances also showed up on Facebook. When one of Belton's sons shared a group photo from Big Lamont's homecoming party, he wrote that he thanked Jesus his family was back together. He missed Demario, Stephen, and Derrick, but he knew his brothers were watching over them.

The post had drawn likes and words of affirmation. But there was one comment different from the others. It wasn't about Jesus, family, or thankfulness. The comment was a terse remembrance of a dealer, a celebration of an ambitious young man who'd seized economic opportunity in a time and place where it was limited. In certain Charlotte neighborhoods, people still hadn't forgotten him.

"Moneyrock," it said. "Legend."

WHERE THEY ARE NOW

Charles Locke, the man who fired first in the 1985 Piedmont Courts shootout, was shot and killed four years later during an argument. He was twenty-five.

Louis "Big Lou" Samuels, twenty-six years old when he squared off with Belton in Piedmont Courts, is now fifty-nine. He was released from federal prison in November 2017 after serving more than twenty years for firearms violations. He was back in jail less than a month later, charged with possessing a firearm as a felon. Samuels told me in a 2012 interview from prison that he held no grudge against Belton Platt and supported his efforts to keep young people out of drug dealing. "Too many kids getting killed now," he said. "The drug game is petty now."

LaMorris Watson, the government informant who testified against Belton in 1989, served less than three years for his drug trafficking conviction. Within months of release, he was charged with trafficking cocaine and again cooperated with the government. He has a predicted federal prison release date of 2024, when he'll be sixty years old.

Since retiring as a judge in 2003, Shirley Fulton has continued volunteer work in Charlotte. In 2018, she launched a mentoring program designed to equip low-income students with social and cultural knowledge helpful for success. She taught skills such as financial literacy, manners, and proper dress, and organizing field trips to expand their horizons, "A lot of these kids have never been out of their neighborhood," she said.

Kimberly Williams Ensley, Belton's oldest daughter, designs wedding accessories and styles photo and movie shoots. She's married to a former police officer who recently ran for sheriff, unsuccessfully, on a platform emphasizing alternatives to incarceration.

Gloria Pruitt, who lost her sons Demario and Derrick in shooting deaths in 2002 and 2009, respectively, was completing her bachelor's degree in psychology in 2018. She hopes to become a therapist.

Big Lamont Davis, thirty-seven, left his job making masonry reinforcement products not long after starting. After months of unemployment, he got a new job making wooden pallets.

Little Lamont Platt, thirty-one, spent 2017 in jail. He was free in early 2018.

Belton Platt, fifty-five, was still preaching at his church in Conway, South Carolina, in 2018, but was planning to move to Charlotte, where he hoped to launch a ministry and a new restaurant. He and Mashandia were waiting for God to let them know when it was time to relocate.

At eighty-two, Carrie Graves has continued overseeing the Trader Joe's food giveaways outside her Southside Homes apartment. She's still babysitting her great-grandchildren and encouraging people to vote.

ACKNOWLEDGMENTS

I couldn't have written this book without the help of dozens of people in Charlotte and beyond who shared their memories and knowledge. Thanks to Shirley Fulton, who provided a keen perspective acquired as prosecutor and judge during Charlotte's big crime years. I am grateful most of all to Belton Platt, Carrie Graves, and family members who described experiences with segregation, cocaine dealing, prophecy, and solitary confinement, to name just a few subjects covered in our conversations. If not for Gordon Platt, I wouldn't have a transcript of Belton's federal trial. After I learned it was missing from U.S. government files, Gordon remembered he had a copy stashed in his bedroom, which he handed over in a shopping bag.

I also relied on a fine first draft of history contained in newspaper stories from the *Charlotte Observer* and *Charlotte News*. Thanks to the reporters who appear in my endnotes. I'm especially indebted to researcher Maria David for countless public records searches and other blessings. She's the one who found Belton Platt's phone number in the first place.

The seed for this book was a series I wrote for the *Charlotte Observer*. It wouldn't have happened if my former editors hadn't allowed me, then the book reporter, to spend more than a year on a project about a former cocaine dealer. Thanks Michael Weinstein, Cheryl Carpenter, and Rick Thames.

I was fortunate to begin this project as a student in Goucher College's nonfiction MFA program. My mentors—Madeleine Blais, Diana Hume George, Jacob Levenson, and Richard Todd—each helped develop my idea and propel me forward. The program's director emeritus, Patsy Sims, and current director, Leslie Rubinowski, have encouraged me throughout. My wonderful online writing group—Goucher alums Jen Adler, Heather Bobula, Jim Dahlman, Theo Emery, Erica Johnson, Thomas Kapsidelis, Carol Marsh, and Kim Pittaway—slogged through and improved many drafts with their critiques.

Thanks to historians and friends Pamela Grundy and Tom Hanchett, always willing to answer questions and help me think more deeply about race in Charlotte. Many friends also helped by reading drafts, commenting, and encouraging. Thank you Liz Chandler, Eric Frazier, Ricki Morell, Kathryn Schwille, Neda Semnani, Melanie Sill, Diane Suchetka, and Betsy Beaven Thorpe. Ever since I began this project, Karen Garloch, Tish Signet, and Nancy Stancill have provided wise counsel. I'm sure they grew weary of hearing me talk about Money Rock, but, being true friends, they hid their feelings well.

My agent, Alia Hanna Habib, understood at once what I hoped to do with this book. I thank her for smart editing and chance-taking on a new author. The same goes for Tara Grove, an editor with a sharp mind and big heart, and her colleagues at The New Press. I'm proud to be one of your authors.

Thanks to my daughter, Emma Foley, my biggest cheerleader, and my son, Jackson Foley, for introducing me to the ten crack commandments. Finally, thanks to Trent Foley for all those years of calm, competent computer troubleshooting, and, most of all, for your love and support.

NOTES

In addition to publications listed in the endnotes, my sources for this book include hundreds of hours of interviews—with the people featured, and with other family members, friends, and acquaintances. I talked to city leaders, academics, historians, police officers, judges, lawyers, court and prison personnel, former prison inmates, former drug dealers, and journalists. I also relied on Belton Platt's prison journals, his unpublished autobiography, personal papers, and photographs, as well as public records, including police reports and court documents. Where I use dialogue in quotation marks, I either heard it myself, used the recollections of the person speaking, or relied on court or law enforcement transcripts. When I don't use quotation marks for dialogue, it means I'm relying on someone who heard the conversation, but not the speaker.

Prologue

1. Shawn Carter, *Decoded* (New York: Spiegel & Grau, 2011), 13.

1. Money Rock and Big Lou

1. Jim Morrill, "A Cycle of Disrepair: Project's Maintenance a Continuing Battle," *Charlotte Observer*, August 3, 1986.

2. Jim Dumbell, "Christmas? It's Tree-Mendous," *Charlotte Observer*, November 27, 1985.

3. Doug Waller, "One Whiff and You've Joined the 'Smart Set,'" *Charlotte News*, August 20, 1977.

4. Ibid.

5. R. Steele, "The Cocaine Scene," *Newsweek*, May 30, 1977, 25–26.

6. Waller, "One Whiff and You've Joined the 'Smart Set.'"

7. Tom Feiling, *The Candy Machine: How Cocaine Took Over the World* (New York: Penguin Books, 2009), 38.

8. Robert Sabbag, *Snowblind: A Brief Career in the Cocaine Trade* (Indianapolis: Bobbs Merrill, 1976), 77–79.

9. Ted DeAdwyler, "Piedmont Courts: A Rougher World Harboring Crime, Poverty, Children," *Charlotte Observer*, October 19, 1985.

10. Jane Gross, "A New, Purified Form of Cocaine Causes Alarm as Abuse Increases," *New York Times*, November 29, 1985.

11. DeAdwyler, "Piedmont Courts: A Rougher World."

12. Dan Morrill, "Slavery in Mecklenburg County," Charlotte-Mecklenburg Historic Landmarks Commission, cmhpf.org/educationslavery.htm.

13. Mary Norton Kratt, *Charlotte: Spirit of the New South* (Winston-Salem: John F. Blair, 1992), 69–70.

14. DeAdwyler, "Piedmont Courts: A Rougher World."

15. Pam Kelley, "Big Lou and Moneyrock: Portrait of a Shoot-out," *Charlotte Observer*, June 22, 1986.

2. Showdown

1. Pam Kelley, "Witnesses to Shoot-out in Piedmont Courts Testify," *Charlotte Observer*, April 16, 1986.

2. Pam Kelley, "5 Shoot-out Victims Can't Identify Shooters," *Charlotte Observer*, April 17, 1986.

3. Nancy Webb, "Shooting Spree Wounds 7, Panics Piedmont Courts," *Charlotte Observer*, December 1, 1985.

4. Ibid.

3. Carrie Platt and the American Dream

1. John Kilgo, "Our Town: Our Plant Life's Gone Mad," *Charlotte News*, September 13, 1963.

2. "The History of Carolinas Medical Center-Mercy," nursinghistory.appstate .edu/sites/nursinghistory.appstate.edu/files/nursing-history-of-mercy -hospital.pdf.

3. Harry Golden, *Only in America* (Cleveland, NY: World Publishing Company, 1958), 121–22.

4. Jerry Shinn, *A Great, Public Compassion: The Story of Charlotte Memorial Hospital and Carolinas Medical Center* (University of North Carolina at Charlotte, 2002), 171.

5. *Presbyterian Hospital: The Spirit of Caring, 1903–85* (Dallas: Taylor Publishing, 1991), 161.

6. Dr. W. Montague Cobb, "The Hospital Integration Story in Charlotte, North Carolina," *Journal of the National Medical Association* 56, no. 3: 226–29.

7. "The Negro and the American Dream: Excerpt from Address at the Annual Freedom Mass Meeting of the North Carolina State Conference of Branches of the NAACP," September 25, 1960, The Martin Luther King Jr. Papers Project, mlk-kpp01.stanford.edu/primarydocuments

/Vol5/25Sept1960_TheNegroandtheAmericanDream,ExcerptfromAddressatt .pdf.

8. Mark Washburn, "A Quiet Step Toward Change—50 Years Ago, Blacks and Whites Joined to Desegregate Charlotte's Restaurants," *Charlotte Observer*, May 17, 2013.

9. Mark Washburn, "Forging Equality Charlotte's Way," *Charlotte Observer*, May 26, 2013.

10. James Reston, "Chapel Hill, N.C.: To the Class of '63 with Love," *New York Times*, June 5, 1963.

11. James K. Batten, "King to Negro Grads: Don't Yield to Lure of Violence," *Charlotte Observer*, May 31, 1963.

12. Bob Slough, "Charlotteans Oppose Civil Rights Bill, Poll Finds," *Charlotte News*, September 9, 1963.

13. Emery Wister, "Ads Promoting Charlotte Set for Wall St. Journal," *Charlotte News*, September 12, 1963.

14. Shinn, *A Great, Public Compassion*, 175–76.

15. Ibid., 192.

16. Minutes from Charlotte Memorial Board of Managers meeting, September 10, 1963.

17. Shinn, *A Great, Public Compassion*, 200.

18. United Press International, "Kennedy Federalizes Guard; Wallace Bows," *Charlotte Observer*, September 11, 1963.

19. United Press International, "Negroes Boycott 3 Schools, Defy Warning by Sanford," *Charlotte Observer*, September 10, 1963.

20. John Hussey, "USC's Integration Is Calm, Orderly," *Charlotte Observer*, September 12, 1963.

21. Thomas W. Hanchett, "Washington Heights," Charlotte-Mecklenburg Historic Landmarks Commission, cmhpf.org/kids/neighborhoods/WashHts .html.

22. Kratt, *Charlotte*, 164.

23. John Vaughan, "Segregation: The Legacy Endures," *Charlotte Observer*, September 14, 1997.

24. "Carrie L. Platt," *Charlotte News*, April 25, 1969.

4. Candy Kingpin

1. Frye Gaillard, *The Dream Long Deferred: The Landmark Struggle for Desegregation in Charlotte, North Carolina* (Chapel Hill: University of North Carolina Press, 1988), 29–30.

2. Ibid., 48.

3. Ibid., 52.

4. John Alexander, "For Kids, No Place to Play on West Blvd.," *Charlotte News*, March 18, 1974.

5. Dennis Rogers, "Dalton Villagers Upset After Girl Hit by Car," *Charlotte News*, October, 13, 1975.

6. Scheryl Gant, "Residents Paint Road In Protest at Dalton Village," *Charlotte Observer*, October 15, 1975.

7. Sherman Harris, "Not Afraid to Patrol in Dalton Village, Police Say," *Charlotte News*, October 29, 1975.

8. Sheilah Vance, "He Does Impossible for Scouts," *Charlotte News*, June 15, 1978.

9. George Will, "An Era of Busing Rolls into School History," *Wilmington Star-News*, November 28, 1999.

10. Pamela Grundy, "A Spirit of Togetherness: Desegregation and Community at West Charlotte High School," in *Yesterday, Today, and Tomorrow: School Desegregation and Resegregation in Charlotte*, edited by Roslyn Arlin Mickelson, Stephen Samuel Smith, and Amy Hawn Nelson (Cambridge, MA: Harvard Education Press, 2015), 41.

11. Tish Stoker, "There's Two Times the Leadership at West Charlotte High School," *Charlotte News*, October 3, 1979.

5. The Dealer's Mother

1. Pat Borden, "Carrie Graves: Voice of the Welfare Mother," *Charlotte Observer*, March 18, 1975.

2. Vanessa Gallman and Patsy Daniels, "Riots Can Occur, Black Leaders Warn at Meeting," *Charlotte Observer*, June 6, 1980.

3. Pat Borden, "For Carolinians, Sisterly Chaos," *Charlotte Observer*, November 20, 1977.

4. Ted Mellnik, John Minter, and Ricki Morell, "Crackdown at Piedmont Courts Ordered," *Charlotte Observer*, December 3, 1985.

6. What Went Wrong with Piedmont Courts?

1. Jim Morrill, "Residents: Solutions Start Inside Piedmont Courts," *Charlotte Observer*, April 25, 1986.

2. Homer Hoyt, *One Hundred Years of Land Values in Chicago* (Chicago: University of Chicago Press, 1933), 316.

3. Laura Shin, "The Racial Wealth Gap: Why a Typical White Household Has 16 Times the Wealth of a Typical Black One," *Forbes*, March 26, 2015.

4. Richard M. Flanagan, "The Housing Act of 1954: The Sea Change in National Urban Policy," *Urban Affairs Review* 33, no. 2 (November 1997): 265–67.

5. Ken Clark, "Planners Take Tour of Area," *Charlotte Observer*, February 4, 1958.

6. Charles Kuralt, "Cut-Rate Urban Renewal: Legislature Paves Way," *Charlotte News*, May 4, 1957.

7. Thomas W. Hanchett, *Sorting Out the New South City: Race, Class, and Urban Development in Charlotte, 1875–1975* (Chapel Hill: University of North Carolina Press, 1998), 250.

8. Jim Morrill and Polly Paddock, "Project's Early Hope Fades to Despair," *Charlotte Observer*, March, 30, 1986.

9. Hanchett, *Sorting Out the New South City*, 224.

10. Stan Brennan, "Alexander Wants New Board for Housing," *Charlotte Observer*, September 19, 1967.

11. Hanchett, *Sorting Out the New South City*, 262.

12. Morrill and Paddock, "Project's Early Hope Fades to Despair."

13. Richard Rothstein, *The Color of Law: The Forgotten History of How Our Government Segregated America* (New York: Liveright Publishing, 2017), 36–37.

14. Ted DeAdwyler, "Piedmont Courts Seeks Better Image," *Charlotte News*, October 22, 1984.

15. Ann Doss Helms, "Picture of Persistence: Ann Bradley Lives by the Principle That Little Steps Add up to Success," *Charlotte Observer*, December 30, 1995.

16. Jim Morrill, "Task Force to Urge Major Changes at Piedmont Courts," *Charlotte Observer*, July 30, 1986.

17. Ibid.

18. David Perlmutt, "Piedmont Courts Celebrates; Once Dangerous Area Has Been Transformed," *Charlotte Observer*, August 5, 1990.

7. State of North Carolina Versus Money Rock

1. Leigh Dyer, "Mystery of 1979 Biker Massacre Still Unsolved," *Charlotte Observer*, July 3, 1999.

2. John Minter, "Piedmont Courts Study Planned," *Charlotte Observer*, February 12, 1986.

3. Kelley, "Witnesses to Shoot-out at Piedmont Courts Testify."

4. Pam Kelley, "Two Men Convicted in Shoot-out," *Charlotte Observer*, June 12, 1986.

5. Kelley, "Big Lou and Moneyrock: Portrait of a Shoot-out."

6. Pam Kelley, "3 Men Convicted on Riot Charges in Shoot-out at Piedmont Courts," *Charlotte Observer*, April 19, 1986.

7. Kelley, "Witnesses to Shoot-out at Piedmont Courts Testify."

8. Ibid.

9. Kelley, "5 Shoot-out Victims Can't Identity Shooters."

10. Ibid.

11. Ibid.

12. Pam Kelley, "Drug Traces Found on Cash in Shoot-out Case," *Charlotte Observer*, April 18, 1986.

13. Ibid.

14. Ibid.

15. Kelley, "5 Shoot-out Victims Can't Identity Shooters."

16. Kelley, "Drug Traces Found on Cash."

17. Kelley, "3 Men Convicted on Riot Charges in Shoot-out at Piedmont Courts."

8. Convictions

1. Pam Kelley, "Brothers Get 35 Years in Piedmont Courts Shoot-out," *Charlotte Observer*, April 24, 1986.

2. Ibid.

3. Pam Kelley, "Shoot-out Defendant Denied Bond During Appeal of Case," *Charlotte Observer*, April 25, 1986.

4. Ibid.

5. Ibid.

6. Janette Thomas Greenwood, *Bittersweet Legacy: The Black and White "Better Classes" in Charlotte, 1850–1910* (Chapel Hill: University of North Carolina Press, 1994), 77.

7. Morrill and Paddock, "Project's Early Hope Fades to Despair."

9. Heavy in the Weight

1. David F. Musto, *The American Disease: Origins of Narcotics Control* (Oxford, UK: Oxford University Press, 1999), 7–12.

2. Joseph F. Spillane, *Cocaine: From Medical Marvel to Modern Menace in the United States, 1884–1920* (Baltimore: Johns Hopkins University Press, 2000), 91–92.

3. Edward Huntington Williams, "Negro Cocaine 'Fiends' Are a New Southern Menace," *New York Times*, February 8, 1914.

4. James A. Inciardi, *The War on Drugs IV: The Continuing Saga of the Mysteries and Miseries of Intoxication, Addiction, Crime, and Public Policy*, 4th edition (London: Pearson Education, 2008), 118.

5. Ryan Grim, *This Is Your Country on Drugs: The Secret History of Getting High in America* (Hoboken, NJ: Wiley, 2009), 70.

6. Chuck McShane, "How Charlotte Got Liquored Up," *Charlotte Magazine*, June 2013.

7. Craig Reinarman and Harry G. Levine, "The Crack Attack: America's Latest Drug Scare, 1986–92," in *Images of Issues: Typifying Contemporary Social Problems*, edited by Joel Best (Piscataway, NJ: Transaction Publishers, 1995), 147.

8. Khary Turner, "A Crack Dealer's Ten Commandments," *The Source*, July 1994.

10. Going Down

1. Carrie tried to fight the restaurant seizure. She had no lawyer, but made a handwritten plea, questioning why the government would take a person's livelihood. "I have not sold drugs," she wrote. "I have a right as an American Citizen I thought to have a business." Government officials closed the restaurant after a U.S. marshal reported finding no bank account, few records, little cash flow, and no evidence of employee pay. "The business did not appear

to have been operated in a business-like fashion," he wrote. The government eventually dropped seizure proceedings after officers confirmed what Belton had asserted—that he was renting the property. He had never owned it, so the federal government couldn't seize it.

11. United States Versus Money Rock

1. Pam Kelley, "By the Law Books: Judge Potter's Sentencing Earns Renown," *Charlotte Observer*, March 8, 1986.

2. Marilyn Mather, "Federal Judge Appointee Cut From Reagan Mold," *Charlotte Observer*, October 31, 1981.

3. "Jim Bakker's Startling Sentence," *New York Times*, October 29, 1989.

4. In 1991, the United States Court of Appeals for the Fourth Circuit threw out Potter's sentence in Jim Bakker's case, ruling Potter was influenced by his religious beliefs. Another federal judge resentenced Bakker to eighteen years, which was later reduced to eight years.

5. Kelley, "By the Law Books."

6. Nancy Webb, "Boy, 11, Charged with Taking Crack to School," *Charlotte Observer*, May 24, 1989; Nancy Webb, "Cocaine Arrest at Courthouse," *Charlotte Observer*, March 23, 1989.

7. Gary L. Wright, "Sherrill Quits, Admits Drug Use," *Charlotte Observer*, March 20, 1990.

8. Nancy Webb, "Cocaine: The Habit, the Hurt," *Charlotte Observer*, January 29, 1989.

9. Richard Oppel, "Ending the Scourge Series Examines Drugs in Charlotte, Surrounding Communities," *Charlotte Observer*, January 29, 1989.

10. Richard M. Smith, "The Plague Among Us," *Newsweek*, June 16, 1986.

11. Peter Kerr, "Extra-Potent Cocaine: Use Rising Sharply Among Teen-Agers," *New York Times*, March 20, 1986.

12. Louis Sahagun, "Former First Lady, Gates on Scene as SWAT Team Carries out Drug Raid," *Los Angeles Times*, April 7, 1989.

13. Reinarman and Levine, "The Crack Attack," 154–56.

14. Richard L. Berke, "Poll Finds Most in U.S. Back Bush Strategy on Drugs," *New York Times*, September 12, 1989.

15. Reinarman and Levine, "The Crack Attack," 147–48.

16. Ibid., 160.

17. Ibid., 155–56.

18. Ibid., 151.

19. The method Judge Robert Potter used to find aggravating factors, including his presumption of Belton's guilt in the Piedmont Courts shooting, was later declared unconstitutional. In 2000, in *Apprendi v. New Jersey*, the Supreme Court ruled that any aggravating factor had to be determined by a jury beyond a reasonable doubt. A related 2005 ruling, *United States v. Booker*, said that a judge could use only a prior conviction or facts admitted by a defendant or proved beyond a reasonable doubt to a jury to exceed the statutory

maximum sentence. Neither of these rulings was retroactive, however, so they didn't help Belton.

20. Nancy Webb, "Drug Dealer Sentenced on Cocaine, Theft Charges," *Charlotte Observer*, May 24, 1990.

12. Coming of Age in a World-Class City

1. Liz Chandler, Ted Mellnik, and Gary L. Wright, "At Charlotte's Core, Violence a Daily Threat," *Charlotte Observer*, June 5, 1994.

2. Rick Rothacker, *Banktown: The Rise and Struggles of Charlotte's Big Banks* (Winston-Salem, NC: John F. Blair, 2010), 15.

3. Charlotte-Mecklenburg Library, *The Charlotte-Mecklenburg Story*, cm story.org/content/1791-washingtons-visit.

4. North Carolina Cities Population Changes in the 1800s, historync.org /NCCityPopulations1800s.htm.

5. W.J. Cash, *The Mind of the South* (New York: Alfred A. Knopf, 1941), 219.

6. Kratt, *Charlotte*, 142.

7. Elizabeth Leland, "Tales of the New South: 'The Little City That Could,'" *Charlotte Observer*, August 26, 2012.

8. Porter Munn, "Welcome, Mrs. Keelan: Midtown Mountain Leveled by Kids," *Charlotte Observer*, June 20, 1963.

9. Leonard Laye, "Charlotte's Win Will Be a Major Upset," *Charlotte Observer*, April 3, 1987.

10. Jack Claiborne, "Put up the Nets—Charlotte's In: Ambition Fulfilled, Charlotte Becomes Major League City," *Charlotte Observer*, April 23, 1987.

11. Scott Fowler, "Hysteria for Hornets Was Real, All Right," *Charlotte Observer*, July 14, 2013.

12. Ed Martin, David Perlmutt, and Foon Rhee, "The Grand Opening: Charlotte Shows off Its New Pride and Joy," *Charlotte Observer*, August, 12, 1988.

13. David Perlmutt, "50,000 Shower Confetti, Thanks on NBA Heroes," *Charlotte Observer*, April 28, 1987.

14. Pam Kelley and Liz Chandler, "Shinn Shares Success Secrets with Students," *Charlotte Observer*, September 1, 1988.

15. Nancy Brachey, "Up or Down? What to Call the Heart of Charlotte Is Still a Source of Debate," *Charlotte Observer*, October 19, 1980.

16. Tommy Tomlinson, "From a Small Town to the Big Time," *Charlotte Observer*, February 20, 2011.

17. Jeff Kunerth, "Charlotte Banks on Its Success," *Orlando Sentinel*, December 6, 1992.

18. Peter Applebome, *Dixie Rising* (New York: Crown, 1996), 151.

19. Liz Clarke, "Carolinas' NFL Dream Comes True," *Charlotte Observer*, October 27, 1993.

20. Mary Elizabeth DeAngelis, "Nobles, Burnette Murder Trial to Start," *Charlotte Observer*, July 5, 1994.

21. Chandler, Mellnik, and Wright, "At Charlotte's Core, Violence a Deadly Threat."

22. Chuck McShane, "1993: Charlotte's Deadliest Year," *Charlotte Magazine*, December 2013.

23. Chandler, Mellnik, and Wright, "At Charlotte's Core, Violence a Deadly Threat."

24. Liz Chandler, "We Want a Place 'Where Our Kids Are Safe,'" *Charlotte Observer*, July 17, 1994.

25. Ricki Morell, "A Street of Despair: Cummings Avenue Languishes in Drugs, Fear, and Crime," *Charlotte Observer*, June 26, 1994.

26. James Redford and Karen Pritzker, "Teaching Traumatized Kids," *Atlantic*, July 7, 2016, theatlantic.com/education/archive/2016/07/teaching-traumatized-kids/490214.

27. Patrick Sharkey, *Uneasy Peace: The Great Crime Decline, the Renewal of City Life, and the Next War on Violence* (New York: W.W. Norton, 2018), 86.

28. Chandler, Mellnik, and Wright, "At Charlotte's Core, Violence a Deadly Threat."

29. Ibid.

30. Bill Arthur, "Business Booms Where a Slum Once Festered," *Charlotte Observer*, May 20, 1973.

31. Liz Chandler and Gary L. Wright, "Hope Amid Despair," *Charlotte Observer*, December 3, 1995.

13. The Christian Inmate

1. Eric Weiner, "The Long, Colorful History of the Mann Act," *All Things Considered*, March 11, 2008.

2. Rebecca Burns, "Al Capone Heads for Atlanta Federal Penitentiary," *Atlanta Magazine*, May 2, 2012.

3. Scott Henry, "Prison Riot!" *Creative Loafing Atlanta*, November 21, 2007.

4. In 2000, the U.S. Supreme Court ruled in *Apprendi v. New Jersey* that the Sixth Amendment right to a jury trial prohibited judges from enhancing sentences beyond the maximum based on factors other than those decided by a jury beyond a reasonable doubt. The ruling wasn't retroactive, however, so it didn't apply in Belton Platt's case.

5. Joseph T. Hallinan, *Going up the River: Travels in a Prison Nation* (New York: Random House, 2001), 38.

6. Nathan James, "The Federal Prison Population Buildup: Options for Congress," Congressional Research Service, May 20, 2016, 22, fas.org/sgp/crs/misc/R42937.pdf.

14. Sentencing a Generation

1. From "Felonies by Race," a 2017 report by the Mecklenburg County Criminal Justice Services Planning Division.

2. Ricki Morell, "A Family Portrait," *Charlotte Observer*, July 27, 1997.

3. North Carolina legislators cut off funding to Mecklenburg County's drug treatment court in 2011. The county took it over and expanded the court's services. Attorney Steve Ward became a consultant, helping judicial districts across the nation launch similar courts.

4. Michael F. Walther, "Insanity: Four Decades of U.S. Counterdrug Strategy" (Carlisle Papers, Strategic Studies Institute, U.S. Army War College, 2012), 2–3, strategicstudiesinstitute.army.mil/pubs/display.cfm?pubID =1143.

5. Ibid.

6. Carrie Levine, "Jones Condemns James' Remarks; Racial Comments Spark Uproar," *Charlotte Observer*, December 2, 2004.

7. James Forman Jr., *Locking Up Our Own: Crime and Punishment in Black America* (New York: Farrar, Straus and Giroux, 2017), 204.

8. Ron Harris, "Blacks Feel Brunt of Drug War," *Los Angeles Times*, April 22, 1990.

9. In 2017, with North Carolina the only remaining state that still automatically prosecuted sixteen-year-olds as adults, the North Carolina General Assembly passed legislation allowing sixteen- and seventeen-year-olds to be prosecuted in juvenile court for misdemeanors and low-level larcenies. The law was to take effect in December 2019.

10. Bill Nichols, "Easing Racial Tensions Gets the Local Touch," *USA Today*, December 1, 1997.

11. Gary L. Wright, "Fulton Announces She's Leaving Bench," *Charlotte Observer*, November, 19, 2002.

12. Ibid.

15. Lost Boys

1. Melissa Manware and Eric Frazier, "Arrests Made in Gang Crackdown," *Charlotte Observer*, March 31, 2007.

2. "Killing Snitches," *Gangland*, April 9, 2009.

3. Peter Smolowitz, "A Different Take on School Discipline," *Charlotte Observer*, November 28, 2006.

4. Elijah Anderson, *Code of the Street: Decency, Violence, and the Moral Life of the Inner City* (New York: W.W. Norton & Company, 1999), 34.

5. Ta-Nehisi Coates, "Beyond the Code of the Streets," *New York Times*, May 5, 2013.

6. Sara Wakefield and Christopher Wildeman, *Children of the Prison Boom: Mass Incarceration and the Future of Inequality* (Oxford, UK: Oxford University Press, 2013), 21–22.

7. Ibid., 157.

8. Dana Goldstein, "10 (Not Entirely Crazy) Theories Explaining the Great Crime Decline," *Marshall Project*, November 24, 2014.

9. Sharkey, *Uneasy Peace*, 57–60.

10. Robert F. Moore, "Disabled Man Killed During Evening Stroll," *Charlotte Observer*, November 14, 2001.

11. Melissa Manware, "3 Charlotte Men Charged in Pair of Armed Robbery Cases," *Charlotte Observer*, October, 11, 2002.

12. Ronald W. Maris, Alan L. Berman, and Morton M. Silverman, *Comprehensive Textbook of Suicidology* (New York: Guilford Press, 2000), 198–200.

16. The Love of His Life

1. T.M. Luhrmann, *When God Talks Back: Understanding the American Evangelical Relationship with God* (New York: Knopf, 2012), xx.

2. Ibid., xxi.

3. Michael Fechter, "W. Virginian Pleads Guilty in Greater Ministries Case," *Tampa Tribune*, April 7, 2001.

4. Ibid.

5. Chuck Fager, "Fraud: Greater Ministries Ministers Get Lengthy Prison Terms," *Christianity Today*, October 1, 2001.

6. John Gorham, "Faith and Mammon," *Forbes*, September 6, 1999.

7. "Federal Officials Charge That Florida-Based, Antigovernment Greater Ministries Is Actually a Criminal Fraud," *Southern Poverty Law Center Intelligence Report*, Spring 1999, Issue Number 94, www.splcenter.org/get-informed /intelligence-report/browse-all-issues/1999/spring/ministry-of-money.

8. Ibid.

9. *The Biblical Examiner*, February 1999, biblicalexaminer.org/MILLER. htm.

10. Belton Platt, *Ministry of the Husband* (Maitland, FL: Xulon Press, 2009), 75.

11. Ibid., 34.

12. Ibid., 193.

17. Freedom

1. Michelle Alexander, "The New Jim Crow: How a War on Drugs Gave Birth to a Permanent American Undercaste," *Mother Jones*, March 8, 2010.

2. Cleve R. Wootson Jr., "Driver Fatally Shot Near Day Care," *Charlotte Observer*, May 16, 2009.

20. Homecoming

1. "Cocaine Arrest; Inmate Gets Violent," *Tabor-Loris Tribune*, December 9, 2009.

2. Ames Alexander, "N.C. to Limit Use of Solitary Confinement for Prisoners," *Charlotte Observer*, July 20, 2017. North Carolina more than halved the number of its inmates in solitary between 2012 and 2017 and began limiting most stays in solitary to thirty days.

3. Deuce Nivens, "Dedication Draws Crowd," *Tabor-Loris Tribune*, August 20, 2008.

21. Life on the Outside

1. "State of the Union," *New York Times*, January 21, 2004.
2. Organizers credited Doug Jones's U.S. Senate victory over Roy Moore in December 2017 partly to efforts to sign up several thousand voters with felonies. Vann R. Newkirk II, "How Grassroots Organizers Got Black Voters to the Polls in Alabama," *Atlantic*, December 19, 2017, theatlantic.com/politics/arch ive/2017/12/sparking-an-electoral-revival-in-alabama/548504/?eType= EmailBlastContent&eId=1cdf32e8-588c-492b-a57d-30254cf202a1.

22. Uprising

1. Richard Fausset and Yamiche Alcindor, "Video by Wife of Keith Scott Shows Her Pleas to Police," *New York Times*, September 23, 2016.
2. Katherine Peralta, "Social Media Plays Growing Role in Police Shootings like the One in Charlotte," *Charlotte Observer*, September 21, 2016.
3. Mark Washburn, Ely Portillo, and Doug Miller, "Trucker to 911 as Looters Close In: They're Coming This Way, Hundreds of Them," *Charlotte Observer*, September 26, 2016, embedded 911 call recording, charlotteobserver .com/news/special-reports/charlotte-shooting-protests/article104279951 .html.
4. Ibid.
5. Erik Spanberg, "Charlotte Mayor Says DNC Changed City Forever," *Charlotte Business Journal*, September 7, 2012.
6. Michael Gordon and Pam Kelley, "The Reviews Are In," *Charlotte Observer*, September 9, 2012.
7. "Mobility, Measured; Class in America," *The Economist*, February 1, 2014.
8. Gavin Off, "New Study: Charlotte's Poor Struggle to Move Up," *Charlotte Observer*, January 23, 2014.
9. Elise Gould, "U.S. Lags Behind Peer Countries in Mobility," Economic Policy Institute, October 12, 2012, epi.org/publication/usa-lags-peer -countries-mobility.
10. Gene Nichol, "What Poverty Looks like in Charlotte," *Charlotte Observer*, July 17, 2016.
11. David Perlmutt, Gavin Off, and Claire Williams, "Poverty Spreads Across Mecklenburg, North Carolina," *Charlotte Observer*, August 2, 2014.
12. Ann Doss Helms, "Schools Ruling Led to a Decade of Change," *Charlotte Observer*, September 10, 2009.
13. Ann Doss Helms, "CMS Data—Hispanic, Asian Student Numbers Increase," *Charlotte Observer*, December 4, 2016.
14. Justin Perry, "We Are at a Crossroads, Charlotte, and That's Good," *Charlotte Observer*, October 18, 2017.

15. Elizabeth Leland, "How Will Charlotte Answer Keith Lamont Scott's Death, Week of Protests?," *Charlotte Observer*, September 24, 2016, embedded video interview with Ophelia Garmon-Brown, charlotteobserver.com/news /local/crime/article103995666.html.

16. "You Were Wrong, Mr. President," *Charlotte Observer*, October 10, 1984.

17. Richard Fausset and Alan Blinder, "Charlotte Officer 'Justified' in Fatal Shooting of Keith Scott," *New York Times*, November 30, 2016.

18. Bruce Henderson, Katherine Peralta, and Ely Portillo, "Protesters March Through Uptown Again," *Charlotte Observer*, December 1, 2016.

23. Southside Homes

1. Hazel M. Trotter, "Project Is Far Cry From Slum Housing," *Charlotte Observer*, January 27, 1952.

2. Greg Lacour, "Charlotte's 'Broken System' Myth," *Charlotte Magazine*, June 2017.

3. "Andy Goh and Andy Smith, "#discussCLT Podcast: Episode 22, 'Two Charlottes' & a Q&A," June 2017, charlottemagazine.com/DiscussCLT/June -2017/discussCLT-Podcast-Episode-22-Two-Charlottes-a-Q-A.

Epilogue

1. Michael Graff, "Hugh McColl's Last Great Investment," *Politico*, December 25, 2017, politico.com/magazine/story/2017/12/25/hugh-mccolls-last -great-investment-216162.

2. Ibid.

3. Anna Douglas and Steve Harrison, "From Charlotte Protester to Politician, Will Braxton Winston's One Voice Matter?," *Charlotte Observer*, November 11, 2017.

4. Rothstein, *The Color of Law*, 197–98.

5. Letter from the Charlotte-Mecklenburg Leading on Opportunity Task Force, leadingonopportunity.org/introduction/letter-from-the-task-force.

6. Ely Portillo, "Aftermath of Keith Scott Shooting—Is City on Track with Affordable Housing Promise? It Depends . . . ," *Charlotte Observer*, September 19, 2017.

7. Greg Lacour, "Is Charlotte Spinning Its Wheels on Affordable Housing?," *Charlotte Magazine*, August 29, 2017, charlottemagazine.com/ Charlotte-Magazine/August-2017/Is-Charlotte-Spinning-Its-Wheels-On -Affordable-Housing.

8. Ashley Mahoney, "Charlotte's Talking, but When Will Change in Social Capital Occur?," *Charlotte Post*, October 25, 2017.

9. Nick Tabor, "55 Ways Donald Trump Structurally Changed America in 2017," *New York Magazine*, December 21, 2017, nymag.com/daily /intelligencer/2017/12/55-ways-donald-trump-structurally-changed-america -in-2017.html.

10. Michael Gordon, "'Police Are Not the Problem,' Sessions Says in Revealing Charlotte Anti-Crime Effort," *Charlotte Observer*, December 20, 2017.

11. Ibid.

12. Greg Lacour, "Digging for the Root of Charlotte's Homicide Spike," *Charlotte Magazine*, January 2018, charlottemagazine.com/DiscussCLT/January-2018/Digging-For-the-Root-of-Charlottes-Homicide-Spike.

13. Jane Wester, Adam Bell, Mark Price, Lavendrick Smith, and Doug Miller, "Charlotte's Homicide Rate Hits Twelve-Year High," *Charlotte Observer*, updated January 31, 2018, charlotteobserver.com/news/special-reports/article183978436.html.

ABOUT THE AUTHOR

A former reporter for the *Charlotte Observer*, **Pam Kelley** has won honors from the National Press Club and the Society for Features Journalism. She contributed to a subprime mortgage exposé that was a finalist for the 2008 Pulitzer Prize for Public Service. She lives in Cornelius, North Carolina.

PUBLISHING IN THE
PUBLIC INTEREST

Thank you for reading this book published by The New Press. The New Press is a nonprofit, public interest publisher. New Press books and authors play a crucial role in sparking conversations about the key political and social issues of our day.

We hope you enjoyed this book and that you will stay in touch with The New Press. Here are a few ways to stay up to date with our books, events, and the issues we cover:

- Sign up at www.thenewpress.com/subscribe to receive updates on New Press authors and issues and to be notified about local events
- Like us on Facebook: www.facebook.com/newpressbooks
- Follow us on Twitter: www.twitter.com/thenewpress

Please consider buying New Press books for yourself; for friends and family; or to donate to schools, libraries, community centers, prison libraries, and other organizations involved with the issues our authors write about.

The New Press is a 501(c)(3) nonprofit organization. You can also support our work with a tax-deductible gift by visiting www.thenewpress.com/donate.